U.S. Interests
in the New Taiwan

U.S. Interests in the New Taiwan

Martin L. Lasater

Routledge
Taylor & Francis Group

NEW YORK AND LONDON

First published 1993 by Westview Press, Inc.

Published 2021 by Routledge
605 Third Avenue, New York, NY 10017
2 Park Square, Milton Park, Abingdon, Oxon OX14 4RN

Routledge is an imprint of the Taylor & Francis Group, an informa business

Library of Congress Cataloging-in-Publication Data
Lasater, Martin L.
 U.S. interests in the new Taiwan / by Martin L. Lasater
  p. cm.
 Includes index.
 ISBN 0-8133-8396-X
 1. United States–Foreign relations—Taiwan. 2. Taiwan—Foreign
 relations—United States. I. Title.
 E183.8.T3L4 1993
 327.73041249—dc20   92-19953
                                                          CIP

ISBN 13: 978-0-3672-1243-8 (hbk)
ISBN 13: 978-0-3672-1524-8 (pbk)

DOI: 10.4324/9780429269929

Contents

Preface

Taiwan is rapidly changing its fundamental character. Very few studies have examined where the new Taiwan is going or what impact developments there will have on Sino-American relations over the next decade. The purpose of this book is to partially fill that intellectual gap. Consequently, the book is oriented toward the future, and I frequently make forecasts. I do so with full awareness of the analytical risks and limitations involved in taking such an approach.

To facilitate the book's readability, I have cited relatively few references. However, many sources have contributed to this work, including more than ten years of personal experience in analyzing the Taiwan issue in Sino-American relations.

Both the Wade-Giles and Pinyin romanization systems have been utilized for Chinese names. In general, the Wade-Giles system has been used for historical names and when referring to Taiwan, and the Pinyin system has been used when referring to mainland China. This reflects current usage by the two Chinese societies.

I am grateful for a research grant from the Institute of International Relations at National Chengchi University and for a publication grant from the Pacific Cultural Foundation, both located in Taipei. The contents of the book, however, are solely my responsibility and represent my opinions.

Martin L. Lasater

Introduction

Called a pariah state by some because of its diplomatic isolation, Taiwan today may be more aptly described as a phoenix rising above its difficulties. Beginning in 1986 and continuing to the present, Taiwan—or, the Republic of China (ROC) as it is called officially—initiated a remarkable series of domestic and foreign policy reforms designed to transform the island-nation into a modern democratic state.

Within a short period of time, forty years of martial law were ended; Taiwan opened its doors for the first time to unofficial contact with its rival, the People's Republic of China (PRC) on the mainland; a major diplomatic offensive, termed "flexible," "pragmatic," or "elastic" diplomacy, was launched; substantial work on liberalizing and restructuring the economy was begun; and advanced locally produced weapons were added to the ROC arsenal, significantly enhancing the island's self-defense capabilities.

These profound changes in ROC policy have created a "new" Taiwan which is remarkably different from the "old" Taiwan of pre-1986. The new Taiwan is a pluralistic society evolving toward a parliamentary democracy. Its market economy, based increasingly on high-tech products rather than labor intensive industry, is largely open to foreign competition. Non-governmental contacts with mainland China are extensive. Effectively using its large financial resources, Taiwan is playing a much more active role in Asian Pacific affairs. Its foreign policy is far more pragmatic and less ideological than in the past, creating opportunities for vastly expanded participation in the international community. The ROC military is stronger than ever before and less dependent on U.S. arms sales.

The new Taiwan is having an important impact on U.S. interests in Asia, an impact which will likely grow in the future. Taiwan's rapid democratization is in U.S. political interests, and Taiwan's free market economy and trade policies follow models long advocated by the United States. Washington considers the increased contacts between Taiwan and mainland China to be in American interests, since the contacts tend to reduce tensions in the Taiwan Strait area. Moreover,

Taiwan's linkages with the mainland appear to have a liberalizing effect on many PRC policies, thus serving U.S. interests in this way as well.

The U.S. generally welcomes wider participation by Taipei in the international community; after all, Taiwan's economic power makes it a de facto part of that community. Taiwan's strengthened self-defense capability is also in the U.S. interests, since indigenously produced weapons tend to reduce the sensitivity of U.S. arms sales to Taiwan as an issue in U.S. relations with the PRC.

But recent policy changes on Taiwan are not all positive from the point of view of U.S. interests. Democracy in Taiwan, for example, has brought to the surface deep ethnic and social divisions long held in check by martial law. The democratic process has placed in office individuals determined to move Taiwan in the direction of national independence. This runs counter to the positions of the ruling Kuomintang (KMT) political party, as well as the Chinese Communist Party, both of which have long insisted that Taiwan is an integral part of China. Since 1972 the U.S. has not taken exception to this Chinese view.

Taiwan's economic success has some negative impact on U.S. interests. A persistent U.S. trade deficit is an obvious example. Taiwan is following in Japan's footsteps by moving into areas of high technology in direct competition with American industries. Billions of dollars from Taiwan are being invested in the U.S., again with mixed feelings among Americans.

Taiwan's economic strength has given its leaders and people much greater confidence. As a result, Taiwan is more independent in its views and less inclined to support U.S. policies when these run counter to Taiwan's own best interests. This attitude is reflected in Taiwan's tougher negotiating positions with the U.S. over a wide range of issues.

Taiwan's ability to produce more of its own weapons also has a down side from the U.S. perspective, because Washington has limited influence over the types of weapons manufactured in Taiwan. Over time, this could weaken U.S. ability to ensure that Taiwan's military forces are armed for defensive rather than offensive missions.

Taiwan's relations with mainland China are of special interest to the U.S. because of the sensitivity of the Taiwan issue in Sino-American relations. There are several developments on Taiwan which deeply concern the PRC and which cloud in varying degrees Washington-Beijing ties. These include ROC efforts to expand its diplomatic presence in the international community, KMT efforts to undermine the legitimacy of the CCP through promotion of the "Taiwan Experience," and Taiwan's support of anti-Chinese Communist movements around the world. Even more threatening to PRC interests is the fact that, as Taipei becomes stronger, it may attempt to prolong indefinitely Taiwan's reunification with the mainland.

Of greatest concern to PRC leaders, however, is the possibility that democracy will bring to power on Taiwan pro-independence elements who will try to make Taiwan a de jure independent country. This would carry high risks of war in the Taiwan Strait, with potentially disastrous results across a wide spectrum of interests in East Asia.

The purpose of this book is to examine the substantial changes that have taken place on Taiwan since 1986 from the perspective of U.S. interests and policy, which are themselves in a state of flux with the ending of the Cold War. The book is organized according to the following plan.

Chapter 1 is an introductory chapter which will provide a brief historical overview of Taiwan and U.S. relations with the ROC through 1986.

Chapters 2 through 5 form Part One of the study, which will examine different aspects of the new Taiwan. Chapter 2, "Taiwan's Political Development," will discuss the origins and evolution of the Kuomintang or Nationalist Party, the process of political liberalization underway on Taiwan, the role of the political opposition, a description of recent political developments, and an assessment of future politics on Taiwan.

Issues addressed in Chapter 3, "Taiwan's Economic Development," include the stages of ROC development and key economic policies; current domestic economic conditions; Taiwan's plans to restructure its economy; Taiwan's economic relations with the mainland; international economic relations, including trade with the United States, Japan, and Western Europe; and Taiwan's likely future economic policies.

Chapter 4, "Flexible Diplomacy," will consider various aspects of ROC foreign policy since 1986, including policies toward the mainland, the United States, Japan, other major countries, and the Third World. The rationale and accomplishments of Taiwan's "flexible diplomacy" will be critically examined.

Chapter 5, "The Security of Taiwan," will review the PRC military threat to Taiwan in terms of military capabilities and political intentions. The chapter will examine possible scenarios of PRC uses of force; the non-military aspects of Taiwan's deterrence strategy; and the role of the United States in Taiwan's security, including arms sales.

Part Two of the book will address U.S. interests in the new Taiwan and policy implications for the United States. Chapter 6, "Beyond Containment in Asia: U.S. Strategy and Policy in the 1990s," will focus on the evolution of U.S. policy in Asia since the end of the Cold War. Discussed will be U.S. interests in the Asian Pacific region as a whole, the foreign policies of presidents Ronald Reagan and George Bush toward East Asia, the impact of the Persian Gulf War on U.S. policies toward the Asian Pacific Rim, and the evolving U.S. strategies of regionalism and integration in the Asian Pacific context.

Chapter 7, "U.S. Interests in the Republic of China on Taiwan," will examine in some detail the various types of interests the United States has with Taiwan. The chapter will discuss U.S. interests in peace in the Taiwan Strait, other U.S. interests in Taiwan, Bush foreign policy operating principles and their applicability toward Taiwan, and U.S. interests in various future scenarios for Taiwan.

Chapter 8, "Policy Recommendations and Conclusions," will integrate the previous discussion by focusing on the challenges that trends on Taiwan bring to American foreign policy in an era of multipolarity and interdependence in Asia. The chapter will address the key issue of how to balance U.S. interests in both Beijing and Taipei in the post-containment period and suggest certain U.S. policy adjustments over the next decade.

1

Historical Background

The Island of Taiwan

Taiwan sits astride the Tropic of Cancer, approximately 115 miles off the coast of Fujian Province, China. Shaped like a tobacco leaf, it is about 250 miles long and eighty miles in width. It has an area of approximately 13,800 square miles. More than half the island is mountainous, with some sixty peaks over 10,000 feet in elevation. Taiwan's mountain peaks are visible from the mainland on a clear day.

The western half of the island is an alluvial plain, a heavily cultivated region where the vast majority of Taiwan's 20.5 million inhabitants live. Because of geological features, transportation on the eastern and central portions of the island is very limited, as are cross island (East-West) rail and road links. Taiwan's climate is subtropical and rainfall is plentiful. The island has considerable forests in the central and eastern mountain regions, but few other natural resources other than coal.

In addition to the island of Taiwan, other islands under the control of the Republic of China include a few small offshore islands near Taiwan, the Pescadores Islands (Penghu) in the Taiwan Strait, and the Quemoy (Kinmen) and Matsu islands groups just off the coast of Fujian Province. Together, these islands contribute about 130 square miles to ROC territory. A few islands in the South China Sea are also occupied by the ROC military, but their ownership is subject to disagreement between several countries.

The population of Taiwan is almost entirely Han Chinese, with a small percentage of aborigines. Prior to World War II, most of the Chinese inhabitants were descendants of emigrants from Fujian and Guangdong provinces, who began arriving around the seventeenth century. Those Chinese who arrived on Taiwan before WWII are often called "Taiwanese," to distinguish them from the nearly two million "mainlanders" who arrived on Taiwan after WWII with Chiang Kai-shek's Nationalist government.

1

Chinese fishermen visited Taiwan regularly for many centuries before much emigration occurred. During the Ming (1368–1644) and Qing (1644–1911) dynasties, Taiwan was a loosely governed outpost of China. The Chinese also sent several military expeditions to Taiwan over the centuries.

As the Europeans sailed into Chinese waters from about the 16th century, many caught sight of Taiwan. The Portuguese called the island "Ilha Formosa," or "Beautiful Island." The local Chinese dialect for the island was "Taiwan," or "Terraced Bay." The Portuguese, Spanish, and Dutch made several attempts to administer the island until 1661. During that year, a Ming leader driven from the mainland by the Qing settled on Taiwan, forcing the Dutch off the island. The Dutch called the Chinese leader "Koxinga." His Chinese name was Kuo Hsing Yeh. Although more than 100,000 Ming followers came to Taiwan, the Qing was finally able to gain control of the island in 1683.

For the next two hundred years the Qing tried to rule the island, but their administration was largely inefficient and the Chinese on Taiwan proved to be a rebellious lot. During this period, fifteen major anti-government insurrections occurred. Meanwhile, the island's commercial importance and population grew rapidly.

The British, Americans, and French tried to establish trading houses on Taiwan after 1842, dealing in opium, camphor, tea, and coal. Taiwan also exported considerable amounts of sugar and rice to the mainland. The increased Western interest in Taiwan caused the Qing to upgrade the island's status to that of province after 1884. The capital was moved from Tainan in the south to Taipei in the north. By 1895 Taiwan had a railway between the northern port of Keelung and Hsinchu, running through Taipei. Taiwan's living standard was considerably higher than that of the mainland.

As a result of its defeat in the 1894–1895 Sino-Japanese War, China ceded Taiwan and the Pescadores to Tokyo in the May 1895 Treaty of Shimonoseki. The Taiwanese attempted to resist the imposition of Japanese control, but they were defeated by military force. Subsequent insurrections by the Taiwanese were also put down, at times very harshly.

With the outbreak of the 1937 Sino-Japanese War, Japan went to extremes to eliminate all vestiges of Chinese culture on the island. All official business had to be carried out in Japanese. Although the Japanese did not prepare the Taiwanese for self-rule, they did provide stability and administrative efficiency which enabled Taiwan's economy to grow rapidly during the colonial period.

The Republic of China (ROC) on the mainland was an American ally during the Second World War. It was stipulated in the Cairo

Declaration of December 1, 1943, that Formosa and the Pescadores would be returned to the ROC following the war. This decision was reaffirmed in the Potsdam Proclamation of July 26, 1945.

As a result, Nationalist troops took over the administration of Taiwan from the Japanese in September 1945. Although Taiwan was heavily bombed by the United States during the final stages of the war, the Taiwanese generally welcomed the arriving Nationalist forces. The island was placed under martial law, however, and its administrator, General Chen Yi, systemically looted the island and mistreated the Taiwanese.

The situation came to a head in February 1947, when island-wide riots erupted over the killing of a local woman selling black-market cigarettes. After Nationalist reinforcements arrived from the mainland, large-scale executions of Taiwanese occurred. According to a report released February 22, 1992, by a special study group commissioned by the ROC government, between 18,000 and 28,000 Taiwanese were killed in suppressing the spontaneous uprising.

ROC President Chiang Kai-shek tried to rectify the situation by removing Chen Yi and most of his associates and by implementing reforms. These reforms intensified, particularly at the economic level, following Chiang's retreat to Taiwan in December 1949 with the remnants of his government and army. Nonetheless, the incident still plagues Taiwanese-mainlander relations, and the report cited above criticized Chiang for failing to punish properly officials responsible for the massacre.

It should be noted at this point that, while both Taiwanese and mainlanders are Han Chinese, there are cultural differences in addition to the normal linguistic differences characteristic of China's several provinces. Largely due to Taiwan's separation from the mainland by over 100 miles of ocean, and its fifty years of Japanese colonial rule, many Taiwanese believe they have a separate culture, although to most foreigners the similarities between the various "Chinese" cultures on Taiwan far exceed their dissimilarities.

Nonetheless, these differences between Taiwanese and mainlanders have contributed to feelings among many Taiwanese that the island ought to be a separate nation from the mainland. These feelings have been exacerbated by the harsh treatment of the Taiwanese by the mainlanders in the immediate post-WWII period, and mainlander discrimination against the Taiwanese in certain fields (especially government service and in the military and security forces) which has persisted until fairly recently. Mainlander-Taiwanese relations will be mentioned throughout the book, because it is one of the major challenges facing Taiwan with serious implications for both the PRC and the United States.

The United States and Taiwan

Although not always given high priority, Taiwan has been an issue in American policy toward East Asia for much of this century. It was partly in response to Japan's seizure of Taiwan from China in 1895 that the United States declared its "Open Door Policy" toward China in the 1899–1900 period. The primary U.S. interest at the time was to prevent the dismemberment of China into foreign-controlled spheres of influence so that American merchants would have equal opportunity in the lucrative China trade.

Later, during World War II, Taiwan was used by Japan as a major staging area for attacks against both the Chinese mainland and Southeast Asia, including the Philippines. Heavily bombed by the U.S., some thought was even given to an American invasion of the island.

During the Chinese civil war and WWII, neither the Nationalists nor the Communists paid much attention to Taiwan. Mao Zedong, for example, was quoted by Edgar Snow as saying in 1936 that Taiwan should be independent of both Japan and China. Mao said, "We will extend to them our enthusiastic help in their struggle for independence."[1]

The U.S. and the Chinese Civil War

In 1928 the U.S. became the first country to recognize Chiang Kai-shek's Nanjing government as the legitimate government of China. Later, after the bombing of Pearl Harbor and the formal U.S. entrance into WWII, the U.S. insisted that the Nationalist regime be considered one of the great Allied powers fighting the Axis coalition.

The principal U.S. interest in China during WWII was to have the Chinese tie down Japanese troops to prevent further aggression and to weaken Japan's deployments throughout the rest of Asia. This was part of an Allied grand strategy to focus first on defeating Germany while fighting a holding action against Japan in Asia. Partly to reward China for its sacrifices, the U.S. and other allied powers in the Cairo Declaration of December 1943 promised the ROC that Formosa (Taiwan) and the Pescadores would be returned to China at the conclusion of the war. With strong U.S. political support, the ROC became one of the five permanent members of the Security Council of the United Nations (UN), formed in June 1945.

In order to concentrate Chinese forces against the Japanese, the U.S. sought repeatedly throughout WWII to mediate differences between the Nationalists and the Chinese Communists. From the point of view of both Chiang and Mao, however, the Japanese invasion was doomed from the start because of the vast size of China and American involvement in the war. Hence, although the Nationalists and Chinese Communists devoted resources to fighting the Japanese, much of their energy was focused on preparing to defeat their domestic rival.

The Nationalists used their status as a formal ally to acquire increased American military support and to prevent such aid from going to the Communists. Due to KMT resistance, the first official U.S. mission to enter Communist controlled territory (the Dixie Mission) did not do so until July 1944. The Communists, on the other hand, stressed their willingness to fight the Japanese in a united front so they could receive U.S. arms and reduce KMT pressure on their positions. After years of frustration in being caught between the two Chinese sides, the United States in January 1945 declared that its policy was to support the ROC government and not to assist any other group.[2]

This decision was not supported by some Americans, however. Several "China-hands" within the U.S. Mission in China and State Department felt the Chiang regime was corrupt beyond redemption and would be unable to govern China after the war. They felt U.S. interests would be served best by maintaining friendly relations with the Communists or, at minimum, keeping U.S. policy options open by not allying too strongly with the Nationalists.

Ambassador Patrick J. Hurley in the spring of 1945 complained publicly that U.S. policy was being undermined from within the State Department by Communist sympathizers. Hurley painted Chiang as a defender of democracy and attributed China's problems to the Communists. Hurley's remarks set off a major U.S. political debate which lasted for decades.

The Nationalist government was an ally of the U.S., but not all American decisions in WWII were beneficial to the ROC. In secret portions of the February 1945 Yalta agreement the U.S. ceded Outer Mongolia to the Soviet Union, along with strategic ports and railroads in Manchuria, in exchange for Moscow's promise to enter the war against Japan. The Manchurian agreement proved costly to the Nationalists, as the Soviets stripped the province of its industrial equipment and turned over vast amounts of captured Japanese arms to the Chinese Communists.

Immediately following WWII, the primary U.S. interests in China were to stabilize the country under a non-Communist government and to prevent China from falling under a Soviet sphere of influence. To this end, the U.S. continued its mediation efforts between the Nationalists and Communists. A brief truce was arranged between the two sides in October 1945, but fighting soon resumed.

In November President Harry S. Truman appointed General George C. Marshall as his special representative to China. Marshall negotiated yet another series of truces in early 1946, but they, too, were broken. Marshall tried unsuccessfully to convince Chiang that a military victory was impossible and that the only way to bring peace to China was through a negotiated settlement with the Communists. To pressure Chiang to accept such a settlement, Marshall even suspended for a time the export to the ROC of U.S. combat equipment which could be used in the civil war. Finally admitting defeat in his mediation efforts, Marshall left China in January 1947 and was named Secretary of State. Marshall reported that the breakdown in KMT-CCP negotiations had been caused by mutual suspicion and radicals on both sides.

Rising concern in the U.S. about possible Soviet domination of Asia and the growing success of the Chinese Communist military campaigns eclipsed further U.S. attempts to mediate a peaceful solution. Instead, policy debates in the U.S. centered on how to assist the Nationalists. In July 1947 Truman sent General Albert C. Wedemeyer to assess what could be done to rescue the Chiang government. Wedemeyer criticized the corruption and inefficiency of the Nationalists, but said that the U.S. should increase its support to the ROC because it would not be in U.S. interests to disengage from China and see it taken over by the Communists.

This recommendation was accepted by the Truman administration, but it was diluted into a policy of providing minimal assistance both to prevent the collapse of the ROC government and to deflect domestic criticism of the President's China policy. American military intervention was considered out of the question, and the last U.S. Marines began to pull out in June 1947.

In 1948 the Nationalists suffered repeated military defeat as the Communists annihilated crack ROC divisions in Manchuria and other parts of Northern China. Chiang pleaded for greater U.S. military and economic assistance, but the Truman administration concluded that the estimated $5 billion cost to rescue the Nationalists would be too high, even if it were properly utilized. The ROC had received more than $2.5 billion in U.S. aid since World War II, but Chiang had not been attentive to American advisers. Only direct U.S. military intervention might save the ROC, and this the U.S. was unwilling (and probably unable) to do.[3]

On the brink of disaster, in January 1949 the Nationalists once again appealed to the U.S. and other western governments, this time to mediate peace with the Communists. The U.S. refused to become involved, and the Communists announced in any case that they intended to finish the fight rather than negotiate. Beijing fell that month. The Yangtze River (Chang Jiang) was crossed in April; Nanjing, Wuhan, and Shanghai fell in April and May. On October 1, 1949, Mao announced the establishment of the People's Republic of China with Beijing as its capital. Later that month Canton fell, and Chongqing fell in November. In late December Chiang Kai-shek joined the tattered remnants of his military and government which had arrived on Taiwan a few months previously.

In the face of this catastrophe, acrimonious debate broke out in the U.S. over who was at fault for the "loss" of China. The State Department blamed the loss on inefficiency within the Chiang government. Secretary of State Dean Acheson wrote in a letter of transmittal accompanying the State Department's White Paper on China policy: "The ominous result of the civil war in China was beyond the control of the government of the United States. Nothing that this country did or could have done within the reasonable limits of its capabilities could have changed that result; nothing that was left undone by this country contributed to it."[4] The White Paper set off a storm of controversy in the Congress, where some Republicans called it a "whitewash of a wishful, do-nothing policy."[5]

The initial reaction of the Truman administration to the collapse of the Nationalist government was to distance itself completely from the ROC and to remain indifferent to an expected imminent Communist attack on Taiwan. Two weeks after Chiang established his new headquarters in Taipei, the State Department cabled American embassies worldwide that Taiwan was expected to fall under the Communists and that Taiwan held "no special military significance" to U.S. security.[6] On December 29, 1949, the newly formed National Security Council decided that "no further action would be taken to assist the Chinese Nationalists to hold Formosa."[7] A few days later, on January 5, 1950, President Truman announced that the U.S. would "not provide military aid or advice to Chinese forces" on Taiwan.[8]

On January 12, 1950, Secretary of State Acheson delivered a famous speech defending the administration's China policy before the National Press Club in Washington. In describing future policy toward Asia, the Secretary declared that the U.S. would be prepared to defend a line running from the Aleutian Islands through Japan and the Ryukyu Islands, thence to the Philippines. Excluded were the Korean peninsula and Taiwan, although the Secretary did say that the defense of these and other areas outside the defined line would depend, first, on the people themselves and, second, on the international community as expressed through the United Nations.

Meanwhile, the administration sent several signals to the PRC that it would consider exchanging diplomatic recognition. This plan, however, was set back because of congressional opposition to recognition of the PRC and Chinese Communist ill-treatment of American diplomats in China.

The Korean War and Taiwan's Role in Containment

Congressional recriminations against the Truman administration were overshadowed dramatically on June 25, 1950, when North Korea launched a surprise invasion of South Korea. Two days later, prompted by concerns that the Korean War might expand and that Beijing might use Taiwan to threaten the U.S. position in Japan, Truman sent the Seventh Fleet into the Taiwan Strait. At the same time, the President authorized military aid to be sent to the Nationalists. Truman viewed the U.S. intervention to be temporary until peace was restored on the Korean peninsula.

Truman's decision to interpose the Seventh Fleet between Taiwan and China was a crucial turning point in U.S. policy, because he reversed U.S. policy of not intervening in the Chinese civil war and instead sought to neutralize military confrontations between the Chinese Communists and the Nationalists. The PRC viewed the U.S. action as an act of aggression against China. But Taipei understandably saw the American action as giving a "second chance" to the Nationalists.

With the outbreak of the Korean War, Taiwan became important to protect the southern flank of U.S. war efforts in Northeast Asia. In fact, some within the U.S. government had argued this point for some time, but they had been overruled in the National Security Council.[9]

The sensitivity of the Taiwan issue was heightened by public condemnation of the Truman administration for having "lost" China and "abandoned" the Nationalists, as well as by oft-quoted statements by the popular General Douglas MacArthur stressing the strategic importance of Taiwan to U.S. interests in the Far East. It was in fact MacArthur's public arguments in favor of expanding the war to the Chinese mainland, including the use of Nationalists troops, that led to his dismissal by Truman in April 1951.

The Truman administration tried to walk a delicate policy line, hoping, despite the intervention of Chinese forces into the Korean conflict, that a way could be found to draw the Chinese away from an alliance with the Soviet Union. To achieve this strategic objective, the Truman administration was willing to limit or even give up its support for Chiang Kai-shek on Taiwan. However, neither the Chinese

Communists nor the political climate in the U.S. permitted such a policy to bear fruit. Because of the desire to achieve this strategic objective, yet the impossibility of doing so under conditions then prevailing, the Truman administration could conceive of no solution for the Taiwan issue which would serve U.S. interests. The State Department said in late 1951, there was "no presently achievable solution for the disposition of Formosa which will satisfy United States policy objectives."[10]

In the 1952 presidential campaign, the Republicans under Dwight D. Eisenhower pursued a tough anti-communist theme and won both the presidency and the two Houses of Congress. President Eisenhower announced in his first State of the Union address that the Seventh Fleet no longer would prevent the Nationalists from attacking the mainland. This announcement, coupled with his July 1953 threat to use nuclear weapons against China, were probably instrumental in convincing Beijing to sign a July 27, 1953, armistice ending the Korean War.

Unlike the Truman administration, Eisenhower deliberately pursued a strategy of pressuring the PRC in order to break Beijing away from its alliance with Moscow and, ultimately, to end communist rule on mainland China.

Under such a strategy, Taiwan assumed great importance as a lever against the PRC, as well as a potential base of military operations against China. Thus, as a result of the Korean War and the ensuing strategy of pressuring China, Taiwan became an important element of U.S. rimland strategy to contain communism in Asia for the next two decades.

U.S. policy was complicated, however, by Chiang Kai-shek's refusal to give up his claims of one day returning to the mainland. Moreover, he insisted that he would defend the small offshore islands of Kinmen (Quemoy) and Matsu, just a mile off the Fujian coast. Such a defense was necessary in Chiang's opinion because it sustained the legitimacy of the ROC claim to be the legal government of China, not just Taiwan. But the U.S. did not want to risk a war with China over small islands in imminent danger of attack.

The matter was brought to a head in September 1954, when the PRC launched a heavy bombardment of Quemoy. This prompted the Eisenhower administration to bring the ROC formally into the U.S. collective security system. In December 1954 the two countries signed the U.S.-ROC Mutual Defense Treaty, giving the U.S. "the right to dispose such land, air and sea forces in and about Taiwan and the Pescadores as may be required for their defense." In an exchange of notes in January 1955, Taipei assured Washington that it would not attack the mainland without prior consultation.

The ROC territory defined under the Mutual Defense Treaty included the islands of Taiwan and the Pescadores (Penghu), but did not include the offshore islands of Quemoy and Matsu. The U.S. attempted repeatedly, always unsuccessfully, to convince Chiang to abandon the offshore islands.

In practice, the U.S. viewed PRC attacks against Quemoy and Matsu as preparatory to an attack against Taiwan itself. Other offshore islands, such as the Ta-chen Islands further north, were not considered essential to the defense of Taiwan and were abandoned by the Nationalists with U.S. logistical support. On January 29, 1955, largely in response to PRC attacks on the Ta-chens, Congress passed the Formosa Resolution giving the President the authority to defend Quemoy and Matsu if he felt it necessary for the security of Taiwan and the Pescadores. American support was given to the ROC during the Quemoy crises of 1954–1955, 1958, and 1962. In the 1955 crisis, the U.S. threatened the PRC with tactical nuclear weapons. In all cases, however, the U.S. was careful not to engage directly PRC military units and to avoid the impression that it was supporting a ROC invasion of the mainland.

As part of its strategy to pressure the PRC, Washington increased political, economic, and military ties to Taiwan. Politically, the U.S. supported ROC representation in the UN and opposed that of the PRC. From 1951 to 1971 annual resolutions against Beijing's admission into the United Nations were adopted by the U.S. Congress. Total U.S. aid to the ROC from 1949 exceeded $5.9 billion, including $1.7 billion in economic assistance and $4.2 billion in military assistance. The United States ended economic assistance to Taiwan in 1965 and phased out military aid in the mid-1970s.

Nixon and China

Prior to the Vietnam War, the U.S. considered its relations with Taiwan to be essential to American objectives to contain China. By the war's conclusion, the U.S. had come to view friendly relations with the PRC as a strategic asset in U.S.-Soviet competition. This was also an era in which the U.S. attempted to pursue a "two Chinas" policy recognizing both Beijing and Taipei as legitimate governments of two separate nations. President Richard Nixon wrote in his memoirs that as late as August 1971 "we had . . . indicated our support of the concept of the 'two Chinas,' Chiang Kai-shek's Republic of China on Taiwan and the communist People's Republic of China, each to have membership" in the United Nations.[11] But when the suggestion of "two Chinas" was raised to the Chiang government, the ROC rejected the idea. The PRC, as well, was firmly against the concept.

One of Nixon's first decisions as president was to direct his National Security Adviser Henry Kissinger to review possible rapprochement with the PRC. For its own reasons, primarily the growing Soviet threat to China's borders, Beijing, too, was willing to consider improved relations with Washington in the 1968–1969 period.

Despite serious disagreements over Taiwan, both the U.S. and the PRC decided to make the issue secondary and to concentrate instead on mutual strategic interests. In November 1969 the U.S. ended its regular Seventh Fleet patrol of the Taiwan Strait. The Chinese demonstrated their willingness to improve relations by meeting secretly with Kissinger in China in July 1971, and then by inviting Nixon to visit the PRC. Kissinger returned to Beijing in October 1971, at the same time that the UN General Assembly voted to seat the PRC as the legitimate government of China. The head of the U.S. delegation at the time was George Bush. As a result of the UN vote and clear trends toward improved U.S.-PRC relations, many nations switched diplomatic recognition from Taipei to Beijing.

During Nixon's February 1972 trip to China, Mao Zedong, Zhou Enlai, Deng Xiaoping, and other Chinese leaders conveyed the impression that the Taiwan issue could wait a considerable length of time before resolution. Kissinger wrote in his memoirs:

> [Mao] delicately placed the issue of Taiwan on a subsidiary level, choosing to treat it as a relatively minor internal Chinese dispute; he did not even mention our military presence there. . . . Neither then, nor in any subsequent meeting, did Mao indicate any impatience over Taiwan, set any time limits, make any threats, or treat it as the touchstone of our relationship. 'We can do without them for the time being, and let it come after 100 years.' 'Why such great haste?' 'This issue is not an important one. The issue of the international situation is an important one.' 'The small issue is Taiwan, the big issue is the world.' These were Mao's thoughts on Taiwan as expressed to us on many visits. (These were also the views of Zhou Enlai and Deng Xiaoping.) But Mao, like Zhou and Deng, spent very little time in our talks on this issue.[12]

The true importance of the Taiwan issue to the PRC became apparent at the end of Nixon's trip, when both sides tried to find mutually acceptable language for a joint communiqué. After several days of intense negotiations, a formula was worked out whereby the two sides agreed to disagree by setting forth their respective positions without any attempt at compromise. In important statements of policy which remain at the bedrock of Sino-American understanding on the Taiwan issue today, the February 28, 1972, Shanghai Communiqué read:

> The Chinese side reaffirmed its position: The Taiwan question is the crucial question obstructing the normalization of relations between China and the United States; the Government of the People's Republic of China is the sole legal government of China; Taiwan is a province of China which has long been returned to the motherland; the liberation of Taiwan is China's internal affair in which no other country has the right to interfere; and all U.S. forces and military installations must be withdrawn from Taiwan. The Chinese Government firmly opposes any activities which aim at the creation of "one China, one Taiwan," "one China, two governments" or advocate that "the status of Taiwan remains to be determined."
>
> ‒   The U.S. side declared: The United States acknowledges that all Chinese on either side of the Taiwan Strait maintain there is but one China and that Taiwan is a part of China. The United States Government does not challenge that position. It reaffirms its interests in a peaceful settlement of the Taiwan question by the Chinese themselves. With this prospect in mind, it affirms the ultimate objective of the withdrawal of all U.S. forces and military installations from Taiwan. In the meantime, it will progressively reduce its forces and military installations on Taiwan as the tension in the area diminishes.

In February 1973 the U.S. and PRC established liaison offices in each other's capitals and gave officials serving there diplomatic immunities and privileges. The intended normalization of Sino-American relations during Nixon's second term in office was prevented, however, by political problems in both countries and by the difficulty in finding an acceptable solution to the Taiwan issue.

Carter and the Normalization of Sino-American Relations

In the spring of 1973 Deng Xiaoping announced three conditions for the normalization of relations with the United States: (1) termination of official U.S. relations with the Republic of China; (2) termination of the 1954 U.S.-ROC Mutual Defense Treaty; and (3) withdrawal of American troops and military installations from Taiwan.

These demands were unacceptable to presidents Nixon and Gerald Ford, but Jimmy Carter entered the White House determined to establish diplomatic relations with China.[13] For mostly strategic reasons, the Chinese were thinking along the same lines. The geopolitical pressures to normalize Sino-American relations increased in January 1978 when Vietnam invaded eastern Cambodia, China's ally, in response to a previous Khmer Rouge attack against Vietnam's Tay Ninh Province. By April Vietnam and China were clashing along their common border. The Soviet Union also began to deploy more modern weapons along the Sino-Soviet border, including SS-20 mobile intermediate range ballistic missiles.

It discussions leading up to normalization of relations, the United States did not press the Chinese for a pledge of nonuse of force against Taiwan. The U.S. did, however, state its intention to continue supplying defensive arms to Taipei. Carter also informed the Chinese that the United States would maintain the Mutual Defense Treaty with Taiwan until it was terminated according to its provisions. He further insisted that Beijing not contradict U.S. statements that the Taiwan issue should be settled peacefully and with patience.

The Communist Party Central Committee met in late November 1978 to consider Carter's proposal for normalization. Two other key issues were on the agenda: the final consolidation of Deng Xiaoping's control over China's modernization and possible military action against Vietnam. In December the PRC softened its rhetoric directed toward Taipei by calling for "peaceful reunification" instead of "liberation."

During Deng Xiaoping's visit to the United States in January 1979, he said two circumstances would cause the PRC not to resolve the Taiwan issue peacefully and with patience: an extended period of no negotiation and Soviet bases on Taiwan.[14]

On December 15, 1978, the United States and the People's Republic of China announced they would exchange diplomatic recognition on January 1, 1979. The official U.S. statement accompanying the joint communiqué said that "as of January 1, 1979, the United States of America recognizes the People's Republic of China as the sole legal government of China." On the same date, the document continued, the U.S. would terminate diplomatic relations with the ROC, give the required one year's notice of termination of the Mutual Defense Treaty, and withdraw remaining American military personnel from the island.

Regarding U.S. relations with Taiwan, the statement explained: "In the future, the American people and the people of Taiwan will maintain commercial, cultural, and other relations without official government representation and without diplomatic relations." To accomplish this, the administration would seek necessary changes in existing law. Regarding the future of Taiwan, the statement said: "The United States continues to have an interest in the peaceful resolution of the Taiwan issue and expects that the Taiwan issue will be settled peacefully by the Chinese themselves."

In its official statement, the PRC expressed confidence that the Taiwan issue had been resolved in principle, but it refused to rule out the use of force as a means of bringing Taiwan back to the control of the mainland.

Taiwan Relations Act

While generally in favor of normalized relations with Beijing, Congress was displeased by the Carter administration's decision to abrogate the U.S.-ROC Mutual Defense Treaty without prior consultation, a request written into the 1979 security aid authorization bill signed by Carter in September 1978. In its hearings on draft legislation submitted by the Carter administration to handle future relations with Taiwan, Congress voiced major concern over the administration's lack of attention to the PRC threat to Taiwan.[15] Over administration objections, Congress rewrote major portions of the legislation in ways favorable to Taiwan. S. 245/H.R. 2479 was passed by more than two-thirds vote of both Houses in late March 1979, and President Carter signed the Taiwan Relations Act (TRA) into law on April 10.

In the absence of diplomatic relations and the Mutual Defense Treaty, the TRA has become the principal legal framework for U.S.-Taiwan relations. The TRA specifically links the future of Taiwan with U.S. security interests in East Asia. Section 2 of the Act states: "The Congress finds that the enactment of this Act is necessary . . . to help maintain peace, security, and stability in the Western Pacific." Section 2 further states that U.S. policy in the Western Pacific is designed:

   (1) to preserve and promote extensive, close, and friendly commercial, cultural, and other relations between the people of the United States and the people on Taiwan, as well as the people on the China mainland and all other peoples of the Western Pacific area;
   (2) to declare that peace and stability in the area are in the political, security, and economic interests of the United States, and are matters of international concern;
   (3) to make clear that the United States decision to establish diplomatic relations with the People's Republic of China rests upon the expectation that the future of Taiwan will be determined by peaceful means;
   (4) to consider any effort to determine the future of Taiwan by other than peaceful means, including by boycotts or embargoes, a threat to the peace and security of the Western Pacific area and of grave concern to the United States;
   (5) to provide Taiwan with arms of a defensive character; and

(6) to maintain the capacity of the United States to resist any resort to force or other forms of coercion that would jeopardize the security, or the social or economic system, of the people on Taiwan.

Section 3 of the Taiwan Relations Act gives specific instructions on the implementation of the above policy. Especially important are the provisions for arms sales to Taiwan:

(1) In furtherance of the policy set forth in section 2 of this Act, the United States will make available to Taiwan such defense articles and defense services in such quantity as may be necessary to enable Taiwan to maintain a sufficient self-defense capability.

(2) The President and the Congress shall determine the nature and quantity of such defense articles and services based solely upon their judgment of the needs of Taiwan, in accordance with procedures established by law. Such determination of Taiwan's defense needs shall include review by United States military authorities in connection with recommendations to the President and the Congress.

(3) The President is directed to inform the Congress promptly of any threat to the security or the social or economic system of the people on Taiwan and any danger to the interests of the United States arising therefrom. The President and the Congress shall determine, in accordance with constitutional processes, appropriate action by the United States in response to any such danger.

Although the TRA was in many respects more specific than the 1954 Mutual Defense Treaty in stating how threats to Taiwan would be against U.S. interests, the PRC reaction to the law was initially muted. This was probably due to President Carter's promise to implement the TRA in a way consistent with the normalization communiqué. The President also imposed a one-year moratorium on arms sales to Taiwan.

The strategic environment in Asia at the time—the Vietnamese occupation of Cambodia in December 1978; the retaliatory Chinese incursion into northern Vietnam in February 1979; increased Soviet access to Cam Ranh Bay shortly thereafter; and the Soviet invasion of Afghanistan in December 1979—was so threatening to U.S. and Chinese security interests that both governments largely ignored Taiwan for a period and focused on solidifying their new relationship. During 1979, Deng Xiaoping openly called for a "united front" between China, Japan, Europe, and the United States to counter Soviet hegemony.[16]

Since the Soviet Union was the principal enemy of the U.S. and the sole country able to threaten U.S. national survival, strategic planners in Washington diligently pursued Deng's tantalizing offer. In this larger geopolitical calculation, Taiwan seemed to lose importance to U.S. interests. There was considerable willingness to narrow U.S. commitments to Taipei in order to secure Beijing's strategic cooperation. This "strategic imperative" even persisted during the first two years of the politically conservative Reagan administration, when a number of concessions were made regarding arms sales to Taiwan.

The PRC Pressures Reagan

President Ronald Reagan came into office in January 1981 on a sour note insofar as Sino-American relations were concerned. In his campaign speeches, Reagan had called U.S. relations with Taiwan "official" and had promised to implement the TRA without the Carter proviso that implementation would be carried out in accordance with the normalization agreement with the PRC. Moreover, the President and many of his top aides were known to be much more friendly toward Taipei than toward the communist regime in Beijing.

The PRC believed that Reagan might undo some of the progress made in Sino-American relations under Carter. This concern seems to have led to a PRC determination to "teach a lesson" to Reagan by pressuring his administration. China did this by threatening to downgrade Sino-American relations, thought strategically important by the new administration because of its overriding concern with the Soviet threat, if U.S. arms sales to Taiwan continued.[17]

The PRC was able to adopt this bargaining strategy because it was in the process of downgrading its assessment of the immediate Soviet threat to China. At the same time, the U.S. was becoming more determined to counter the Soviet Union. One of the best pieces of evidence of this PRC reassessment of the strategic balance of power is a December 1983 statement by Huan Xiang, then director of China's Institute for International Affairs. In response to questions from *Der Spiegel* as to why China was pursuing an "independent" foreign policy in 1983 when in 1979 Deng had been calling for "coordinated measures" with the U.S. against Moscow, Huan explained:

> What has changed is the international situation. In the early seventies the Soviet Union had very strongly expanded toward the outside militarily and had become a threat to everybody. For this reason China offered cooperation to each state that felt threatened by the Soviet Union.
> Near the end of the Carter administration's term and at the beginning of the term of the Reagan administration, the Americans determinedly and energetically put up a front against the Soviet Union politically and militarily in the struggle for superiority in nuclear armament, in the

matter of the European intermediate range weapons, in the Caribbean region, in the Middle East and, finally, also in Asia. This stopped the Soviet Union, and the rivalry of the two superpowers considerably intensified throughout the world. It seems that the Russians still do not feel strong enough to react to the U.S. offensive. In our view, a certain balance between the two has emerged, especially in the military field.[18]

Because of the strong U.S. response to Soviet hegemony following the invasion of Afghanistan, China no longer had to be in the forefront of anti-Soviet united front activity. The U.S. assumed this activist role. As the U.S. strengthened its deterrent posture in Asia to counter the Soviets, the PRC found it enjoyed increased diplomatic flexibility since both superpowers wanted to solidify their relations with Beijing in order to concentrate on Soviet-American rivalries. This gave the PRC an advantageous bargaining position in the "strategic triangle," particularly on bilateral issues such as Taiwan.

This reassessment of the balance of power between the U.S. and the USSR also led to China's determination, announced formally at the 12th Party Congress in September 1982 by General Secretary Hu Yaobang, to pursue improved relations with the USSR as part of a new "independent" foreign policy.[19]

The PRC took advantage of U.S. and Soviet rivalries to improve relations with Beijing to strengthen China's bargaining position over "obstacles" in Sino-Soviet and Sino-American relations. In the case of the Soviet Union, China demanded concessions on the "three obstacles" as the price for normalization of relations.[20] In the case of the U.S., China demanded concessions on U.S. relations with Taiwan, particularly arms sales.

The Reagan administration was unaware of this shift in PRC strategic perceptions. Determined to counter the growing Soviet threat, the new administration pursued a strategic relationship with the PRC even more vigorously than the Carter administration. Because of its preoccupation with the Soviet Union and misreading of PRC intentions, the Reagan administration made significant concessions to Beijing over Taiwan. Most notable of these were the 1982 decisions not to sell Taiwan the FX replacement fighter and to sign the August 17 U.S.-PRC Joint Communiqué limiting future weapons transfers to Taipei.

The FX Fighter Issue

In June 1980 the U.S. government permitted Northrop and General Dynamics to go to Taiwan to discuss the sale of their versions of a new fighter, the so-called "FX." The FX was designed by both companies with Taiwan specifically in mind. Taipei wanted to modernize its air force with purchases from the U.S., but nothing in the U.S. inventory was thought to be suitable. Washington did not want to sell Taipei weapons posing an offensive threat to the PRC for fear of jeopardizing Sino-American relations. Consequently, the Department of Defense and State Department approached Northrop and asked that company to design a new air defense fighter with limited range and ground attack capability for export to Taiwan and similar countries.

Northrop designed the F-5G (or F-20, as it later became known) as a follow-on model to the F-5E/F fighters it coproduced on Taiwan. The F-5G sale was approved in principle by both the Department of Defense and Department of State, but the sale was delayed because Congress decided to give General Dynamics an opportunity to compete for the potentially lucrative contract. General Dynamics' version of the FX, the F-16-J79, was a lower performance version of the U.S. Air Force's front line fighter, the F-16.

The PRC interpreted U.S. efforts to sell an advanced fighter to Taiwan as a serious threat to Beijing's efforts to isolate and weaken Taipei and force it into reunification on terms favoring the PRC. Beijing feared that if Taiwan acquired the new interceptor, it would delay reunification indefinitely by means of the island's enhanced deterrent capabilities. Air superiority had long been identified as the key to Taiwan's security, and the FX would give Taipei that superiority for at least ten years.

Concerned that the Reagan administration would sell the FX and other advanced weapons such as the antiship Harpoon missile to Taiwan, PRC leaders threatened to downgrade Sino-American relations unless Washington changed its arms sales policy. The Reagan administration was caught on the horns of a dilemma. It wanted to expand Sino-American strategic cooperation against the Soviet Union, but the administration's conservative political base was strongly in favor of the FX sale.

After months of intense lobbying and internal debate, the issue was finally decided in January 1982, when the State Department announced that "no sale of advanced fighter aircraft to Taiwan is required because no military need for such aircraft exists."[21] The administration did promise, however, to extend the F-5E/F coproduction line on Taiwan for additional aircraft.

The administration hoped the FX decision would mollify the Chinese and lead to increased strategic cooperation. However, the PRC seemed angry over the F-5E/F coproduction extension and mounted even greater pressure for a resolution of the arms sales issue. Shortly after the January 1982 announcement, the U.S. and the PRC began several months of very difficult negotiations over what became the August 17, 1982, U.S.-PRC Joint Communiqué on arms sales to Taiwan.

August 17 Communiqué

As word leaked out that an agreement limiting future arms sales to Taiwan was being negotiated, U.S. supporters of Taiwan began to raise loud objections. Coming on the heels of the administration's refusal to sell the FX, such an agreement was seen to be a sell-out of Taiwan. Details of the negotiations were kept secret, so rumors of the talks had the effect of fueling even greater suspicions among Taiwan's friends.

In early July 1982 the *Washington Times* reported that the State Department had prepared at least two versions of a secret communiqué limiting future arms sales to Taiwan. Senator Barry Goldwater, a leading supporter of Taiwan in the Congress, asked the State Department about the versions. He was told no such drafts had been prepared. The White House also queried the State Department and received a similar response.

Later, it was found that the State Department had indeed secretly prepared the draft communiqués. As Goldwater commented when all of this became public: "It was clear to me and to the White House that President Reagan, Vice President Bush, and National Security Adviser William Clark had been lied to by the State Department about what they were planning."[22] The withholding of information about the communiqué drafts directly influenced the timing of Alexander Haig's resignation as Secretary of State.

Conservatives were outraged at what they considered to be, once again, the State Department's manipulation of U.S. China policy to the detriment of the ROC.[23] At this point, President Reagan personally intervened to ensure that no further compromise to the Chinese would be made on the arms sales issue, particularly on a specific cutoff date.

On July 14 the administration gave several key assurances to Taipei. As described in the official ROC statement on the August 17 Communiqué, Washington told Taiwan that the U.S.:

    1. has not agreed to set a date for ending arms sales to the Republic of China,

    2. has not agreed to hold prior consultations with the Chinese communists on arms sales to the Republic of China,

    3. will not play any mediation role between Taipei and Peiping,

    4. has not agreed to revise the Taiwan Relations Act,

    5. has not altered its position regarding sovereignty over Taiwan,

6. will not exert pressure on the Republic of China to enter into negotiations with the Chinese communists.

The administration took several other steps to bring the issue to closure: it publicly announced its intention to proceed with the sale to Taiwan of the additional F-5Es promised in place of the FX; it proposed to China an agreement containing assurances that in the future it would not sell Taiwan weapons of higher quantity or quality than those sold in the past; and the President and his top advisers told key congressional supporters that the assurances given Beijing were deliberately vague in order to give the U.S. the freedom to adjust its mix of arms sales in the future to allow for inflation, technological advances, and increased threats from the mainland.[24]

Beijing twice rejected the new proposal, but when it became apparent that the U.S. would sell the F-5Es regardless of whether an agreement had been signed, China accepted.

The August 17 Communiqué contained important language which affected U.S. relations with Taiwan. In paragraph five the United States, after emphasizing the importance it attaches to Sino-American relations, reiterated that "it has no intention of infringing on Chinese sovereignty and territorial integrity, or interfering in China's internal affairs, or pursuing a policy of 'two Chinas' or 'one China, one Taiwan'." The U.S. said that it "understands and appreciates" China's fundamental policy of "striving for a peaceful resolution of the Taiwan question." Because of China's policy of peaceful reunification, the U.S. noted that a "new situation . . . has emerged with regard to the Taiwan question" which created an environment in which the arms sales issue might be resolved.

Paragraph six contained substantive and controversial commitments by the U.S. It stated:

> Having in mind the foregoing statements of both sides, the United States Government states that it does not seek to carry out a long-term policy of arms sales to Taiwan, that its arms sales to Taiwan will not exceed, either in qualitative or in quantitative terms, the level of those supplied in recent years since the establishment of diplomatic relations between the United States and China, and that it intends to reduce gradually its sales of arms to Taiwan, leading over a period of time to a final resolution.

In an important explanation of the U.S. interpretation of the ambiguously worded communiqué, Assistant Secretary of State John Holdridge told Congress that the U.S. agreement to limit future arms sales to Taiwan was predicated on the continuation of China's peaceful approach to reunification. He said:

> Let me summarize the essence of our understanding on this point: China has announced a fundamental policy of pursuing peaceful means to resolve the long-standing dispute between Taiwan and the mainland. Having in mind this policy and the consequent reduction in the military threat to Taiwan, we have stated our intention to reduce arms sales to Taiwan gradually, and said that in quantity and quality we would not go beyond levels established since normalization. . . . While we have no reason to believe that China's policy will change, an inescapable corollary to these mutually interdependent policies is that should that happen, we will reassess ours. Our guiding principle is now and will continue to be that embodied in the Taiwan Relations Act: the maintenance of a self-defense capability sufficient to meet the military needs of Taiwan, but with the understanding that China's maintenance of a peaceful approach to the Taiwan question will permit gradual reductions in arms sales.[25]

Questions immediately arose over whether the August 17 Communiqué would take legal precedence over the Taiwan Relations Act, which in Section 3(1) conditioned U.S. arms sales to those "necessary to enable Taiwan to maintain a sufficient self-defense capability." State Department Legal Advisor Davis Robinson explained to the Senate Judiciary Committee on September 27 that the TRA would remain the law of the land. He said:

> [The August 17 Communiqué] is not an international agreement and thus imposes no obligations on either party under international law. Its status under domestic law is that of a statement by the President of a policy which he intends to pursue. . . . The Taiwan Relations Act is and will remain the law of the land unless amended by Congress. Nothing in the joint communiqué obligates the President to act in a manner contrary to the Act or, conversely, disables him from fulfilling his responsibilities under it.[26]

Thus, the Reagan administration attempted to minimize the damage done to Taiwan's security by the August 17 Communiqué by interpreting the agreement as lacking precedence over the TRA and by linking future arms sales to the continuation of China's policy of peaceful reunification. More practically, the administration sold Taiwan adequate military equipment to limit the immediate adverse effects of the communiqué. Details of these sales will be discussed in Chapter 5.

Sino-American Relations in the Post-Communiqué Period

Despite significant differences in U.S. and PRC interpretations of the August 17 Communiqué, the agreement had the effect of enabling both sides to back away from harsh rhetoric and to concentrate on more pragmatic policies. After the communiqué, the U.S. adopted a more realistic assessment of China's value to U.S. interests, particularly the limitations inherent in Sino-American strategic cooperation.

The U.S. began to pursue policies which earlier were rejected on the grounds they might damage U.S.-PRC relations. This included substantial arms sales and technology transfers to Taiwan, as well as serious disagreements with the PRC over several issues. During the 1983–1986 period, these included disagreements over human rights violations in Tibet, nuclear technology transfers to Pakistan, arms sales to Iran, quotas imposed on China's textile exports to the U.S., and U.S. advanced technology transfers to the PRC.

The August 17 Communiqué also cleared the way for a more "normal" U.S. relationship with Taiwan. The Reagan administration was careful to couch its contacts with Taipei within the confines of the three U.S.-PRC communiqués and the TRA, but within those parameters substantial flexibility existed. The administration generally exercised that flexibility to the benefit of Taiwan. Washington extended diplomatic privileges to Taiwan's representatives, established separate immigration quotas for Taiwan residents, signed numerous executive agreements covering a broad range of what normally would be considered state-to-state relations, often supported Taipei's participation in international organizations and events, maintained an informal but high level dialogue with Taiwan officials, and promoted ever broader commercial relations with Taiwan.

Policy Reviews on China's Reunification in 1985 and 1986

Despite the friendly relationship between Washington and Taipei, there were substantive reviews of U.S. policy toward Taiwan during 1985 and 1986. In particular it was asked whether the U.S. should assume a more active role in assisting the reunification of China.

The issue was first raised by Deng Xiaoping, who sent a message to Ronald Reagan through British Prime Minister Margaret Thatcher following her signing in Beijing of the U.K.-PRC Agreement on the future of Hong Kong in December 1984. The message requested that the U.S. "do something" to further contact between the mainland and Taiwan.

Prior to the signing of the Hong Kong Agreement, there was little consideration given in the United States to playing a role in China's reunification. Taipei was firmly against U.S. involvement; Beijing's focus was on stopping U.S. interference through the repeal or revision of the Taiwan Relations Act and curtailing arms sales to Taiwan; and Washington could see no advantage or moral justification in nudging Taipei into closer contact with the PRC.

But the signing of the Hong Kong Agreement introduced a new element in policy debates in the U.S. By making it clear that the Hong Kong settlement was intended to be a model for Taiwan and by demonstrating an arguably sincere effort to preserve Hong Kong's way of life after 1997 through the "one country, two systems" formula, the PRC strengthened its image of flexibility and pragmatism on the Taiwan issue in the eyes of some U.S. officials.

Thus, when China approached the U.S. in early 1985 to ask for its assistance to resolve the Taiwan issue, there was a willingness to examine U.S. policy to see if indeed something could be done to remove this long-term problem in U.S.-PRC relations.

During the ensuing policy discussions, arguments were advanced both for involvement and noninvolvement in China's reunification. Arguments supporting U.S. involvement often stressed the timeliness of reunification. Ageing leaders on both sides, particularly Deng Xiaoping and Chiang Ching-kuo, were thought to share a vision of one China and to possess the necessary political power to make the concessions required to achieve a peaceful, workable reunification. Also, in the case of the mainland, the PRC had embarked on a path of pragmatic economic modernization which made Beijing appear more flexible in working out reunification arrangements with Taipei.

In the case of Taiwan, the emergence of a native Taiwanese political force on the island made a settlement of the reunification issue more urgent. Mainlanders on Taiwan believed in "one China," but the possibility existed of a Taiwanese-dominated government deciding to pursue independence at some time in the future. Moreover, East Asia was peaceful at the time, both Chinas were stable politically, and the PRC and ROC economies were strong. Some in Washington felt the PRC would do almost anything to solve the Taiwan issue, if only Taipei would accept the PRC's sovereignty and fly the PRC flag. It was thought that a unique opportunity was presenting itself for Washington to help resolve the Taiwan issue in such a way as to improve relations with China without sacrificing ties to Taiwan or the lifestyle and well-being of its people.

Despite the logic of these arguments, there were compelling reasons for the U.S. to retain its existing policy of noninvolvement.

First, although the PRC had indicated a desire to reunify with Taiwan in the near future, Taipei had on no occasion signalled its willingness even to discuss reunification. In fact, Taiwan had asked the U.S. to stay out of the issue. There was little sentiment in the Reagan administration to apply pressure on Taipei on this matter.

Second, no one knew for certain whether the reform policies initiated by Deng Xiaoping would continue beyond his death. China's peaceful reunification policy was part of the reform policy package introduced in December 1978. If that package became unraveled for some reason, then the policy of peaceful reunification might be changed as well. Also, it made little sense to push Taiwan into reunification before a reasonable period passed to see how Beijing upheld its part of the Hong Kong Agreement.

Third, there was concern that a move by the U.S. to nudge Taiwan into reunification could undermine Taiwanese confidence in their future and result in social, political, or economic instability on the island. This possibility was serious in an era of liberalization, when Taiwanese were becoming more politically active and the ability of the KMT to dominate ROC policy toward China was weakening. A U.S. move to help Beijing achieve peaceful reunification might in fact backfire, resulting in a move toward independence and possible PRC intervention by force.

Fourth, conservative supporters of the Reagan administration would strenuously object if the administration became involved in China's reunification. Conservatives were not altogether happy with friendly U.S. relations with Beijing, although most recognized the strategic importance of Sino-American relations. As long as the U.S. helped Taiwan remain free of Chinese Communist control, the Reagan administration could claim that its China policy was "balanced" and thus deserving of support. Liberals, too, would object to U.S. involvement in reunification because of their strong support for the right of the Taiwan people to determine their own future. Thus, any U.S. involvement in China's reunification ran the risk of alienating both conservatives and liberals and of undermining the broad consensus then supporting U.S. China policy.

Fifth, there was deep suspicion that even if the Taiwan issue were resolved to Beijing's satisfaction, it would make very little substantive difference in Sino-American relations. China would continue to pursue its independent foreign policy, to maintain friendly ties with the U.S. while rejecting a strategic alliance, and to improve relations with the Soviet Union. Beijing would neither renounce socialism, nor expand its economic and political reforms. The tone of Sino-American relations might improve somewhat, but the substantive issues would remain.

Finally, most Asian allies of the U.S. supported Washington's "dual-track" China policy of pursuing friendly official relations with

Beijing and friendly unofficial ties with Taiwan. None of China's neighbors were anxious to see China unified because of the increased national power that would bring to Beijing. A stronger China would be one better able, even if not necessarily more willing, to resume its traditional role of regional hegemon.

For these and other reasons, including President Reagan's personal friendship toward the ROC and the Taiwanese people, the U.S. decided in the spring of 1985 not to accept Deng's request to help expedite China's reunification.

Another far-reaching review of U.S. policy toward Taiwan took place in mid-1986 as part of a larger inquiry into U.S. policy toward Asia in the wake of Soviet General Secretary Mikhail Gorbachev's speech in Vladivostok in July 1986.[27] In this address Gorbachev made several sweeping pronouncements and proposals which signalled a marked departure from previous Soviet policy toward Asia.

Gorbachev announced that the Soviet Far East would become export-oriented and open to foreign investment and joint enterprises. He proposed to limit the arms race in Asia and promised to improve bilateral relations with all regional countries. He suggested that the Soviet Union and the U.S. reach an understanding over the future of the Pacific, one that would include the Soviet Union in any future Pacific Basin economic community. He reiterated the old Soviet plan to establish an Asian regional cooperative security system. He called for the normalization of Sino-Vietnamese relations and the establishment of closer ties between the countries of Indochina and the Association of Southeast Asian Nations (ASEAN). He proposed limiting nuclear weapons in the region, reducing U.S. and Soviet naval fleets, and cutting back regional conventional forces.

Perhaps most important were his proposals for improved Sino-Soviet relations. Gorbachev announced the withdrawal of six Soviet regiments from Afghanistan. He disclosed that "the question of withdrawing a considerable number of Soviet troops from Mongolia is being examined." And he held out the prospects for major troop reductions along the Sino-Soviet border, saying that, "the USSR is prepared to discuss with the PRC specific steps aimed at a balanced reduction in the level of land forces."

Gorbachev also held out several carrots to the PRC, including favorable references to the Chinese, hopes that relations would improve in the future, calls for increased trade, and concessions on border issues. To emphasize the importance of Gorbachev's speech, the Soviet Union dispatched high-ranking officials to China and Asia to reiterate that the Soviet proposals were meant to reflect a new direction in Moscow's foreign policy toward the region.

Beijing took Gorbachev's proposals seriously since they indicated a possible shift in Soviet strategy toward the PRC. Although cautious, the Chinese responded favorably to the prospects of improved Sino-Soviet relations.

This became clear in Deng Xiaoping's September 1986 interview on the CBS TV program, "60 Minutes." Regarding relations with the Soviet Union, Deng stated: "If Gorbachev takes a solid step towards the removal of the three major obstacles in Sino-Soviet relations, particularly urging Vietnam to end its aggression in Kampuchea and withdraw its troops from there, I myself will be ready to meet him."

As for the U.S., Deng said: "There is one obstacle in Sino-U.S. relations. That is the Taiwan question, or the question of China's reunification of the two sides of the Taiwan Straits. . . . I hope that President Reagan will, during his term in office, bring about further progress in Sino-U.S. relations, including some effort in respect of China's reunification. I believe that the United States, President Reagan in particular, can accomplish something with regard to this question."[28]

In the months following Gorbachev's speech, major studies were undertaken in the U.S government to determine the impact of the Soviet initiative on U.S. interests in Asia and whether a change in U.S. policy, including that toward Taiwan, was necessary. After extensive review, the administration concluded that while the Gorbachev speech indicated a more active role for the Soviet Union in Asia, the U.S. should not overreact. The U.S. enjoyed a strong position in the Asia-Pacific region and could set its own policy agenda without being forced into action by Moscow. Gorbachev's initiatives in Asia were not seen as threatening U.S. interests, save under those circumstances where American policy mistakes opened targets of opportunity for Moscow.

Some within the administration were apprehensive that the Soviets might be able to take advantage of the Taiwan issue and Beijing's paranoia over the influx of Western "spiritual pollution" to drive a wedge between the U.S. and the PRC. Most U.S. policymakers, however, believed Moscow had very limited ability to achieve a strategic realignment with Beijing. The administration thus concluded that although some improvement in Sino-Soviet relations could be expected, relations would not improve to the point where significant damage would occur to U.S. interests. In fact, limited Sino-Soviet rapprochement could be in U.S. interests insofar as it reduced regional tensions.

These assessments minimizing the Soviet challenge to U.S. interests in Asia led to the determination that U.S. policy should remain essentially the same. The preservation of the status quo remained in U.S. interests, although more attention should be paid to the Soviet role in Asia and Sino-Soviet relations should be monitored closely. In regards to Taiwan, no reason could be seen to change existing U.S. policy.

These policy reviews in 1985 and 1986 had the effect of further stabilizing Washington-Taipei relations. In was in this relatively secure international environment that the ROC government began a remarkable series of reforms in 1986 which created the "new" Taiwan. The story of these reforms through 1991 are the subject of the next section. Part Two of the book will once again take up U.S. interests in Taiwan as the reforms were being implemented.

Notes

1. Edgar Snow, *Red Star Over China* (New York: Modern Library, 1944), p. 96.

2. An account of this interesting period of Sino-American relations, from both the U.S. and PRC perspectives, can be found in Harry Harding and Yuan Ming, eds., *Sino-American Relations, 1945-1955: A Joint Reassessment of a Critical Decade* (Wilmington, DE: Scholarly Resources, Inc., 1989).

3. Some of the factors weighing against U.S. military intervention were the lack of political support in the U.S. for such intervention, demobilization of American armed forces after WWII, the growing crises in Europe and the Mediterranean, and reluctance on the part of American political and military leaders to be drawn into a land war on the Chinese mainland.

4. U.S. Department of State, *United States Relations with China with Special Reference to the Period 1944-1949* (Washington, D.C.: Government Printing Office, 1949), p. xvi.

5. Quoted in *China: U.S. Policy Since 1945* (Washington, D.C.: Congressional Quarterly, Inc., 1980), p. 87.

6. *Ibid.,* p. 88.

7. Omar Bradley and Clay Blair, *A General's Life* (New York: Simon and Schuster, 1983), p. 533.

8. *China: U.S. Policy Since 1945*, p. 88.

9. George F. Kennan, head of the Policy Planning Staff in 1949, suggested that the U.S. seize control of Taiwan in the name of protecting the native population from both the Nationalists and the Communists Chinese. Noted in Robert L. Messer, "Roosevelt, Truman, and China: An Overview," and Wang Hsi, "The Origins of America's 'Two China' Policy," in Harding and Yuan Ming, eds., *Sino-American Relations, 1945-1955*, pp. 74, 199. See also George F. Kennan, *Memoirs, 1950-1963* (Boston: Little, Brown, 1972), p. 254.

10. An examination of the Truman and Eisenhower strategies to drive a wedge between China and the Soviet Union during this period can be found in John Lewis Gaddis, "The American 'Wedge' Strategy, 1949-1955," in Harding and Yuan Ming, eds., *Sino-American Relations, 1945-1955*, pp. 157-183. The State Department document was quoted on p. 167.

11. Richard M. Nixon, *RN: The Memoirs of Richard Nixon* (New York, NY: Grosset and Dunlap, 1978), p. 556.

12. Henry A. Kissinger, *White House Years* (Boston, MA: Little, Brown and Co., 1979), p. 1062.

13. For Carter's views on relations with China, see Jimmy Carter, *Keeping Faith: Memoirs of a President* (New York, NY: Bantam Books, 1982), pp. 186–211.

14. *Ibid.*, pp. 209–210.

15. An excellent account of the congressional handling of the Taiwan Relations Act can be found in Lester L. Wolff and David L. Simon, *Legislative History of the Taiwan Relations Act* (New York, NY: American Association for Chinese Studies, 1982).

16. See, for example, Deng Xiaoping's interview in *Time*, February 5, 1979, p. 34.

17. For a discussion of how the PRC was able to manipulate American strategic perceptions to gain concessions from the Reagan administration over the Taiwan issue, see Martin L. Lasater, *The Taiwan Issue in Sino-American Strategic Relations* (Boulder, CO: Westview Press, 1984).

18. *Der Spiegel*, December 26, 1983, in Foreign Broadcast Information Service, *Daily Report: China*, (henceforth *FBIS-China*), December 29, 1983, pp. A7–A8.

19. Hu Yaobang, "Create a New Situation in All Fields of Socialist Modernization," *The Twelfth National Congress of the CPC* (Beijing: Foreign Languages Press, 1982), pp. 58–59.

20. The "three obstacles" were massive deployment of Soviet forces along the Sino-Soviet and Sino-Mongolian borders, the Soviet occupation of Afghanistan, and Soviet assistance to the Vietnamese occupation of Cambodia.

21. "No Sale of Advanced Aircraft to Taiwan," *Department of State Bulletin*, February 1982, p. 39.

22. *Washington Times*, July 2, 1982, p. 1; *Washington Post*, July 2, 1982, p. A26.

23. On July 9 representatives from 28 conservative groups met in Washington and warned the President that he would receive an "extremely acrimonious" backlash from his supporters if he agreed to any cutoff of arms to Taiwan. See *Washington Post*, July 9, 1982, p. A5.

24. *New York Times*, July 31, 1982, p. A2.

25. Holdridge's testimony on the August 17 Communiqué can be found in U.S. Congress, House of Representatives, Committee on Foreign Affairs, *China-Taiwan: United States Policy* (Washington, D.C.: GPO, 1982), pp. 2–29.

26. Prepared statement of Davis R. Robinson, Legal Advisor, Department of State, given before U.S. Congress, Senate, Committee on the Judiciary, Subcommittee on Separation of Powers, September 27, 1982, pp. 1–2, ms.

27. Gorbachev's July 28 speech can be found in *FBIS-Soviet Union*, July 29, 1986, pp. R1–R20.

28. Embassy of the People's Republic of China, "Deng Xiaoping on Sino-U.S. Relations" and "Deng Xiaoping on Sino-Soviet Relations," Press Release, September 6, 1986, pp. 1–3.

PART ONE

The New Taiwan

2

Taiwan's Political Development

From 1949 until very recently, Taiwan was under a system of martial law which tightly controlled all political activity. Beginning in 1986, however, the pace of Taiwan's political development increased rapidly. In the space of five years, martial law was lifted, over sixty new political parties were formed, restrictions on the press and bans on street demonstrations were lifted, a native-born Taiwanese was elected President of the Republic of China and Chairman of the ruling Kuomintang, several elections were held with freely competing political parties, senior parliamentarians who had held office without reelection since 1947 were retired, and for the first time the people of Taiwan were free to debate openly the future of their country.

The process of democratization is continuing on Taiwan. But in a remarkably brief period, Taiwan moved from an authoritarian regime dominated by the KMT to a multiparty democracy in which the KMT still rules, but by majority vote and must compete for power against several active opposition parties.

The Kuomintang, or Nationalist Party

Most observers were surprised at the rapidity with which political reforms were implemented on Taiwan after 1986. In fact, however, the KMT has always had an ideological commitment to democracy.

The Nationalist Party evolved from various revolutionary groups active in the overthrow of the Qing, or Manchu, dynasty in October 1911. The party's name was adopted in 1924, when Dr. Sun Yat-sen, founder of the Republic of China, reorganized the KMT along Leninist lines with the help of Soviet advisors. Dr. Sun formed the KMT as the instrument to achieve his Three Principles of the People (*San Min Chu-i*): national independence, political democracy, and social well-being.

In the KMT ideology, nationalism means an equal and independent status for China in the world; an equal status for all ethnic groups in China; and the restoration and renaissance of traditional Chinese culture. Democracy is intended to ensure that all Chinese people have civil liberties, including "political power." Social well-being, sometimes called "people's livelihood," implies a welfare state with a prosperous economy and a just society. This third principle advocates a free enterprise economic system with strong elements of government planning so that national wealth can be rapidly accumulated and equitably distributed. The *San Min Chu-i* remains the ideological foundation of the KMT today.

The ROC government is organized into five branches, or yuan. Three were adopted from western political traditions: the Executive Yuan, Legislative Yuan, and Judicial Yuan. Two were adopted from traditional Chinese political systems: an Examination Yuan to select members of the civil service and a Control Yuan to enforce standards of behavior among government officials.

According to the 1947 ROC Constitution, which is in the process of being amended, legislative responsibilities are shared by the Legislative Yuan, whose members serve three-year terms and who are directly elected; the Control Yuan, whose members serve six-year terms and who are indirectly elected; and the National Assembly, whose members serve six-year terms and who are directly elected.

The 1947 ROC Constitution provides for a National Assembly to elect the president and vice president, recall the two officials, amend the Constitution, and vote on proposed amendments to the Constitution submitted by the Legislative Yuan by way of referendum.

The Legislative Yuan is the highest legislative organ of the state, having the power to decide by resolution statutory or budgetary bills and bills concerning martial law, amnesty, declaration of war, conclusion of peace or treaties, and other important affairs of state.

The Constitution gives the Control Yuan the power to review the actions of public functionaries and to impeach those found guilty of violating the law or neglecting their duty.

As the ruling party, the KMT conducts its relations with the government in a parliamentary fashion by implementing policies through party members working in the government. Political cadre in the government include appointed ministers and vice ministers in the Executive Yuan and elected representatives in the National Assembly, Legislative Yuan, Control Yuan, and the provincial, municipal, county, township, and village assemblies and councils. The KMT selects the individuals for these posts and, if necessary, trains them for government service. The KMT also assists its nominated candidates in running for office.

In 1990 the KMT's membership was about 2.5 million, approximately twelve percent of Taiwan's total population of 20.5 million. The KMT's supreme organ is the National Congress, which convenes every four years or so. When the Congress is not in session, the KMT is governed by a Central Committee, which meets every year in plenary sessions. Day-to-day activities are overseen by the Central Standing Committee, which meets weekly. The Central Standing Committee is headed by a chairman (usually the President of the ROC). He is assisted by a group of party counsellors, the secretary general of the party, and three deputy secretary generals. Below the central level are congresses for provinces, counties, cities, and districts.

History of KMT

Sun Yat-sen theorized that the ROC would go through three stages of development to implement the *San Min Chu-i.* The first would be a military administration to unite the country. The second would be political tutelage under the KMT to educate the Chinese people in exercising their political rights. The third and final stage would be constitutional democracy.

The actual history of the ROC parallels this theoretical pattern of development. During the early 1920s, the KMT was organized along Leninist lines with the help of Soviet Comintern agents to be a revolutionary party. It military arm was headed by General Chiang Kai-shek, who took over the party leadership following Dr. Sun's death in 1925. From 1927 to 1947, Chiang ruled the ROC as a military dictator in constant warfare against various warlords, the Chinese Communists, and the Japanese.

Elections were held in 1947 in those parts of China under Nationalist control, and a constitution guaranteeing civil liberties was adopted. Shortly thereafter, however, martial law was declared because of deteriorating conditions brought about by the civil war being fought between the Nationalists and the Communists. From 1948 until 1987 the ROC was under an often benign form of martial law, but with gradually expanding political participation carefully controlled by the KMT. Martial law was lifted in July 1987, although a National Security Law was subsequently passed which gave the government strong powers to counter perceived sedition threats. In May 1991 the "Period of Mobilization for the Suppression of Communist Rebellion" on the mainland was ended, with appropriate changes made in the ROC Constitution to reflect the end of the civil war between the KMT and the Chinese Communist Party.

Since the lifting of martial law in 1987, the KMT has moved Taiwan rapidly toward the democracy promised in the 1947 Constitution and the *San Min Chu-i.* The KMT and fifteen other political parties competed for seats in the December 1989 elections. By the end of 1991, there were over sixty political parties on Taiwan. although only two, the KMT and its principal opposition, the Democratic Progressive Party (DPP), were politically powerful. As it stood at the end of 1991, the ROC political system could be described as having a multi-party, but single-party dominant, representative government.

Following the transfer of the ROC government to Taiwan in late 1949, the KMT undertook a comprehensive self-examination and reformation. This was essential for Nationalist survival, because it was recognized that ineffective KMT policies had contributed directly to the loss of mainland China and that its occupation policies on Taiwan had seriously undermined native Taiwanese support for the ROC government.

One key decision reached at that time was a shift in KMT strategy from trying to use military means to defeat the communists on the mainland, to using political and economic means to undermine Beijing and regain the support of the Chinese people. According to this strategy, Taiwan would be made into a model province of the *San Min Chu-i*. This strategy remains in place today, although often denigrated by detractors of the "return to the mainland" goal of the KMT.

Once this strategy was adopted, KMT priorities shifted from military confrontation with the PRC to the economic, social, and political development of Taiwan. This meant raising the standard of living of the Taiwanese people, improving the quality of their life, and gradually implementing the democracy called for by Sun Yat-sen.

The economic foundation of this process was established by a successful ROC land reform program during 1949–1953, transferring ownership of farmland from large landlords to the farmers actually tilling the land. A large portion of the stocks and bonds received by the landlords in payment for their land was invested in industry and business, giving these sectors of the economy an important boost.

One result of the decision to make Taiwan a model province was a unique arrangement whereby national politics was dominated by the mainlanders (roughly fifteen percent of the population) while private sector economic power rested almost entirely in the hands of the Taiwanese (eighty-five percent of the population). The Taiwanese also controlled local and provincial Taiwan politics. Since martial law prevented the emergence of new political parties, local Taiwanese politicians were mostly members of the KMT, although some were independents.

This arrangement, despite its social inequities and human cost, worked reasonably well for several decades and contributed to political stability on the island. The few Taiwanese who criticized fundamental KMT policies were dwelt with harshly under martial law, often being jailed for lengthy sentences. A number of Taiwanese political activists fled to Japan and the U.S. to take up anti-KMT causes. Many of these dissidents advocated that Taiwan should become an independent nation, free from mainlander control, whether by the KMT or the communists.

Liberalization and Taiwanization

Another major change in KMT direction began in the late 1970s, when a series of internal and external pressures caused the Nationalists to liberalize Taiwan's political system. These forces for political change included:

- the rise of Taiwan's middle class and a well-educated public, both of which demanded more political freedom

- the rise to power of reform-minded KMT leaders, who believed that the political system needed to be liberalized

- the increasingly antiquated ROC parliament, obviously in need of reform

- a more open attitude toward the discussion of sensitive political issues on Taiwan

- the growing consensus within Taiwan that martial law had fulfilled its purpose of stabilizing the island and that its continuation was harmful to ROC and Taiwan interests

- lower perceptions of the PRC military threat to Taiwan

- the mounting criticism of martial law and human rights violations from foreigners, especially Americans

- the increased isolation of the ROC in the international community, including the shift in U.S. diplomatic recognition from the ROC to the PRC in 1979

- the need to counter the rise in prestige and influence of the ROC's rival regime in Beijing.

Chiang Kai-shek died in 1975, and his son Chiang Ching-kuo succeeded to the leadership of the KMT and ROC. The younger Chiang was instrumental in the process of political reform on Taiwan.

Cognizant of the pressure building for change in the ROC, Chiang Ching-kuo began the process of "Taiwanization" of the ruling party and central government in the late 1970s. Before his death in 1988, this key reform resulted in KMT membership becoming over seventy percent Taiwanese and party and government officials being over fifty percent Taiwanese. The process of Taiwanization—which has yet to be fully implemented in a few professions—more closely linked the long-term interests of the Taiwanese and the KMT. The KMT no longer is a party dominated by Chinese from the mainland. The ruling party's fate, and that of the ROC itself, lies increasingly in the hands of Chinese born and raised on Taiwan, most of whom have roots on the island extending back for centuries.

Another important step introduced by Chiang Ching-kuo was the recruitment of Western-trained Chinese technocrats into positions of power and responsibility in the government and party. Many of these individuals used their positions to recommend and implement political reform modelled on Western democracies. In addition, a significant number of Overseas Chinese experts in the social sciences from the U.S. and other Western countries returned to Taiwan to assume high-ranking posts. These specially recruited individuals played an important role in the democratization process.

Elections on Taiwan Through 1986

One of the best ways to track democratic progress on Taiwan is to review the elections held on the island. While democracy at the national ROC level has been of a tutelage variety, its pace tightly managed by the ruling party until recently, democracy was established early at the local grassroots level. Township, city, and provincial elections have been held regularly since 1950–1951. Voter turnout rarely falls below seventy percent of registered voters, and Taiwanese members of the KMT win virtually every seat.

Elections at the national level have posed a major dilemma for the ROC government. On the one hand, the KMT wanted to democratize the political system as part of its program to make Taiwan a model province. This required increasingly open elections. On the other hand, the central government's elected bodies had to reflect the ROC claim that they represented not just Taiwan Province but all of China. Otherwise, the KMT and the ROC government would lose their legitimacy in the eyes of domestic and international audiences.

This dilemma was set aside temporarily by martial law provisions permitting those elected on the mainland to continue to hold office without reelection on Taiwan. Inevitably, this resulted in the gradual ossification of the legislative bodies and their irrelevancy in policy-making. The executive branch assumed control of policy with few checks and balances from elected representatives.

To increase the vitality of the elected bodies, to introduce at least a measure of true democracy, and to reflect more accurately the importance of Taiwan to the ROC, a series of "supplementary" elections were held from 1969 to expand the size of Taiwan's representation in the National Assembly, Legislative Yuan, and Control Yuan. About eighty percent of the newly elected representatives to the Legislative Yuan were Taiwanese members of the KMT.

The formation of new political parties on Taiwan was not permitted under martial law, although the KMT was riddled with factions, usually based on family loyalties. Beginning in 1977, however, more open competition emerged between KMT and non-KMT candidates. Opposition to the KMT took the form of non-party independents, or *tangwai* ("non-party"). Although the *tangwai* labored under martial law restrictions and were very disorganized and faction-ridden themselves, the *tangwai* made an impressive showing.

In the 1977 elections, the *tangwai* captured twenty-seven percent of the Provincial Assembly seats, twenty percent of the county magistrate and city mayor seats, and sixteen percent of the Taipei City Council seats. The strong *tangwai* showing caused a major reaction within the KMT, with some leading party reformers receiving blame for the Nationalist setback.

Political competition increased in the 1980 supplementary elections, held in the wake of the January 1, 1979, derecognition of the ROC by the U.S. and the Kaohsiung riot in December of that year. In the latter incident, a *tangwai* rally turned into a riot in which a number of policemen were injured. Shortly thereafter, several major opposition leaders were arrested and sentenced to lengthy prison terms by military courts.

In preparation for the elections, some progressive KMT members worked with various *tangwai* to evolve a set of ground rules to permit a more meaningful election process. The resulting "Public Officials Election and Recall Law" of May 1980 favored the KMT, but it also provided for much greater freedom for the opposition. Still banned from forming a political party, many of the opposition organized into a political "association" with a common platform.

Included in the *tangwai* platform were demands for more seats to be placed up for elections in the National Assembly, Legislative Yuan, and Control Yuan; popular elections for the governor of Taiwan province and the mayors of Taipei and Kaohsiung; more Taiwanese to be appointed to government positions; new political parties to be allowed to form; more freedom of the press, speech, and assembly; less restrictions on election campaigns; abolishment of the "Temporary Provisions"; and the release of political prisoners.

In the elections the KMT won about eighty percent of the contested seats, while the *tangwai* won about seventeen percent. Several individual *tangwai,* however, received the highest number of votes for any of the candidates.

KMT-*tangwai* competition became more open in the December 1983 supplementary elections. The KMT won eighty-five percent of the seats and the *tangwai* and other candidates won only fifteen percent. This election was characterized by a highly organized KMT and a *tangwai* badly split between various factions.

The election of December 1986 represented yet another step forward in the evolution of Taiwan's democracy, because it saw the emergence of a genuine (but as yet illegal) opposition party to the KMT: the Democratic Progressive Party (*Min-chu chin-pu tang*).

This election took place during the initial stages of major political reform initiated by President Chiang Ching-kuo.[1] At his urging, the KMT created a special task force in April 1986 to study the possibility of lifting the "Temporary Provisions," legalizing the formation of new political parties, strengthening the system of local self-government, reinvigorating the national parliament, and implementing internal reform within the KMT.

Convinced that trends toward political liberalization were now irreversible, several leading *tangwai* formally organized the Democratic Progressive Party (DPP) in September 1986. Although this was an illegal act, the government decided not to intervene. The next month President Chiang told *Washington Post* chairperson Mrs. Katharine Graham that the ROC would soon lift martial law and allow new political parties to be formed.

In November 1986 the DPP adopted a platform which included the following major points:

- Allow all residents of Taiwan to determine Taiwan's future. Oppose any talks between the KMT and communists on this issue as a violation of the principle of self-determination by the Taiwan people.

- Cease confrontation between the two sides of the Taiwan Strait. They should compete with each other on an equal footing to preserve peace in the region.

- Adopt more flexible and active measures to rejoin the United Nations.

- Cut the size of the nation's armed forces and shorten the length of compulsory military service.

- Close down all existing nuclear power plants within ten years and develop alternative sources of energy.

- Adopt a national health insurance program and an unemployment insurance program covering all citizens.

The most controversial items on the DPP platform were calls for Taiwan's "self-determination" and "equal footing" between Taiwan and the mainland. To many people, these terms meant an independent Taiwan. Advocating Taiwan independence was an illegal act in the ROC, and the PRC had repeatedly threatened to preempt by military force any move toward Taiwan's independence. In the December 1986 elections KMT candidates received sixty-nine percent of the vote and over eighty percent of the available seats in the National Assembly and Legislative Yuan. DPP candidates received twenty-one percent of the vote and fifteen percent of the seats in both bodies.

Controversy over the DPP

More than a few KMT members viewed the growing strength of political opposition as a threat to Nationalist goals and a danger to ROC security. Most KMT, however, thought opposition political parties were an essential ingredient in a democratic system because of their useful role in ensuring meaningful checks and balances on the government.[2] In reality, the DPP had both positive and negative impact on Taiwan's evolving democracy.

On the positive side, the DPP became fairly effective as an opposition party in the Legislative Yuan and in presenting alternative proposals which had popular appeal. It was particularly successful in articulating consumer interests, environmental concerns, and the need for government accountability. Without question, the DPP broke the "rubber-stamp" image the legislative branch had earned under KMT domination. Taiwan's democracy thus benefitted.

On the other hand, many DPP legislators were highly disruptive of parliamentary procedures, sometimes using verbal or physical abuse to "freeze" the legislative process for extended periods of time. This made it difficult for the government to pass needed legislation. Also, some DPP parliamentarians openly encouraged strikes and demonstrations, contributing to a general decline in social order and staining the image of democracy in the eyes of many Chinese who traditionally value social harmony and government efficiency.

But the DPP had serious internal weaknesses which limited its power. One weakness was the DPP's small size. Membership in late 1989 was about 20,000. Other weaknesses included lack of coordination between leaders and their supporters, lack of experience in politics and international relations, weak organization, too narrow an appeal base among the population, and lack of strong central leadership.

The most damaging weakness was a serious ideological split between moderates, who wanted to work within the existing system to bring about gradual reform, and the radicals, who wanted to apply heavy pressure on the system to cause it to change quickly. The issue of Taiwan's independence deeply divided these two groups. Moderates wished to play down this issue in order to coordinate reforms with the KMT; many radicals demanded the ouster of the KMT regime and immediate moves toward Taiwan independence.

Although larger in number, the moderate faction was unable to control the DPP, since moderate leaders were not unanimously accepted and the radicals controlled most opposition media. The radicals were skilled at organizing street demonstrations in support of DPP programs, thus gaining mass media attention otherwise inaccessible to the DPP because of KMT control over most of these channels of communication. The radicals forced many moderate DPP leaders to adopt confrontational tactics to ensure their political survival within the party.

The confrontational strategy of the DPP caused intense debate within the KMT. Some Nationalist officials felt the DPP were little more than common criminals and that they posed a greater security threat to the ROC than did the Chinese communists. Most KMT leaders, however, viewed the DPP as necessary for Taiwan's political evolution. In time and with increased experience and responsibility, these officials thought, more reasonable opposition leaders would emerge, or else the DPP would self-destruct because of its alienation from the majority of Taiwanese.

The KMT attempted to cooperate with moderate DPP to define areas of policy consensus; at the same time, the ruling party tried to isolate radical DPP and render them ineffective. One highly successful KMT tactic to ensure its continued role as leading party was to adopt opposition proposals when these appeared to be popular with the public. Because of the KMT's organizational strength and tendencies toward radicalism within the DPP, most KMT strategists believed the Nationalist Party would continue to dominate the government of Taiwan for well into the twenty-first century.

Political Reform Under Lee Teng-hui

Wielding enormous political power within the ROC government and the KMT, President Chiang Ching-kuo was able to push through reform in sensitive areas such as Taiwan politics and policy toward the mainland. Without his personal support for these reforms, it is doubtful such sweeping policy changes could have been implemented on Taiwan in such a short period of time. But on January 13, 1988, President Chiang Ching-kuo died. Before passing, however, he expressed his wish that no member of his family should succeed him. His death ended the Chiang dynasty in ROC history and on Taiwan a new political era began.

Vice President Lee Teng-hui, a native Taiwanese with a Ph.D. in agricultural economics from Cornell University, assumed the presidency in procedures stipulated by the Constitution. Lee assured his countrymen that he would continue the policies of Chiang, including the democratization of Taiwan.

Because Lee was Taiwanese and did not have an extensive network of support within the party, government or military, there was some doubt whether he had the political clout to implement the democratic reforms initiated by his predecessor. Powerful conservative forces within the KMT, held in check by their loyalty to the Chiang family and their healthy respect for the enormous power of Chiang Ching-kuo, now openly said the reforms were proceeding too fast and warned that Taiwan's security and stability were being threatened. Moderates within the KMT leadership backed Lee, however, arguing that change was inevitable and that the only way to ensure the KMT's political survival was to be in the forefront of necessary change.

During the Thirteenth KMT Party Congress in July 1988, various party conservatives attempted to have someone other than Lee elected Chairman of the KMT. After heated debate and much maneuvering, the Congress finally elected Lee as Chairman, the first Taiwanese to hold that position. A new Central Standing Committee was also elected, of which sixteen were Taiwanese and fifteen were mainlanders, the first time Taiwanese held a majority in that decision-making body. Like Lee, almost half of the members had received advanced degrees in the U.S. When Lee formed a new Cabinet the following week, Taiwanese comprised eight of the thirteen newly appointed members.

In late 1988 the Legislative Yuan became the center of political attention as KMT and DPP members literally fought over several bills designed to reform Taiwan's political system. These bills included proposals for the voluntary retirement of senior parliamentarians holding office since 1947 and for the legalization of new political parties.

The most serious confrontations between the KMT and DPP occurred over the Voluntary Retirement of Senior Parliamentarians Bill. The bill proposed paying each retiring official a pension of NT $3.74 million.

A cost of living index was later added, raising the value of the pension to NT $4.5 million (US $167,000). DPP members strongly opposed the plan, demanding instead that a general election be held to force the lawmakers out of office without pension. Using disruptive tactics, the DPP stopped all legislative action in the Parliament as a way of forcing the KMT to drop the bill.

After several weeks of unsuccessful attempts to compromise, KMT legislators in December 1988 sent the bill into committee over heated DPP protests. The action sparked melees in the Legislative Yuan. DPP members stormed the speaker's podium, ripped out microphones, hurled chairs, and scuffled in the aisles with KMT legislators. Despite the protests, the voluntary retirement bill became law on February 3, 1989.

The law signalled an important step toward democracy on Taiwan. At the time of the bill's passage, about 900 of the 1,000 members of the National Assembly and about 200 of the 300 members of the Legislative Yuan were senior representatives "frozen" in office since 1947. The voluntary retirement bill convinced some, but not all, of the senior parliamentarians to retire. Many stayed on, especially in the National Assembly responsible for electing the president and amending the Constitution.

Another important bill passed by the Legislative Yuan in early 1989 was a Civic Organizations Law legalizing the formation of new political parties. Although the law made forming a new political party relatively easy, it prohibited political parties from violating the Constitution, advocating communism, or supporting Taiwan independence. It further stipulated that political groups must be organized and function in accordance with democratic principles.

Since the enactment of the Civics Organization Law, more than sixty political parties have registered on Taiwan. With the exception of the KMT, DPP, China Democratic Socialist Party, China Youth Party, and the National Democratic Independent Political Alliance, most of these parties reflected specialized interest groups such as labor, business, environmentalists, and Chinese nationalists. Some of the new parties included the Labor Party, Workers Party, China Tatung Democratic Party, China Hung Ying Patriotic Party, China Democratic Party, China Democratic Justice Party, China Republican Party, China United Party, China New Socialist Party, China Popular Party, China Chungho Party, China Unification Party, Unification Democratic Party, and the China Loyal Virtue Party.

An important personnel change occurred in June 1989, when Premier Yu Kuo-hwa resigned and was replaced by Lee Huan, a senior KMT leader noted as a political reformer. At the same time, another important reform leader within the KMT, Dr. James Soong, was named Secretary-General of the Kuomintang. Soong, who has a Ph.D. from Georgetown University, said at the time of his appointment that the most urgent task facing the KMT was to adjust the party's structure and to rejuvenate its spirit to make it more responsible and efficient. He said that the two major goals of the party would be to better reflect public opinion in government policies and to strengthen the party's organizational and mobilizing capabilities.[3]

A further indication of ROC and KMT policy direction came from President Lee Teng-hui in his address to the KMT Party Congress in June 1989. Lee pointed out that the newly passed Civic Organizations Law legalized a competitive, multi-party system in the ROC which would force the KMT to complete with new ideas and an efficient work attitude. As an urgent task, Lee called for the review and revision of the "Temporary Provisions," which gave to the president extraordinary powers and which in the eyes of many constituted a major obstacle to democracy.[4]

In addition to the liberal political policies announced by President Lee Teng-hui, Premier Lee Huan, and James Soong in the summer and fall of 1989, their statements also indicated a shift in ROC social priorities from rapid economic growth to social stability and a more equitable distribution of wealth. This reflected public concerns about the need to improve their quality of life, as well as to enjoy more economic prosperity. In fact, this growing concern over the quality of life on Taiwan dominated the election campaigns of December 1989.

December 1989 Elections

On December 2 elections were held for 293 seats in the ROC national, provincial, and local governments.[5] Of the seats, 101 were for the Legislative Yuan, 77 for the Provincial Assembly of Taiwan, 51 for the Taipei City Council, 43 for the Kaohsiung City Council, 16 for county magistrate seats, and 5 for mayoral seats.

The elections were an important step in the development of democracy on Taiwan: they were the first to be held since the lifting of martial law, the first since the legalization of additional opposition parties to the KMT, and the first in which most of the candidates were selected through primaries. They were also exceptional in terms of the large number of seats open for competition and the large number of candidates.

The ruling party believed the elections would greatly influence the future of the ROC. If the KMT won a sufficiently large number of votes and seats, then the reforms instituted since 1986 would be vindicated. If the KMT did poorly in the elections, then blame would be laid either on remaining hardliners within the party or on the reformers. If the hardliners were held accountable for the loss, they would be forced to retire early. If the reformers were discredited, they would lose power and there would be an opportunity for conservatives to make a political comeback.

Both the KMT and DPP held primaries on July 23 to choose their respective candidates. The primaries were a major step in the ruling party's own democratization, since most KMT-sponsored candidates in the past were chosen by the party leadership. Based on the primary results, the KMT sponsored 222 candidates. About half the nominees were incumbents, 181 were Taiwanese, and 41 were first or second generation mainlanders.

In addition to these 222 KMT-sponsored candidates, another 104 party members registered as candidates on their own. These individuals did not win in the primaries, nor did the KMT request that they run. In fact, thirteen faced expulsion from the party because they ran against officially sanctioned candidates for mayors and county magistrates.

The DPP also held primaries to select its candidates. Before the primary process began, however, DPP chairman Huang Hsin-chieh publicized a list of his preferred candidates for county magistrates and city mayors. The existence of the list was controversial because of sharp differences between the two main DPP factions. The more moderate "Formosa" faction, led by Huang Hsin-chieh, advocated a gradual change in the nation's political system. Its goals were democracy first, Taiwan independence second. The Formosa faction believed that too much emphasis on Taiwan independence would alienate middle-class voters who wanted social stability and economic growth.

The more radical "New Movement" faction (sometimes also referred to as "New Wave" or "New Tide"), led by former DPP chairman Yao Chia-wen, regarded Taiwan independence as its most important policy objective. New Movement leaders wanted to "purify" the DPP of all not accepting its ideology. For a time, the New Movement faction threatened to break away from the DPP, but this did not occur.

The DPP primaries resulted in the official nomination of 145 opposition candidates. Eighteen DPP members ran in the elections on their own. The Formosa faction won the largest number of positions for its candidates.

To win its goal of at least seventy percent of the vote, the KMT appealed to voters on the basis of past accomplishments and promises of future reform. The theme of the KMT platform was the pursuit of constitutional democracy while ensuring national security.[6]

The platform promised to promote the "Taiwan Experience" and to continue to work toward the reunification of China. The KMT said it would:

- support political democratization on mainland China to oppose the communist dictatorship

- promote economic liberalization on the mainland, including the private ownership of property, the free enterprise system, and a market-oriented economic system

- promote social pluralization on the mainland, including respect for basic human rights and equal educational opportunity

- promote traditional Chinese values on the mainland and support opposition to Marxism-Leninism

- encourage more grassroots exchanges across the Taiwan Strait and the creation of anti-communist united fronts at home and abroad

- amend mainland trade policy to place equal emphasis on national security and economic benefits

- support racial minority groups in border areas fighting against the communists

- publicize the "Taiwan Experience" as a means of achieving a "reunified, democratic and prosperous new China."

Despite advantages by virtue of being the ruling party, the KMT was often on the defensive in the election campaign. It was plagued by negative images caused by four factors: the continued presence of senior statesmen in the National Assembly and Legislative Yuan; the lack of separation between the KMT, the government, and the military; the fact that it had been unable to solve the most visible, pressing problems facing Taiwan in 1989, namely, pollution, traffic, and crime; and frequent allegations of bribery and vote buying on the part of KMT candidates.

The DPP, on the other hand, was noticeably on the offensive as it tried to win a larger role in Taiwan politics. The DPP did not publish a specific platform for the 1989 elections, although its policy intentions were widely publicized throughout the election campaign. The DPP's unofficial platform advocated a political order based on democracy and freedom in which the nation rested on the free will of the majority of the people and respected the principle of self-determination.[7] The party called for peaceful and independent defense and foreign policies, suggesting that the government:

- develop its relations with other countries based on the principles of equality, reciprocity, independence, and self-determination

- assume more flexible and active measures to handle problems related to Taiwan's status in the international community

- seek to resolve international disputes by peaceful means, including support for worldwide disarmament talks, control of military equipment, and destruction of nuclear and chemical weapons

- cut the size of the military and upgrade their quality through more purchases of air and naval weapons systems; diversify the sources of military procurement; and strengthen domestic production of weapons

- place the armed forces, which should be politically neutral, under the jurisdiction of civilian government authorities, including the parliament.

Regarding the key issue of Taiwan's future, the DPP said that the government should allow all residents of Taiwan to determine the future of Taiwan and its political affiliation. The governments on the two sides of the Taiwan Strait should cease confrontation and solve their problems based on the principles of humanity, equality, peace, self-determination, and the interests of the Taiwan people.

On the question of Taiwan independence, DPP officials emphasized four points. First, people living on Taiwan have the exclusive right to determine their future relationship with China. Second, although the DPP advocates self-determination, it does not specifically suggest what that decision should be. Third, the people of Taiwan should be allowed to discuss openly their future, whether it be independence, unification, or some other arrangement between Taiwan and China. And fourth, there was no urgency to make a decision on the self-determination issue.

Despite this reasoned explanation given to foreign observers by the DPP headquarters staff, there were significant differences of opinion among DPP candidates over the issue of Taiwan independence. A few weeks prior to the elections, thirty-two DPP candidates from the New Movement faction formed a "New Nation Alliance," which openly advocated "a new nation, a new parliament, and a new constitution."

The Alliance platform was deemed illegal, but members publicly campaigned for a new nation anyway.

The DPP rightly complained that even if they won 100 percent of the popular vote, they would still only occupy about one-third of the seats in the Legislative Yuan. The KMT would retain control of the parliament because of the senior parliamentarians frozen in office since 1947.

Having no hope of winning a majority in the Legislative Yuan, DPP strategy focused on winning county magistrate and city mayor posts. Because local executives maintain fairly large discretionary powers in terms of budgets and implementation of national policies, DPP strategists felt their control of local areas could be used to bargain with the KMT on national issues. The DPP also hoped that by winning local offices, its candidates could demonstrate their competence to voters. This would enable DPP candidates to win more seats in future elections. As more offices were occupied by DPP members, the KMT would splinter and various factions would work with the DPP on specific issues. The DPP felt that, if successful, its local strategy could result in a major change in power in seven to twelve years.

To implement this strategy, the DPP persuaded many of its best-known members, including incumbents in the Legislative Yuan, to run in the local elections. Assuming that the electorate would give the opposition party its "rightful" share of seats in the legislature, less well-known members were asked to run for the Legislative Yuan.

Voter turnout was over 75 percent of Taiwan's 12 million eligible voters. In a political setback, the KMT won only 60 percent of the vote instead of its anticipated 70 percent. The DPP won about 31 percent, while independents won most of the remaining 9 percent. Political parties other than the KMT and DPP fared poorly. In terms of total seats, the KMT won 70 percent, the DPP won 22 percent. and independents won most of the remaining 8 percent.

Since DPP strategy focused on county magistrates and city mayors, these elections attracted a great deal of attention. The DPP won six of the sixteen county magistrate seats, while the KMT won ten. The KMT, however, won four of the five mayor seats, and an independent, closely allied with the DPP, won the other mayorship.

The DPP gained considerable political power by winning these county magistrate positions. Those counties won by the DPP were Hsinchu, Changhwa, Ilan, Kaohsiung, Pingtung, and Taipei County. Taipei County is the island's most important political center. In terms of local politics, the DPP governed roughly half of the territory of Taiwan and thirty-five percent of its population.

The 1989 elections ushered in a new era of party politics on Taiwan. The KMT remained the ruling party, but the DPP emerged as a significant opposition, at least at certain levels of government.[8]

Since DPP membership was only about 20,000, most individuals voted for the opposition for reasons other than party affiliation. Numerous interviews on Taiwan after the election suggested that the motivations of these voters were several. A large number voted DPP out of sympathy for candidates persecuted by the KMT in the past. Others voted against the KMT because they did not like the ruling party, or because they believed the KMT had too much power. Many decided to vote DPP because they were dissatisfied with the KMT's performance, especially its failure to solve pollution, traffic, and crime. Some voters felt the DPP probably would do no better than the KMT, but since the Nationalists had ruled for forty years, why not give someone else a chance. Still others voted for the DPP because they believed Taiwan had reached a stage of development where it should have its own government, not a government controlled by mainlanders.

While the election outcome reflected dissatisfaction with the KMT, it also meant that if the DPP was to become a permanent fixture in Taiwan politics, it had to find a way to draw these circumstantial supporters into a stronger commitment to DPP policies. Otherwise, the KMT might be able to attract some of these independent voters in future elections.

Political Events in 1990

One of the major difficulties facing the KMT during the December 1989 elections was the continued presence of senior parliamentarians in the national legislative bodies. Those holding office since 1947 proved to be an embarrassment to many KMT candidates in the elections, some of whom even denounced the senior leaders in their campaign speeches.

KMT reformers in the party leadership had to handle carefully the senior parliamentarians, however, because they controlled the National Assembly and could, if offended, elect someone other than Lee Teng-hui for ROC president at the forthcoming Assembly meeting in March 1990. The senior parliamentarians maintained strong alliances with KMT factions believing that democratization was proceeding too fast and that the DPP was undermining Taiwan's social stability and security.

Election of Lee Teng-hui as President

In early February 1990 the KMT Central Standing Committee unanimously agreed to nominate Lee in the scheduled March 21 presidential election in the National Assembly. Sharp disagreement arose, however, over who would be nominated as vice president. A poll of National Assembly members in early February reflected strong support for General Wego Chiang to be vice president. Gen. Chiang was the youngest son of Chiang Kai-shek and secretary-general of the National Security Council. Others mentioned in the polls were Li Yuan-zu, secretary-general to the President, Premier Lee Huan, and former Premier Yu Kuo-hwa.[9]

In mid-February the Central Standing Committee approved Lee Teng-hui's choice of Li Yuan-zu to be the vice presidential nominee, but Lee's choice was challenged in an indirect fashion. Several members of the Committee, including Premier Lee Huan, former Premier Yu Kuo-hwa, and Judicial Yuan President Lin Yang-kang, argued that the method of selection should be through secret ballot rather than the traditional show-of-hands which had been decided upon by KMT secretary-general James Soong. The vote on this procedural question, seen as a challenge to the reformers' control of the party, was fairly close. Those approving the show-of-hands method won 90 to 70.[10]

The rather delicate control of the party by the reformers was further challenged by events later that month, when the DPP organized several violent demonstrations in Taipei against the process of nominating and electing the ROC President and Vice President. The DPP protested the fact that nearly ninety percent of the 752-member National Assembly had been frozen in office for more than four decades.

These demonstrations humiliated President Lee and threatened his election. In one incident televised live throughout the island, DPP members of the Legislative Yuan overturned dinner tables at a banquet hosted by the President for National Assemblymen. Other violent protests, with injuries and considerable property damage, occurred outside the Legislative Yuan.

The demonstrations proved to many conservatives that Lee was unable to maintain stability on the island. Perhaps to ward off that growing sentiment among senior KMT leaders, the President assumed a much tougher line on demonstrations. In a statement to the press, Lee said the government would henceforth take "stern, legal action" and that in the future "no political ideas will be advocated through illegal or violent means" on Taiwan.[11]

Political opposition to Lee mounted. In early March an alternative presidential-vice presidential ticket was circulated, comprised of Lin Yang-kang and Wego Chiang. There was considerable support for this ticket among National Assemblymen because of dissatisfaction over Lee's administration and the perception that Lee did not have a strong enough commitment to the ROC goal of China's reunification.

Lee, proving to be a capable politician, worked very hard to dispel this perception. In the days leading up to the March 21 election, Lee and Li Yuan-zu visited many senior National Assemblymen. The President constantly reaffirmed his commitment to a reunited China. On one occasion, he told a group of Assemblymen: "I anticipate an opportunity for the Republic of China to return to the mainland in the next six years." He also stated, "Taiwan, as a part of the Republic of China, can never be separated from China." He emphasized that stability on Taiwan could not be maintained if there existed the possibility of secession. Such an idea would only lead the destruction of Taiwan, he said.[12]

Partly because of Lee's lobbying and partly because of appeals from senior KMT leaders to preserve party unity, Lin Yang-kang and Wego Chiang announced during the second week of March that they would not accept their names being placed into nomination. Their withdrawal resolved the issue of the election of the President and Vice President, but then another political crisis arose which gave Lee an opportunity to turn the tables on his conservative opponents. During the third week of March, a KMT screening committee in the National Assembly passed several proposals to be voted upon by the full Assembly. These proposals widened the power of the National Assembly and gave it considerable authority to manage the direction of Taiwan's policies. The proposals included holding Assembly sessions yearly instead of once every six years and giving the Assembly the power to introduce laws and veto bills passed by the Legislative Yuan. There was also a proposal granting a fourfold increase in the attendance fees paid to National Assemblymen.

When the proposals became known to be public, there was a largely spontaneous and peaceful demonstration of over 15,000 people at the Chiang Kai-shek Memorial in downtown Taipei. The demonstrators demanded that the KMT proposals be rejected. The fact that several thousand students from over twenty Taiwan universities participated in the demonstrations added a moral dimension to the protest, since the ROC government did not want any parallels made to the June 4, 1989, massacre of students that occurred in Tiananmen in Beijing. In response to the protests, the KMT withdrew the unpopular proposals.

The students, however, continued to stay at the Memorial through the Assembly's presidential and vice presidential votes.

When the vote for President took place on March 21, Lee received 641 of the 668 votes cast. The following day, Li Yuan-zu received 602 out of 644 votes cast for Vice President. Immediately after the vote, Lee called student representatives to his office and promised them that a timetable for political and constitutional reform would soon be announced. Thereupon, the students packed their sleeping bags and returned to the campuses.

In his formal acceptance speech to the National Assembly, Lee announced that he was making preparations for a "national affairs conference" at which a broad spectrum of views from all quarters would be solicited regarding the issues of constitutional reform and national unification. Aware of perceptions that he might be leaning in the direction of Taiwan independence, Lee stated categorically: "Although many different concepts are now being advocated, and the desire for change is urgent, our national entity will not countenance change, our national territory must not be divided, and our objective of reunifying our country must in particular not waver." Outside of these areas, President Lee said, any proposals will be welcomed.[13]

KMT-DPP Relations After Lee's Election

Soon after the National Assembly election, Lee met with DPP chairman Huang Hsin-chieh to invite opposition participation in the National Affairs Conference scheduled for July 1990. Lee urged the DPP chairman to restrain his members from advocating Taiwan independence. For his part, Huang brought several proposals setting forth the DPP's priorities for the 1990s. The proposals, along with Lee Teng-hui's response, were as follows:

- Approve the direct election of the ROC President before March 31, 1993. [Lee said this issue would be discussed in the National Affairs Conference.]

- Radio and television broadcasting must be liberalized. [Lee said this issue would be studied.]

- Retire all senior parliamentarians before September 1, 1990. [Lee said this issue would be resolved within two years.]

- Terminate by July 1, 1990, the powers given the ROC government by the "Mobilization During the Period of Communist Rebellion" edict. [Lee said the issue would also be resolved in two years.]

- Hold general parliamentary elections before December 31, 1990. [Lee said this issue would be resolved within two years.]

- Hold direct elections of the provincial governor and the mayors of Taipei and Kaohsiung before June 30, 1991. [Lee said this would be resolved within two years.]

- Pardon all political prisoners and restore their civil rights. [Lee said the feasibility of this would be considered.]

- Put into operation a national health insurance program before 1992. [Lee said this would be fully implemented by 1992.][14]

Lee invited four DPP leaders to join the 25-member committee being organized to plan the National Affairs Conference. The opposition party, however, announced that it would participate only under certain conditions, one of which was that "the future of Taiwan and the future of the island's relationship with the China mainland should be discussed under the principle of self-determination." According to press reports, this condition, clearly unacceptable to the KMT, was set because the DPP's New Movement faction did not want the party to participate in any discussions regarding the possibility of future reunification of Taiwan and mainland China.[15]

On May 20, 1990, Lee Teng-hui was sworn in as President of the Republic of China. In his inauguration speech, Lee announced that the 42-year old "Period of Mobilization for Suppression of the Communist Rebellion" would soon be terminated. This would end the long-standing ROC policy toward the mainland of the "three nos" (no contact, no compromise, and no negotiation with Beijing). Lee said, "completely open academic, cultural, economic, trade, scientific and technological exchanges" with the mainland would be possible if the PRC met three conditions:

- promote democratization and economic liberalization

- renounce the use of force against Taiwan

- stop trying to isolate the ROC in the international community of nations.[16]

More about this change in ROC policy toward the mainland will be discussed in Chapter 4, but it is important to note in terms of political developments on Taiwan that Lee was using his speech to once again demonstrate his determination to work toward China's eventual reunification. A clear statement of such intentions was necessary to solidify KMT support behind his administration.

Appointment of General Hau Pei-tsun as Premier

Another important step taken by Lee to consolidate his power by addressing the concerns of conservative critics was his appointment in early May of General Hau Pei-tsun, then Defense Minister and former Chief of the General Staff, to the position of Premier to replace Lee Huan. Hau Pei-tsun was a mainlander with a reputation as a "military strongman" who highly valued "law and order."

Lee said he nominated Gen. Hau because of the public's demand for a return to political and social stability. These concerns were prevalent among virtually all segments of society and were heard frequently in the 1989 election campaign. During the month of April 1990, over 1,000 PRC manufactured firearms were seized by police in an island-wide crackdown on serious crime. Burglaries and robberies were common, and serious crimes increased dramatically as the country became more liberalized with the lifting of martial law. Lee may have had other motivations in nominating Hau: to reward the General for his support during KMT internal power struggles, to send a signal that as President he intended to uphold the principle of China's reunification, and to replace Lee Huan, who had emerged as a serious political rival over the past year.

In accepting the nomination, Hau Pei-tsun stressed that President Lee and he agreed on "upholding the lofty goal and sacred mission" of reunifying China, opposing communism, supporting Taiwan democracy, and opposing any efforts to separate Taiwan from mainland China.[17]

The nomination of General Hau was strongly opposed by the DPP, not only because of his mainlander origins but also because of his well-known opposition to Taiwan independence. Hau maintained powerful connections throughout the ROC military, security, and KMT party apparatus. Many DPP feared that Hau would slow or even halt democratic reform on Taiwan.

Hau answered these criticisms in several public appearances, stating that he supported constitutional democracy, but opposed "abnormal" democracy. He defined this as being democracy without rule of law. "Very simply put," he said, "democracy is based on the rule of law, and the rule of law means the majority must care about the minority and the minority must respect the wishes of the majority."[18]

In an interview somewhat later, Premier Hau stated that "political instability is mainly to blame for social disorder." The Premier went on to explain:

> [T]he present social disorder is a result of the maladjustment of the government's political and social functions...Much of the police manpower is consumed in political tasks, and this reduces the personnel available

for maintaining social order. Harmonious political operation is essential in solving the problem. To that end, the ruling and opposition parties should seek a consensus regarding political reforms. The decline of government authority contributes to social disorder....Some economic phenomena are also at the center of the problem. We see environmental protection issues, labor unrest, and rampant gambling and speculation in our society. We will endeavor to provide a sound environment for economic development by working out constructive financial and economic policies.[19]

Through these and other statements, Hau indicated that he would support democratic reform but strictly enforce the law. His "law and order" stance won Hau superior ratings in public opinion polls, although the DPP viewed his policies as a threat to their efforts to press for rapid political change on Taiwan. To ease concerns that the military was intervening in domestic politics, Hau gave up his four stars as general.

The Legislative Yuan approved Hau's nomination on May 29 by a vote of 186 to 27. Two weeks later, the new Premier outlined his plans for restoring social order with priority placed on firearms control and curtailing smuggling, gambling, prostitution, organized crime, and un- authorized or violent demonstrations.

In his first administrative report to the Legislative Yuan in mid-June, Hau said that certain contradictions had arisen during the course of the ROC's development which had caused obstacles to social stability and harmonious progress. He listed these contradic- tions as: rapid economic growth marred by environmental pollution; high development of education accompanied by a confusion of values; the emergence of social pluralism together with a breakdown of social discipline; and political democratization without due respect for the rule of law.[20]

In his presentation to the 86th session of the Legislative Yuan in late September 1990, Hau outlined a six-year "national construction plan" which would coordinate the ROC's efforts to become one of the world's foremost modernized democracies. Specific targets in- cluded a higher national income, a lower crime rate, a more law-abiding citizenry, better protection for the people's mental and physical health, a balanced socio-economic order, good traffic control, and an improved natural environment. Also included in the plan was Hau's definition of the role of government as "chief of staff" to help chart the course of development of Taiwan's market economy.[21] More will be said about this six-year plan in the next chapter on Taiwan's economy.

National Affairs Conference

President Lee had promised in March 1990 that a National Affairs Conference would be called to discuss the major issues facing Taiwan. The purpose of the National Affairs Conference (NAC) was to arrive at public consensus on key issues. The NAC's agenda was set in late April, with a focus on parliamentary reform, the central and local government systems, methods of revising the ROC Constitution, and relations between the two sides of the Taiwan Strait. Lee said that consensus in any of these areas would become part of future national policies.

A few days prior to the July 28–July 4, 1990 conference, the Council of Grand Justices reached a decision with far-reaching implications. The Council is the judiciary body charged with the constitutional authority to interpret the Constitution. The Justices ruled thirteen to two that the senior parliamentarians frozen in office to represent mainland constituencies would have to vacate their office by December 31, 1991. The decision affected seventy-six percent of the members of the nation's legislative bodies, including 612 members of the National Assembly, 138 members of the Legislative Yuan, and eighteen members of the Control Yuan. The ruling also stipulated that those senior parliamentarians not able to perform their duties or who had not done so on a regular basis would have to retire immediately.

A few days after this monumental decision, President Lee Teng-hui opened the National Affairs Conference with 140 scholars, legislators, political party representatives, and others in attendance. Several important areas of consensus and disagreement emerged.

First, there was consensus supporting the Grand Justices' decision that all mainland-elected parliamentarians should retire. There was disagreement, however, over when their retirement should take place. The various timetables depended on when elections for a new parliament were to be held.

Second, there was consensus that the next ROC president should be elected by popular vote. Opinion was divided, however, on whether the president should be directly elected by the people or indirectly elected through an electoral college system similar to that in the United States. If the latter was adopted, many felt the existing National Assembly could be restructured to serve that purpose.

Third, there was consensus that the Period of Mobilization for the Suppression of the Communist Rebellion should be ended, along with necessary revisions made to the ROC Constitution. The majority felt that the existing Constitution could be adequately amended, but a vocal minority (mostly DPP) wanted a new constitution. A small group demanded that the Constitution be replaced by a "Grand Charter for Democracy" previously drafted by the DPP.

Fourth, there was consensus that the PRC had no right to exercise sovereignty over Taiwan or other territories controlled by the ROC. The delegates felt that priority should be given to the well-being of the people of Taiwan, but that Taiwan should help the people on the mainland achieve freedom and democracy. The delegates wanted clearer guidelines from the government on policies toward the mainland. The majority of delegates felt that the ROC and PRC were equal governments with jurisdiction over Taiwan and the mainland respectively.

Fifth, there was consensus that local government in the ROC should be characterized by democracy and autonomy, placed within a legal framework, and given a larger share of central government revenues. The majority of delegates were not satisfied with the present division of the ROC into a central government, Taiwan provincial government, various county and city governments, and township and town offices. A majority of the delegates favored direct, democratic-style elections of the Taiwan provincial governor and the mayors of Taipei and Kaohsiung.

Consensus was not reached on the question of whether the ROC government should be a presidential system, a cabinet system, or a combination of the two. No agreement was reached on whether the President, Executive Yuan, or Legislative Yuan should be the supreme power.

Immediately after the NAC meetings, President Lee appointed various committees in the government and ruling party to study ways to implement the recommendations. The KMT committee to study the key issue of constitutional reform was headed by Vice President Li Yuan-zu.

In November 1990 Li Yuan-zu's committee reached a decision on how to reform the legislative bodies affected by the ruling of the Grand Justices requiring all parliamentarians elected on the mainland to retire at the end of 1991. The KMT committee recommended that at the end of 1991 there should be an election for 375 new members of the National Assembly. These new members would serve four-year terms ending in January 1996 and would join the eighty members previously elected in supplementary elections to form a 455-member Second National Assembly (the First National Assembly being elected on the mainland in 1947). The new National Assembly would undertake the necessary revisions of the ROC Constitution during its first session in 1992.

The constitutional reform committee also recommended that by February 1993, 150 members would be elected to the Second Legislative Yuan to serve a three-year term. By the same date, fifty-four members would be elected to the Control Yuan for six-year terms. Under this plan, the transformation of Taiwan's legislative bodies would be completed by the end of February 1993.

The issue of constitutional reform was fundamental to the future of the KMT and the Republic of China. Great care was taken to establish guidelines that would permit needed reform but also preserve the mission of the ROC as envisioned by earlier leaders. In January 1991 KMT secretary-general James Soong set forth five principles which would be used to guide constitutional reform. Soong said the KMT would insist on:

1. ROC legitimacy as derived from the Constitution,
2. the basic principle of the reunification of China,
3. the primary framework of a quintuple-power Constitution,
4. revision of the Constitution, rather than promulgating a new Constitution, and
5. preserving the original content of the Constitution, and revising it by the addition of new articles.[22]

The following month, the KMT Central Standing Committee proposed a consensus on a two-staged plan to reform the Constitution. The first stage would involve the convening of an extraordinary session of the National Assembly in April 1991. This session, dominated by senior parliamentarians elected on the mainland, would prepare the legal framework necessary for the dissolution of the First National Assembly and its replacement by the Second National Assembly in 1992. Members of the Second National Assembly would be elected at the end of 1991. Until then, the First National Assembly would study and debate proposed constitutional amendments.

The second stage of constitutional reform would begin in 1992 when the Second National Assembly convened. At that time, the Assemblymen would consider the original proposals, the advice and counsel of the First National Assembly, and then decide on constitutional amendments as authorized by the Constitution.

Most of the proposals for constitutional reform related to President Lee's suspension of the period of mobilization against the communists in May 1991. His decision to end the state of war technically existing between the KMT and CCP nullified eleven amendments added to the 1947 Constitution which were collectively called the "Temporary Provisions Effective During the Period of Communist Rebellion." These gave the ROC President extraordinary powers to handle the crisis with the communists, powers which resulted in martial law being in effect until 1987.

National Unification Council

Another important committee established by President Lee was the National Unification Council (NUC). The NUC, about which more will be said in Chapter 4, was created to be an advisory body to the policy-making Mainland Affairs Commission in the Executive Yuan. Headed by Lee Teng-hui himself, with Li Yuan-zu and Hau Pei-tsun as deputies, the new council signalled the ROC's commitment to the reunification of China.

Lee invited DPP chairman Huang Hsin-chieh, former legislator Kang Ning-hsiang, and other opposition party and independent leaders to join the NUC. Huang refused, saying, "Unification is beneficial only to the mainland...Taiwan would be hurt by reunification. Forming a unification committee would be Taiwan's admission of Communist China's sovereignty, and would hurt Taiwan's international image."[23] Kang Ning-hsiang, who was an advisor to the DPP, agreed to become a member but the DPP fired him as a result. The NUC was formally established on October 7 with thirty government officials, political party leaders, industrialists, civic leaders, scholars, and journalists as members. In opening the NUC, President Lee stressed that unification was no longer an "unreachable dream," that "Taiwan independence is not a viable option," and that China "must be reunified as quickly as possible."[24]

At the same time that the NUC was being inaugurated, the DPP passed a resolution at its Fourth National Congress stating that Taiwan's sovereignty cannot be extended to mainland China. The resolution said: "Taiwan's de facto sovereignty claim does not include the territory of the People's Republic of China and the Mongolian People's Republic." DPP chairman Huang Hsin-chieh insisted, "the proposal does not claim independence."[25] However, many viewed the declaration as bordering on a declaration of Taiwan independence, since the ROC does claim sovereignty over the mainland. To claim sovereignty just over Taiwan would in fact affirm that Taiwan and the mainland were two separate entities and not two parts of one country.

A declaration in open support of Taiwan independence was an illegal act according to the 1990 Law on Organizations of Civic Groups, punishable by disbandment of the group. Not deterred, the DPP central standing committee voted in November to form a "Taiwan Independent Sovereignty Campaign Committee." The ROC government promptly announced that it would investigate the campaign committee to determine if it violated laws against organizing pro-independence activities.

Yet another effort by President Lee to signal his willingness to work toward unification was announced in November 1990 with the establishment of the Foundation for Exchanges Across the Taiwan Strait. The purpose of the foundation, whose activities will be described in Chapter 4, was to serve as an unofficial organization to handle various exchanges between the two Chinese sides. DPP legislator Lin Cheng-chieh agreed to serve as adviser to the foundation, although the DPP itself refused to accept a seat on the foundation's executive board.

Public Opinion Polls

One of the institutions accompanying the development of democracy on Taiwan is the appearance of public opinion polls. Polls are taken frequently on the island and cover a wide range of subjects. Chinese traditionally have been reluctant to disclose their true thoughts on sensitive issues, especially politics, but with a higher educational level and widespread media exposure to current issues, the people of Taiwan have become more forthright in expressing their views.

In October 1990 a poll conducted by the Across the Strait Research Fund focused on Taiwan-mainland China relations.[26] A total of 1,013 people were contacted throughout the island. Because of the sensitive nature of the questions, a large percentage of respondents voiced no opinion. However, those openly favoring Taiwan independence totalled 16.2 percent, while those opposed totalled 62.7 percent. About 21 percent said they had no opinion. About 80 percent of those who said they were members of the KMT opposed independence, while 50 percent of those who said they were DPP supported independence.

Asked whether they thought the PRC would attack Taiwan if it became independent, 49.4 percent said yes, while 20 percent said no. About 30 percent had no opinion. As to whether the ROC should give up mainland China, 9.7 percent agreed and 60.4 percent said no. Nearly 30 percent voiced no opinion.

A fairly significant percentage of those polled were in favor of increased contact with the mainland. Those favoring party-to-party talks between the KMT and the Chinese Communist Party totalled 49.6 percent (opposed 22.7 percent, no opinion 27.8); those favoring Taipei-Beijing government-to-government talks were 56.7 percent (opposed 15.5, no opinion 27.9); those favoring direct trade with the mainland totalled 65.3 percent (opposed 19.4, no opinion 15.4); and those favoring direct sea and air links with the mainland totalled 66.4 percent (opposed 19.8, no opinion 13.8).

In December 1990 the Public Opinion Research Foundation conducted a poll of 1,067 Taiwan homes to ask residents to rate the ROC government's performance during the last half of the year. The results were compared to responses received for the first half of the year.[27]

According to the poll, the overall administration of the government was given a 67.8 percent approval rating for the second half, a slight increase over the previous period. The public's approval rating of the government's policy on social order was 69.3 percent. This was a marked increase from 43.9 percent for the previous six months, probably reflecting approval of the steps taken by Premier Hau Pei-tsun to establish social order on the island.

The government received a 51.9 percent approval rating for public health for the last half of 1990, a 50.4 percent approval in steps taken to protect labor interests, a 42.3 percent approval on environment protection, a 40.2 percent approval for the handling of economic affairs, and a low 28.8 percent approval for solving Taiwan's notorious traffic problems. In the area of foreign affairs, the government had a 49.7 percent approval rating, down from 54.0 percent earlier in the year. In national defense, the government had a 46.2 percent approval rating, down from 50.5 percent during the first half of 1990.

Continued DPP Disruption of Legislative Yuan

During the 85th session of the Legislative Yuan, ending in July 1990, only seven bills were passed or amended in an extended 148-day session. This was largely due to DPP filibustering tactics, as well as some violence such as smashing microphones and shoving other legislators. Because of the turmoil, the Legislative Yuan was seen by the public as being weak and unable to respond to the need for effective legislation.[28]

The difficulty of finding a workable compromise between the KMT and DPP was demonstrated once again in December 1990, when the ruling party, after repeated unsuccessful efforts to convince the opposition to allow consideration of several needed bills, finally forced votes on two bills concerning employment, evaluation, salary, and bonuses for government civil servants. The votes were 105 to 18, and 119 to 24, in favor of passage. Despite their minority standing, DPP members went on a rampage, destroying microphones, screaming insults, and jumping on top of tables.

Indicating that the KMT was tiring of the exercise, an exasperated ruling party's spokesman said that the party had tried to work with the DPP, but that it had been unable to reconcile differences in regards to Taiwan independence and the need for respect for the rule of law.[29]

Taiwan's Political Goals for the 1990s

In several speeches toward the end of 1990, President Lee Teng-hui outlined ROC goals over the next decade. In his October 10, 1990, speech on the occasion of the seventy-ninth anniversary of the ROC, Lee said four basic tasks would pre-occupy his administration over the next several years: accelerating constitutional reform to implement democracy, creating a new economic miracle on Taiwan, expanding diplomatic relations through pragmatism, and reaching a consensus on achieving national reunification.[30]

President Lee's 1991 New Year's message also set forth the goals of the ROC during the coming decade.[31] In the speech, Lee said the coming decade would be characterized by the conclusion of the Cold War, pluralism in international politics, and movement toward the establishment of a new world order. He especially noted that communism was a failure worldwide. These changes in the international community were beneficial to the ROC, Lee said, and proved the correctness of the Three Principles of the People and the ROC goal of achieving the eventual unification of China under the principles of democracy and freedom.

Lee said the 1990s would be a decade in which constitutional democracy will approach full maturity on Taiwan. He promised that the "Period of Mobilization for Suppression of the Communist Rebellion" would soon be concluded, officially ending the war with Beijing. In addition, Lee promised that the rejuvenation of the national legislative bodies and appropriate revisions in the Constitution would proceed.

Lee said the 1990s would be a decade of comprehensive development in the ROC. Certain imbalances in society, culture, and the environment would be corrected. A massive "Six-Year National Development Plan" would be put into effect to enable Taiwan to enter the ranks of developed nations. Taiwan's industry would be assisted in ways to help them compete internationally yet not harm Taiwan's environment. The six-year plan had as well the objective of improving the quality of people's life and their social environment. Lee promised the 1990s would be a decade of cultural development on Taiwan. This would include the promotion of traditional Chinese culture, as well as improving social ethics and morality.

Also, according to the President, the 1990s would be a decade for the promotion of China's reunification. The security of Taiwan and the well-being of its people would remain the central concerns of the ROC government, but its responsibility toward all of China would not be forgotten. Lee said the desire of the Chinese people for democracy, freedom, and prosperity were the strongest forces propelling the nation toward reunification. In this effort, he said, the Chinese people themselves must find the solution.

More immediate goals for the ROC government were set by Premier Hau Pei-tsun in his January 1991 report. The Executive Yuan document said the government would accelerate democratic and constitutional reform in keeping with public sentiment and the rule of law; continue to work for the peaceful, democratic reunification of China while staying cognizant of the welfare of the people of Taiwan; and steadily develop the nation's economy. Various priorities were assigned:

- Interior Affairs: Strictly enforcing constitutional democracy; strengthening the self-government system; mapping social welfare plans; expediting public construction.
- Foreign Affairs: Expanding maneuvering space for ROC diplomacy by establishing ties with nations which have no official relations with the ROC.
- National Defense: Expediting research and development of high-performance jet fighters and defensive missiles.
- Finance: Amplifying financial regulation systems; enhancing the balanced financial development of central and local governments.
- Economic Development: Promoting the Six-Year National Development Plan; promoting economic liberalization and disciplines; enforcing fair trade policies; encouraging foreign investment in high-tech industries.[32]

Developments in 1991

The ROC continued its rapid political reform in 1991. Several accomplishments were especially noteworthy:

- Official Guidelines for National Unification were adopted.
- The initial stages of constitutional reform were completed by the First National Assembly.
- The period of emergency mobilization against the Chinese Communists rebellion was terminated.

- The emergency powers given the President during the civil war were ended.
- All senior parliamentarians frozen in office since being elected on the mainland were retired.
- Elections for the Second National Assembly were held.

Guidelines for National Unification

A significant document governing ROC policy toward the reunification of China was adopted in February by the National Unification Council (NUC) and approved by the Executive Yuan the following month. The document outlined three stages in a process leading to eventual unification. Stage one was short-term, with an emphasis on exchanges and reciprocity. Stage two was mid-term, with steps designed to establish mutual trust and cooperation. Stage three was a long-term goal of formal consultation between the two Chinese governments and unification.

More will be said of these guidelines in subsequent chapters, but it is important to note here that they served several important political purposes:

1. The guidelines helped to defuse PRC concerns over Taiwan independence, while at the same time appeasing conservative KMT fears that Lee's government was moving in the direction of Taiwan independence.
2. The guidelines reaffirmed the ROC goal of a united China under democratic principles and set forth specific economic and political reforms which the PRC had to take before unification could occur.
3. The document allayed Taiwanese concerns about their interests being "sold out" by KMT unification advocates.
4. The guidelines improved the ROC's international image by presenting Taipei as now assuming the initiative in trying to resolve the reunification issue in a peaceful, reasonable way.

Amending the Constitution

On April 8, 1991, President Lee Teng-hui called into session an extraordinary session of the National Assembly to begin work on proposed constitutional changes and amendments. The session convened with sharp controversy over procedures. The eight members of the DPP, who had insisted that amendments could only be considered by a new National Assembly elected on Taiwan, walked out of the session in protest on April 16. The next day the opposition party organized a fifteen-hour march of more than 10,000 people in downtown Taipei to protest mainland elected assemblymen taking part in the amendment process.

In an effort to calm emotions and head off a possible militant confrontation between the demonstrators and police, President Lee Teng-hui addressed the nation on television on April 17. He emphasized that "constitutional reform is not revolution." He explained that the purposes of the constitutional amendments being considered were, first, to deal with the emergency powers granted him by the period of national mobilization and, second, to prepare the legal framework for the new National Assembly which would consider additional amendments.[33]

The President's speech calmed public concerns; and the National Assembly, with the DPP still boycotting, passed a series of amendments on April 22. These

- terminated the extraordinary emergency powers given to the ROC president to combat the Chinese Communist threat

- mandated that all senior deputies in the three legislative branches of the ROC government would retire at the end of 1991

- reduced the number of deputies in the National Assembly from 593 to 327, and the size of the Legislative Yuan from 230 to 161

- provided that in the future all delegates would be elected in Taiwan, but that one-third of the seats in both the National Assembly and Legislative Yuan would be reserved for delegates representing overseas and mainland Chinese

- gave the president the right to issue emergency orders in times of national security crises, but mandated that these be confirmed by the Legislative Yuan within ten days or cease to be valid

- gave the president the authority to establish a National Security Council and National Security Bureau, and the Executive Yuan the authority to establish a Central Personnel Administration

- authorized the government to regulate relations with mainland China through the passage of laws.[34]

Termination of Emergency Powers

On April 30 the President enforced the constitutional amendments and proclaimed an end to the ROC's hostility toward the PRC. The President stated:

I have already signed the document authorizing the termination of the Period of National Mobilization for Suppression of the Communist Rebellion as of 00:00 hours, May 1, 1991.

At the same time, in accordance with resolutions adopted at the Second Extraordinary Session of the First National Assembly, I will proclaim tomorrow the abolishment of the Temporary Provisions Effective During the Period of Communist Rebellion and the enactment of constitutional amendments of the Republic of China.

With the proclamation of the end of the mobilization period, we again affirm unequivocally that we will not use force to achieve national unification.[35]

National Assembly Elections

On December 21 elections were held for a new National Assembly. To make way for those newly elected on Taiwan, nearly 470 Assemblymen elected on the mainland retired.

The total number of members in the Second National Assembly was 403. Of these, seventy-eight deputies were elected in the 1986 Taiwan supplementary election and carried over into the new Assembly until their terms expire in January 1993. A total of 225 deputies were directly elected by the people of Taiwan in December 1991, while another 100 deputies were selected as representing "nationwide" and "overseas Chinese." The latter two categories were proportioned between the parties according to party share of their votes in the December elections.

The one-ballot, proportional representative system was adopted by the Legislative Yuan in July 1991. Other changes in election procedures required ROC voters and candidates to reside in Taiwan for at least six months prior to elections; allowed political parties to campaign on television; and forbade state-run enterprises and corporations to donate funds to candidates.

The KMT's platform in the election emphasized the need to amend the existing Constitution, to oppose Taiwan independence, to revise the present method of electing the president, and to promote civilian exchanges and step-by-step realization of unification through the Guidelines for National Unification.

The DPP's platform advocated the adopting of a new "Basic Law" to replace the 1947 Constitution, founding an independent sovereign "Republic of Taiwan," supporting the presidential system of government for Taiwan, adopting direct elections of the president, and eliminating the Control Yuan, Examination Yuan, and the National Assembly.

The most controversial issue in the election was Taiwan independence. The DPP in its Fifth Party Congress in October 1991 voted to include in its platform a call for the establishment of a Republic of Taiwan independent from China. The leader of the moderate Formosa faction, Hsu Hsin-liang, narrowly defeated the radical New Movement faction leader Shih Ming-te by 180 to 163 votes. Nonetheless, the New Movement faction won for the first time a majority on the DPP Standing Committee, having six members to four for the Formosa faction and one independent.

In quick response to the DPP platform clause, both President Lee Teng-hui and Premier Hau Pei-tsun warned that there could be only one China and that the ROC government would not tolerate irresponsible efforts to undermine the country.[36] An investigation was launched to determine if the DPP should be banned.

Although the DPP action was clearly illegal, Premier Hau Pei-tsun met with opposition leaders and worked out a compromise of sorts: Hau promised not to take action against the DPP until after the elections, and the DPP agreed in principle that the PRC threat to Taiwan in case it declares independence should be taken seriously.

In the December 1991 elections, the KMT won 71 percent of the votes, winning 179 of the regional seats, 60 of the nationwide seats, and 15 of the Overseas Chinese seats. This represented a total of 254 of the available 325 seats. The DPP won 24 percent of the vote, or 41 of the regional seats, 20 of the nationwide seats, and 5 of the Overseas Chinese seats. Only 5 seats were won by other parties or independents.

Since 64 KMT deputies had been elected in 1986, along with 9 DPP and 5 other party and independent deputies, the new 403-member Second National Assembly was comprised of 318 KMT (79 percent), 75 DPP (19 percent), and 10 other parties and independents (2 percent).

The December 1991 elections represented a significant comeback for the KMT, which won only about sixty percent of the vote in the 1989 elections. Similarly, the 1991 elections were deemed a loss for the DPP, which dropped about seven percentage points. Many analysts attributed the outcome of the vote to the public's negative reaction to the DPP's perceived efforts to turn the election into a plebiscite on Taiwan independence. Lin Cho-shui, the radical leader who masterminded the DPP's adoption of the controversial party platform, was defeated. Only two New Movement members were elected.

The election outcome strongly implied that the people of Taiwan do not want to move in the direction of Taiwan independence, at least not under conditions prevailing in late 1991. Other factors were no doubt involved in the DPP defeat, including sharp disagreement between the Formosa and New Movement factions, the irritation caused by constant DPP disruption of normal government functions, the significant progress the KMT had made in democratic reform, the retirement of the senior parliamentarians, and the highly effective KMT political machine which concentrated on winning this election in order to seat three-fourths of the Assembly's members. Such a majority was necessary to ensure that KMT-sponsored amendments to the Constitution could not be blocked by the opposition.

Conclusion

For the remainder of this century, Taiwan will be making the difficult transition from an authoritarian regime to a democracy. One of the principal problems confronting Taiwan in this transition is that democratization occurred very rapidly, without adequate legal and procedural mechanisms in place. Just as the ROC needed infrastructure to "take off" economically, so Taiwan needs a legal and political framework to "take off" politically if its new democracy is to work effectively.

The tasks of amending the 1947 Constitution and passing implementing legislation are essential to create this framework for democracy. As such, one of the greatest threats to Taiwan's democracy is the destruction of this process of legal construction by the DPP. Being new, Taiwan's democracy is fragile. Efforts to paralyze the Legislative Yuan and National Assembly, to keep needed legislation from passing, to use violence to prevent free and open debate on issues, and to refuse to abide by majority rule are destructive of democracy and likely to result in one of two outcomes: the loss of public support for the DPP or the reversal of democratic trends on Taiwan.

A democracy requires a viable opposition, effective checks and balances, and mutual tolerance and respect between majority and minority members of the government. The KMT, for its part, has demonstrated a willingness to play by democratic rules. It is extremely unlikely the people of Taiwan will allow the KMT to reverse this direction without just cause. Thus, if the opposition decides to pursue its interests through legitimate democratic means, then democracy will probably flourish on Taiwan.

The fundamental problem in ROC politics is that the KMT and DPP cannot agree on their country's name, constitution, or flag. By refusing to swear allegiance to a common nation and to serve the interests of a common national identity, the ruling and opposition parties find cooperation frustratingly difficult.

Political change on Taiwan will force the KMT and the DPP to make painful choices about their future roles in Taiwan politics. First among these choices for the KMT will be a redefinition of the nature of the party. The historic mission of the KMT has been that of a revolutionary party dedicated to the unification of China under a democratic government. More recently, it has stressed the growth of democracy on Taiwan as a political example for the mainland. Most KMT leaders believe the party continues to have a dual role as both a revolutionary and a democratic party, and hence a dual responsibility on Taiwan of both leading public opinion and following public opinion.

But balancing these dual roles and responsibilities is more easily said than done. To accomplish this in a democracy, the KMT will have to convince the Taiwan people that it is in their best interests to pursue a policy of eventual reunification. Convincing the Taiwanese people that such is the case may not be an easy task, especially when one considers that the KMT has already had nearly forty years of control over most forms of public information and education on the island. The DPP's platform of self-determination is proof that reunification is not acceptable to a significant portion of Taiwanese.

Just as the KMT must redefine itself as a result of the political transformation underway on Taiwan, so the DPP must determine what type of political party it should become. If the DPP is serious about becoming the ruling party of Taiwan through democratic elections, then it must act responsibly and appeal to mainstream voters by helping to solve the many immediate and practical problems facing the nation. The tactics of disrupting the National Assembly and Legislative Yuan are not in keeping with this requirement. Nor can the DPP succeed in a pluralistic society if it remains identified as a party solely for the Taiwanese. It must attract mainlanders as well.

The DPP is plagued by internal divisions. Its policies are heavily influenced by a strong minority of radicals who want to bring about an immediate change in the country's direction rather than to work within the system according to democratic rules to bring about gradual change. Eventually, the DPP may divide into two distinct groups, moderate and radical, in which case new coalitions will be formed in Taiwan politics.

The probability of the DPP or another opposition party gaining control of Taiwan's government is small for the remainder of this century. Nonetheless, the emergence of the DPP and its promotion of self-determination for the Taiwan people have introduced elements of uncertainty in Taiwan politics.

The issue of whether to seek eventual reunification or Taiwan independence will probably remain at the core of Taiwan politics for much of the 1990s. Yet even with this divisive issue, the political evolution on Taiwan seems firmly set toward representative democracy.

Notes

1. A discussion of political reform in Taiwan from 1986 until early 1988, with excellent background information, can be found in Hung-mao Tien, *The Great Transition: Political and Social Change in the Republic of China* (Stanford, CA: Hoover Institution Press, 1989).

2. In addition to the KMT, the ROC brought members of two other political parties to Taiwan from the mainland, the Young China Party and the China Democratic Socialist Party. These two parties were very weak and did not serve as an effective opposition to the KMT in the legislative bodies.

3. *Free China Journal,* June 5, 1989, p. 1. Hereafter referred to as FCJ.

4. FCJ, June 29, 1989, p. 5.

5. For an analysis of these important elections, see Martin L. Lasater, *A Step Toward Democracy: The December 1989 Elections in Taiwan, Republic of China* (Lanham, MD: University Press of America, 1990).

6. See "Platform of the Kuomintang of China," *Getting to Know the KMT Series,* no. 10 (Taipei, Taiwan: China Cultural Services, 1989).

7. Taken from *DPP: Democratic Progressive Party* (Taipei, Taiwan: DPP, 1989).

8. The DPP was less successful in smaller elections. For example, on January 20, 1990, local elections were held for 842 seats on county, city and town councils, and 309 local executive positions. The KMT won 70 percent of these positions, while the DPP won only 6 percent of the council seats and 2 percent of the executive posts. Independents won most of the other seats. A similar pattern of voting arose in the June 1990 elections for town and village representatives. The KMT won 77 percent, independents won 21 percent, and the DPP won 2 percent. In elections for neighborhood and ward leaders, the KMT won 73 percent of the total, independents won 24 percent, and the DPP won 1 percent.

9. FCJ, February 8, 1990, p. 1.

10. FCJ, February 15, 1990, p. 1.

11. FCJ, February 26, 1990, p. 1.

12. FCJ, March 15, 1990, p. 1.

13. FCJ, April 2, 1990, p. 2.

14. FCJ, April 5, 1990, p. 1.

15. FCJ, April 12, 1990, p. 2.

16. FCJ, May 24, 1990, p. 1.

17. FCJ, May 7, 1990, p. 1.

18. FCJ, May 14, 1990, p. 2.

19. FCJ, June 14, 1990, p. 2.

20. FCJ, June 18, 1990, p. 1.

21. FCJ, October 1, 1990, p. 1.

22. FCJ, January 24, 1991, p. 2.

23. FCJ, September 17, 1990, p. 1.

24. FCJ, October 11, 1990, p. 2.

25. FCJ, October 11, 1990, p. 2.

26. The results of the poll were printed in FCJ, October 18, 1990, p. 1.

27. FCJ, December 6, 1990, p. 1.

28. See *Far Eastern Economic Review,* January 31, 1991, p. 24.

29. FCJ, December 24, 1990, p. 2.

30. The text of Lee's speech can be found in FCJ, October 11, 1990, p. 1.

31. For the text of Lee's speech, see FCJ, January 7, 1991, p. 5.

32. FCJ, January 28, 1991, p. 1.

33. FCJ, April 22, 1991, p. 1.

34. FCJ, May 7, 1991, p. 7.

35. FCJ, May 2, 1991, p. 1.

36. For the texts of statements by the President and Premier, see FCJ, October 18, 1991, p. 1.

3

Taiwan's Economic Development

Because of its dynamic economy, Taiwan is considered a Newly Industrialized Country (NIC) and one of the "four little dragons of Asia" along with South Korea, Hong Kong, and Singapore. At current prices, its per capita Gross National Product (GNP) in 1951 was $145. In 1991 Taiwan's per capita GNP was over $8,000, surpassed in Asia only by Japan, Australia, Hong Kong, and Singapore. Taiwan was the world's fifteenth largest trading nation in 1991, and it held the world's largest foreign exchange reserves.

The average annual growth rate of Taiwan's economy from 1952 until 1989 was 8.9 percent, compared to 3.5 percent for industrialized countries and 5 percent for developing countries. In 1990 Taiwan's growth rate dropped to 5 percent, in part because of the slowdown in the world's economy due to the Persian Gulf crisis which arose in August. But in 1991 Taiwan's growth rate increased to 7.2 percent, while the world economy experienced a negative 0.3 percent growth rate.

At the same time that Taiwan's economy was rapidly growing, the ROC government was implementing policies to distribute national wealth. In 1953 the ratio of the population by income of the top 20 percent to the bottom 20 percent was 20.5 to 1. By 1988 that ratio was 4.85 to 1, one of the world's most equitable and a reflection in part of the *San Min Chu-i* principle of social well-being.

The "Taiwan model" of economic development has attracted wide attention in the Third World. Several communist countries, including the PRC, have carefully studied the Taiwan model and adopted some of its strategies to develop and improve their own economies.

This chapter briefly describes Taiwan's economy, with special emphasis placed on economic conditions in 1991, trade relations with the United States and other major trading partners, economic interaction with the PRC, and ROC goals and policies which will guide Taiwan's economic development over the next few years.

Stages of Development and Key Economic Policies

One characteristic of Taiwan's economy is the close relationship between government and private business to develop preferred sectors of the economy. As such, Taiwan's economic development has gone through four general phases since World War II.

The first stage occurred from 1945–1952 and focused on rehabilitation and recovery from the devastation caused by Allied bombing and blockade. During this stage, the ROC concentrated on stabilizing prices and restoring agricultural production and existing industries.

The second stage was between 1953 and 1960, when two major four-year economic development plans were implemented. The increase of agricultural and industrial production was the primary objective, as was continued effort toward consumer price stabilization. U.S. economic assistance, which totalled nearly $2 billion through 1965 when it was phased out, combined effectively with government policy to achieve a growth rate of over 7 percent. Per capita GNP grew more slowly because of a 3.6 percent rise in population.

During this phase of economic development, the government adopted a policy of import substitution. Foreign exchange was limited, and raw materials and equipment had to be imported. Taiwan's import needs were so high that a continuous trade deficit was experienced. The major exports were agricultural goods.

The third stage of economic development occurred between 1961 and 1972, when the third, fourth, and fifth four-year plans were implemented. The economy grew more than 10 percent annually, with savings, investment, and exports increasing rapidly. Labor productivity increased and unit labor costs fell, giving Taiwan a significant export advantage. This was a period of sustained economic growth because of increasing demands for Taiwan's exports. Stable commodity prices worldwide kept the cost of imports within predictable bounds.

The fourth stage of Taiwan's economic development began in 1973 and continued through 1991. It was characterized by heavy dependence on stability in the international marketplace and an economy driven by expanding exports. During times of worldwide recession, such as the early 1970s due to rapid oil price increases, the ROC initiated major infrastructure projects which pumped billions of dollars into the domestic economy. These policies compensated for falling exports and shrinking private investment. Taiwan experienced continued high levels of growth throughout this period.

Key Economic Strategies

Taiwan's economic strategies have been designed to balance competing pressures. One key strategy was the balanced development of agriculture and industry. The restoration of agriculture production was the first economic priority of the ROC during its early period of rule on Taiwan. By concentrating on agriculture, the ROC created a sound economic base from which to industrialize later.

As part of its agricultural policies, Taiwan implemented a highly successful land reform program which gave land to the farmers and took it out of the hands of absentee landlords. An increase in farm production soon followed, which provided the first raw materials for budding industries. Growing farm incomes led to increased demand for locally produced manufactured goods, as well as needed funds for investment.

Other key economic strategies balanced light and heavy industry. As surplus farm labor became available due to higher agricultural productivity, the government shifted this labor pool into light, labor-intensive industries such as textiles, plastic products, paper, wood products, and electrical appliances. These industries did not require too great of a capital outlay, but provided a fairly quick return in profits.

After 1960 more emphasis was placed on industries requiring higher levels of investment capital, such as refrigerators, washing machines, televisions, and motorcycles. Toward the end of the decade, accumulated capital and management expertise reached the point where the government began to implement policies favoring the development of heavy and chemical industries. More recently, high-tech and service industries have been given priority by the government.

A balance also was maintained between policies promoting import substitution and export expansion. After its initial post-war recovery, import substitution was necessary to conserve scarce foreign exchange. By the late 1950s, however, Taiwan's domestic market was saturated with light consumer goods. Steps were then taken to build industries geared to exports. This strategy proved exceptionally successful, and by the end of the 1960s manufactured goods had replaced agricultural products as Taiwan's chief export. The rapid expansion of industrial exports has remained a vital engine of Taiwan's economic growth.

Yet another balance had to be struck between manpower and technology. The Chinese are a talented, intelligent people who traditionally possess a strong work ethic. These qualities have been enhanced on Taiwan by a universal system of education. Wages on Taiwan, however, have been relatively low until recently. Taiwan's cheap, high quality labor gave its exports a significant price advantage in international markets.

Taiwan's labor cost advantage has eroded, as other developing countries have built their own labor-intensive industries. Unable to compete with cheaper labor costs, Taiwan in recent years has turned increasingly to high technology to improve the quality and sophistication of its products. The introduction of advanced technology in turn has necessitated educational reform and large-scale retraining programs. These reforms resulted in higher wages for a better trained, more professional work force, but at the same time they contributed to a severe shortage of manual labor on the island.

The government's strategy of using public construction to stimulate the economy should also be noted as a key factor in Taiwan's economic development. Taiwan's infrastructure was heavily damaged in World War II. These facilities were soon repaired, but by the mid-1960s the inadequacies of the existing infrastructure were constraining economic growth. Public construction projects pushed forward by Premier Chiang Ching-kuo rapidly improved the island's transportation, communications, and port facilities. In 1979 and 1985 additional major public construction projects were started, including the construction of a subway system in Taipei and a mass rapid transit system along the island's densely populated west coast. Under President Lee Teng-hui, a $303 billion Six-Year National Development Plan has been implemented, one facet of which is a $37 billion commitment to improve Taiwan's land transportation system.

Viewed from the perspective of ten-year intervals, the percentage of Gross Domestic Product (GDP) produced by agriculture was reduced from nearly 33 percent during the 1950s to less than 8 percent during the 1980s. Industry contributed a little over 20 percent to GDP in the 1950s and nearly 45 percent in the 1980s. Services contributed a fairly consistent 46 percent during this forty-year period.

During the 1950s, the ratio of exports to GNP was about 9 percent, increasing to over 53 percent in the 1980s. The percentage of imports to GNP was 15.5 percent in the 1950s and 44 percent in the 1980s. Whereas the trade balance/GNP ratio was a negative 4 percent during the 1950s, that ratio changed into a positive 11 percent in the 1980s.

Taiwan has consistently enjoyed a trade surplus since the mid-1970s, but it experienced a trade deficit for many years prior to then. In the five years between 1987 and 1991, Taiwan's trade surplus totalled nearly $70 billion, helping to create unparalleled prosperity on the island but also causing problems with its most important trading partner, the United States.

Domestic Economy

Four major trends characterized Taiwan's economy over the past decade. First, increasingly large foreign exchange reserves were accumulated due to trade surpluses. This put intense pressure on the exchange value of the New Taiwan Dollar (NT$), causing it to appreciate from about NT $40 to US $1 in the early 1980s to NT $25 to US $1 in 1991. Second, both domestic consumption and domestic investment fell behind production, leaving savings very large. This resulted in large-scale overseas investment, particularly in the United States, Southeast Asia, and mainland China. Third, the share of the manufacturing sector in total GNP reached its peak by the middle of the 1980s, signalling a structural change in the economy. Since then, much greater emphasis has been placed on high-tech and service industries. And fourth, the government shifted toward more liberal economic policies, resulting in the removal of most trade barriers and in movement toward privatization of state-owned enterprises.

1991 Economic Data

Taiwan's GNP in 1991 was $180.1 billion, the twenty-first largest in the world. Per capita income was $8,810, ranking number thirteen in the world.[1] Between 1986 and 1991, Taiwan's GNP increased over 230 percent, while its per capita GNP more than doubled. The 1992 per capita GNP is forecast to be in excess of $10,000.

Taiwan had a very high GNP growth rate of 7.3 percent in 1989, a fair rate of 5.0 percent in 1990, and a high rate of 7.2 percent in 1991. These growth rates, coupled with the low increase in consumer prices (3.6 percent in 1991), very low inflation (0.2 percent), the low unemployment rate (1.5 percent), and high labor productivity (increasing 11.33 percent over 1990), meant that Taiwan's residents enjoyed a visibly improving standard of living. Cash was plentiful. In 1991 domestic savings reached $57.3 billion, 30 percent of the nation's total GNP.

Taiwan's foreign exchange reserves at the end of 1991 were over $82 billion, the largest in the world. Its external public debt was a very low $800 million. Taiwan's current accounts balance was $9.5 billion in 1991, down from $10.8 billion in 1990 and $11.4 billion in 1989.

Export trade remained an important foundation for Taiwan's economy, totalling $76 billion in 1991 and accounting for 42 percent of GNP. About 30 percent of those exports were purchased by Americans. Foreign investment in Taiwan from 1952–1991 totalled $15 billion, 28 percent of which ($4.3 billion) came from the United States.

Taiwan's growth rate of 7.2 percent in 1991 compared favorably to Hong Kong's 4 percent and South Korea's 6 percent, although it fell behind Singapore's 8 percent growth rate. The principal factors behind Taiwan's economic growth in 1991 were:

- heavy public investment in large infrastructure projects
- an increase in domestic investment

- increased domestic demand for locally produced goods
- a significant improvement in exports caused mainly by exports of intermediate goods to production bases in Southeast Asia and on mainland China.

Taiwan's trade in 1991 totalled $139 billion, the world's fifteenth largest, with $76.2 billion in exports and $62.9 billion in imports. Exports grew 13 percent over 1990, while imports increased 15 percent. Taiwan's global trade surplus increased 6.4 percent to $13.3 billion. The most important growth factor in exports was transshipment of goods via Hong Kong to the PRC. Exports to Hong Kong increased 45 percent to $12.4 billion. Taiwan's $10.5 billion trade surplus with Hong Kong in 1991 surpassed the ROC trade surplus with the United States for the first time.

Mainland China and Southeast Asia have become significant bases for Taiwan-owned factories assembling goods for export to third countries. Most of these overseas production facilities were established in the 1987–1990 period, when the rapid appreciation of the New Taiwan Dollar and rising costs for production on Taiwan drove industrialists and investors offshore to find low labor and land costs. This resulted in a drop in domestic investment on Taiwan of over 8 percent in 1990. In 1991, however, the trend reversed, with a nearly 5 percent increase in domestic investment. This was largely due to a dynamic local market and opportunities inherent in the government's $303 billion six-year economic development plan.

Foreign investment on Taiwan was down 23 percent in 1991. Investments from Japan, which totalled about 30 percent of all foreign investment, dropped 36 percent. U.S. investments increased by 5 percent. Most foreign investors looked elsewhere for labor-intensive manufacturing opportunities, although investment in Taiwan's high-technology and capital-intensive industries increased.

Several important economic trends emerged on Taiwan during the five-year period of 1987–1991. First, while Taiwan's economy continued to be trade-oriented, much of its actual growth was driven by rising consumer demands. Domestic demand grew from 81 percent of GNP in 1987, to 90 percent in 1990, and to 93 percent in 1991.

Second, significant structural change in the economy took place. By 1988 the service sector began to contribute a larger share to Taiwan's GDP than did industry; meanwhile, agriculture's share continued to fall. The service industry has thus become the main force in Taiwan's economy. According to the Republic of China Yearbook, 1990–1991, the service sector contributed 5.3 percent to the 9.9 percent annual economic growth rate experienced by the ROC from 1986 to 1989. Industrial production contributed 4.2 percent.[2] In 1991 service firms grew 8.6 percent, while manufacturing firms grew 6.4 percent and agriculture grew 0.7 percent. Light and heavy industry grew 8 percent and 5 percent, respectively.

Third, important structural change occurred in industry itself. The conventional mainstay of the Taiwan economy, labor-intensive industries, shrank while heavy and technology-intensive industries expanded. This was necessary because of the sharp appreciation of the New Taiwan Dollar,[3] a growing labor shortage, rising wages on Taiwan, and increased competition from mainland China and developing countries in Southeast Asia. In 1989 labor-intensive industries accounted for 44.2 percent of manufacturing on Taiwan, down from 52.6 percent in 1985. Over the same period, capital- and technology-intensive industries rose from 47 percent to 55.8 percent.

Economic Problems

Taiwan's rapid economic growth has brought negative as well as positive results. There is too much idle capital on the island, and this has contributed to a serious erosion of Taiwan's famous work ethic. Real estate prices have skyrocketed, especially in crowded Taipei which is now one of the world's ten most expensive places to live. Because the price of housing often doubles within a few months, many residents have become millionaires overnight. Others have become wealthy through Taiwan's volatile stock market or numerous lotteries. The example of the nouveaux riches has prompted many others to take time off work to speculate in real estate, gamble on the stock market, or play the lotteries. Believing that money can be earned faster and easier through these non-productive endeavors, many are refusing to work with their hands. People are working fewer hours because wages are higher. Increasingly, businesses are closed at night and over the weekends. Fewer taxis can be found during off-hours.

The combination of a weakening work ethic, low wages in labor intensive sectors of the economy, and frequently inadequate working conditions has contributed to a serious labor shortage on Taiwan. Many government construction projects have their bids go unanswered because construction firms cannot find workers. The labor shortage has led to a rapidly growing illegal work force on Taiwan. Most illegal workers come from Southeast Asia. In February 1991, for example, there were an estimated 60,000 Filipinos working illegally in Taiwan. In 1990 roughly half of the textile industry's production lines were dependent on illegal foreign laborers.

The government has tried to solve the problems of labor shortages and illegal workers by adopting a quota system. About 30,000 workers from Southeast Asia were approved in the fall of 1991 to work in public construction projects, textiles, basic metal processing, metal products, machinery, electric and electronic products, and general construction.

A more serious problem with security overtones is that a growing number of illegal workers are coming from mainland China. A small percentage of these are probably agents deliberately inserted into Taiwan by the PRC to engage in sabotage, assassination, riots, and other disruptive activities in the event of a military crisis in the Taiwan Strait.

Taiwan's more democratic atmosphere has led to acceptance of the right to strike. In mid-1988, for example, bus and train workers went on strike for higher wages. Paralysis of the island's transportation system was avoided only because the military used its buses for public transportation. The DPP and other opposition political parties sometimes encourage labor to demand higher wages and to strike for worker rights.

Partly as a result of greater attention being paid to worker demands, wages on Taiwan are steadily increasing. In 1991 wages rose an average of 10 percent. Increased wages improve the lifestyle of Taiwan's workers, but higher wages also increase the per unit cost of Taiwan's products. Since most Taiwan businesses traditionally maintain a low profit margin to gain advantage in domestic and international markets, rising labor costs have forced many labor-intensive industries and smaller trading firms to go out of business.

Many Taiwan industrialists are faced with a choice of either relocating their factories to other countries or upgrading their existing plants to produce higher quality goods. A large number have moved their production lines overseas. The government's preferred solution is to establish new higher-value added industries on Taiwan. However, this requires massive retraining of displaced workers or higher unemployment rates.

In its rush to industrialize, the government allowed Taiwan's environment to deteriorate seriously. Taipei, Kaohsiung, and other major cities are heavily polluted. Since the lifting of martial law, the public has begun to severely criticize the government for its neglect of the environment. This has had some adverse impact on Taiwan's economic growth. Plans for a fourth nuclear power plant and two naphtha crackers were postponed for years because of protests by environmentalists, causing concern among officials that Taiwan could face an energy shortage in the near future. Also, Taiwan residents now frequently refuse to allow new factories to be built in their neighborhoods for fear of added pollution. It is common for people to refuse to sell their land to the government for major infrastructure projects such as road construction.

The appreciation of the New Taiwan Dollar, higher labor costs, labor shortages, increased land costs, anti-pollution requirements, political uncertainty, and the rising crime rate have driven many Taiwan investors overseas. At the end of 1991, Taiwan investments overseas totalled $19 billion, making Taiwan the world's ninth largest supplier of investment capital. After Japan, Taiwan is the world's second largest investor in Southeast Asia. Between 1987 and 1990, Taiwan investments in Southeast Asia rose 420 percent. One example is Malaysia. By early 1992 Taiwan had invested nearly $5 billion in that country, mostly in electronics, textiles, and petrochemicals.

In general, banking and the insurance sectors were the most popular areas for Taiwan enterprises relocating capital or operations overseas, followed by electronics and electrical appliances. Other major investments went to plants producing machinery, textiles, sporting goods, footwear, petrochemical products, and toys.

The emigration of export industries from Taiwan to Southeast Asia and mainland China in 1990 resulted in negative growth in Taiwan's industrial production for the first time in fifteen years. In 1991, however, the trend toward overseas investment reversed suddenly, and local businessmen returned to Taiwan. Private domestic investment grew 4.7 percent in 1991, while overseas investments fell dramatically. Most of the domestic investments went into capital- and technology-intensive enterprises to take advantage of opportunities associated with the government's six-year economic development plan.

Economic Restructuring

Taiwan reached a point in the early 1980s when major restructuring of its economy had to occur. Two areas of needed restructuring were identified. First, domestic demand as a percentage of GNP had to increase so the economy would not be overly dependent upon exports for growth. Greater consumerism was encouraged and public expenditures for various infrastructure, environmental, cultural, and other projects were increased. To a certain extent, this restructuring effort was successful; a larger percentage of GNP is now produced domestically. However, since Taiwan's population is too small to sustain a high level of economic growth through consumerism, export trade continues to play a vital role in the economy.

The second area identified for restructuring is even more difficult to achieve: Taiwan's businessmen must be convinced to form larger, more efficient enterprises so the country's products can remain competitive in international markets. In 1989–1990, over 90 percent of Taiwan's enterprises were small to middle-sized, as were 98 percent of all local manufacturers.[4] These nearly 780,000 businesses accounted for 60 percent of the island's total work force and 55 percent of its GNP. The companies and their employees paid nearly 70 percent of the total taxes on Taiwan and produced over 60 percent of its total exports. In 1989 Taiwan's two largest trading firms accounted for only 0.33 percent of Taiwan's trade, while some 3,230 medium-and small-sized firms managed 65 percent of the island's trade.

The government has attempted to persuade smaller businesses to merge into larger enterprises and to change from labor-intensive industries to capital- and technology-intensive industries. Special tax breaks are given to those who invest in such fields as information technology, civil aviation, energy, telecommunications, production automation, and biotechnology. Despite these and many other incentives, the Chinese tradition of every man wanting to be his own boss presents an almost insurmountable obstacle to merger. Indeed, many businessmen have elected to relocate their factories to other countries rather than to give up their autonomy on Taiwan.

Six-Year National Development Plan

In February 1991 the government approved an ambitious Six-Year National Development Plan to bring Taiwan into the ranks of developed nations by the year 2000. Specific goals were to make the ROC the world's tenth largest trading nation and to boost per capita income to $14,000 by 1996. The costs of the plan were estimated to be $303 billion. Government investment will be about 14 percent. Other investments will come from public bonds, tax hikes, private investment, and investments from state-owned enterprises.

Some 775 projects composed the plan, covering a wide range of economic, educational, cultural, medical, environmental, and social areas. The plan assumed a 7 percent annual economic growth rate and an annual inflation rate of 3.5 percent. A total of $193 billion will be spent on public construction, with investments from the government and state-run enterprises amounting to 80 percent of the total.

The plan aimed to privatize and internationalize many state-run enterprises. Privatization will be accomplished through issuing stock, a certain percentage of which foreigners can purchase. Internationalization will be enhanced by floating corporate bonds abroad.

One high-priority item in the six-year plan was the cleaning up of the environment. A total of $37 billion was earmarked for this purpose, of which the government will spend $19 billion with the remainder evenly split between state-run and private enterprises.

Much depends on the success of the six-year development plan. Based on past experience with guiding economic transitions on Taiwan, the government believes that massive public and private investment, carefully targeted on key projects, can restructure the economy while at the same time improve the quality of life on Taiwan. There are substantial risks involved in the $303 billion plan, not the least of which is whether the government and private sector can afford to spend so much money. On the other hand, Taiwan's economy needs a "jump-start" to propel it into the ranks of developed nations. The Six-Year National Development Plan, despite its uncertainties, is the ROC's strategy to prepare the Taiwan economy for the challenges of the twenty-first century.

International Economic Relations

With few natural resources other than a talented and hard-working population, Taiwan has made trade the mainstay of its economy. Expanding exports are essential to Taiwan's continued economic growth, indeed, to the ROC's very survival. Because of its dependency on international markets, Taiwan is extremely vulnerable to the vagaries of trade.

In the highly competitive world of trade, Taiwan has done exceptionally well. International lenders rank Taiwan as one of the most credit-worthy countries in the world, generally higher than either Hong Kong or South Korea and just beneath Singapore. Taiwan's southern city of Kaohsiung is expected to pass Hong Kong as the world's largest container port by the year 2000.

In 1991 Taiwan's exports increased 13 percent over 1990 to $76 billion, while imports grew 15 percent to $63 billion. Taiwan's surplus of $13 billion was an increase of 6.4 percent over 1990. Taiwan's trade grew despite the fact that much of the global economy was in recession. The main reason for the expansion was increased trade with Southeast Asia and transshipment via Hong Kong to mainland China. In both cases, exports were mostly to Taiwan-owned factories, the result of overseas investments in recent years. Another bright spot was the increase of exports to Europe, which increased 14.5 percent to $14 billion in 1991, giving Taiwan a $4 billion surplus. This represented an increase of 52 percent over Taiwan's trade surplus with Europe in 1990.

Several patterns can be seen in Taiwan's trade since 1987. First, there is continued growth in the value of total trade, increasing from $88.6 billion in 1987 to over $139 billion in 1991, a 57 percent increase over five years.

Second, Taiwan's annual trade surplus has shrunk and now seems stabilized at around $12–$14 billion. Taiwan's surplus in 1987 was $18.6 billion, while in 1991 it was $13.3 billion.

Third, exports have increased less rapidly than imports. In 1987 Taiwan's exports were $53.6 billion. In 1991 exports were $76.2 billion, a 42 percent increase. Taiwan's imports in 1987 were $35.6 billion, while in 1991 imports were $62.9 billion, an 80 percent increase.

Fourth, the trade to GNP ratio has been steadily declining. In 1987 that ratio was 91 percent; in 1991 it was 77 percent. The ratio of exports to GNP has also dropped. In 1987 the ratio was 55 percent. In 1991 the ratio had declined to 42 percent. While still vital to Taiwan's economy, exports are becoming a less significant engine of growth for the ROC.

Fifth, Taipei has taken major steps to diversify its export markets to reduce dependence on the United States. This effort has been fairly successful. In the period between 1989 and 1991, the U.S. share of ROC exports shrank from 36.2 percent to 29.3 percent. Taiwan no longer maintains the second largest trade surplus with the United States after Japan, its place having been taken in 1991 by the PRC. In 1991 Taiwan's exports to Europe accounted for 18.4 percent of total ROC exports; Hong Kong accounted for 16.1 percent (of which at least 6 percent was transshipped to the mainland); Japan accounted for 12.1 percent; and Southeast Asia accounted for 9.7 percent.

Trade with the United States

Using trade figures cited in the March 1992 *FET: Taiwan,* U.S.-Taiwan trade for 1989 totalled $36 billion.[5] Exports from Taiwan totalled $24 billion and imports from the United States totalled $12 billion. The U.S. share of Taiwan's exports was 36 percent, while the U.S. share of its imports was 23 percent. Taiwan's trade surplus of $12 billion represented 8 percent of the ROC's $150.3 billion GNP for 1989.

In 1990 trade between the United States and Taiwan was valued at $34.4 billion, with exports being $21.7 billion and imports $12.6 billion. The U.S. share of Taiwan's 1990 exports was about 32 percent, while its share of imports was 23 percent. The $9 billion trade surplus enjoyed by Taiwan was 5.6 percent of the ROC GNP of $161.7 billion for 1990.

In 1991 U.S.-Taiwan trade was $36.4 billion. Exports to the United States totalled $22.3 billion, while imports amounted to $14.1 billion. The ROC trade surplus with the United States was $8.2 billion, or 4.6 percent of Taiwan's GNP of $180.1 billion. In 1991 exports to the United States accounted for 29.3 percent of Taiwan's total exports, while imports were 22.4 percent of Taiwan's total imports.

These figures suggest several trends in U.S.-Taiwan trade. First, the value of trade between the two countries is steadily increasing, but not at alarming rates. Overall, the increase in Taiwan's trade from 1987 to 1991 was 57 percent, while the increase in U.S.-Taiwan trade was 16 percent.

Second, the United States is purchasing a lower percentage of Taiwan's total exports. In 1987, for example, the United States purchased 44 percent of Taiwan's total exports, whereas in 1991 the United States purchased 29 percent.

Third, despite ROC government efforts to encourage the purchase of American products, Taiwan is purchasing only a slightly larger percentage of its total imports from the United States. In 1987 the percentage of American goods and services purchased by Taiwan was 21 percent of total Taiwan imports. In 1991 that percentage was 22 percent.

Fourth, Taiwan's trade surplus with the United States has been declining steadily. In 1987 Taiwan enjoyed a surplus of more than $16 billion with the United States. In 1991 that amount had fallen to a little over $8 billion, a 50 percent reduction. Between 1989 and 1991 alone, Taiwan's trade surplus with the United States decreased nearly 32 percent.

Fifth, the percentage of Taiwan's GNP attributable to Taiwan's trade surplus with the United States has also decreased significantly. In 1987 the ratio between the ROC trade surplus with the United States and Taiwan's GNP was 16.5 percent. By 1991 it was 4.5 percent, a 73 percent reduction over the five-year period.

Many of these trends reflect deliberate efforts by Taipei to solve trade difficulties with the United States which arose during the last three years of the Reagan administration (1986–1988). U.S. trade deficits with Taiwan during this period exceeded $40 billion, leading to strong congressional pressure to impose protectionist legislation against Taiwan products and to force Taiwan to purchase more American goods. U.S. negotiators demanded that Taipei eliminate unfair trading practices such as counterfeiting American products or dumping Taiwan-made goods at below-market prices in the United States. Other demands included appreciation of the ROC currency, removing tariff and non-tariff barriers, and purchasing big-ticket items such as airplanes from American manufacturers. Taiwan, along with South Korea, Hong Kong, and Singapore, were graduated from the U.S. Generalized System of Preferences (GSP) in early 1989.

In May 1989 the Bush administration included Taiwan, along with seven other countries, in a "priority watch list" for possible violations of intellectual property rights under the "Super 301" provision of the 1988 Omnibus Trade and Competitiveness Act. However, Washington soon eased up on its pressure tactics when Taiwan announced a Trade Action Plan, promising to reduce its trade surplus with the United States by at least 10 percent a year. Since then, the U.S. trade deficit with Taiwan has decreased to levels more politically palatable to Washington.

In addition to its Trade Action Plan, Taiwan appreciated the value of the New Taiwan Dollar by over 50 percent, lifted trade barriers to U.S. goods and services, actively promoted the purchase of U.S. products on the Taiwan market, extended favorable treatment to Americans seeking business opportunities in Taiwan, sent more than a dozen "Buy America" missions to the United States to purchase in excess of $11 billion of American products, and made major purchases of U.S. goods and services for ROC public works and state-owned enterprises.

These efforts on Taiwan's part to accommodate U.S. concerns over its trade deficit were deeply appreciated in Washington. Many contrasted Taipei's behavior to that of Tokyo, where Washington was experiencing great frustration over annual trade deficits in the $40–$50 billion range.

Over the past few years there have been numerous agreements signed between the United States and Taiwan governing trade and other commercial matters. In January 1989 an Agreement for the Protection of Copyright was signed, and in May of that year an Agreement on Audio-Visual Copyright Protection was approved by both sides. These agreements have helped to resolve many of the copyright and intellectual property right complaints lodged by American citizens and companies. In 1990 there were more than thirteen major rounds of trade talks between the United States and Taiwan, more than with any other U.S. trading partner.

One unintended result of Washington's pressure on Taiwan to redress its large trade surplus was massive Taiwanese investment in mainland China and Southeast Asia. Many labor-intensive industries were relocated, especially in apparel, footwear, toys, umbrellas, and simple electronic goods. By 1991 completed factories had begun to import goods from Taiwan for final assembly. These Taiwan-owned factories then exported their products to the United States under the host country's label. This resulted in a lower surplus for Taiwan in its trade with the United States, but a sharp increase in U.S. imports from mainland China and Southeast Asia.

Businesses remaining on Taiwan are rapidly upgrading their manufacturing operations and expanding their interests to include capital- and technology-intensive industries in areas such as advanced electronic goods, automobiles, and aeronautical equipment. The upgrading of Taiwan's industry and the implementation of the six-year development plan have increased dramatically Taiwan's need for imported machinery, equipment, and technical services.

According to the *FET: Taiwan* report of March 1992, major opportunities existed for U.S. businesses in the following areas: pollution control, computers and peripherals, computer software, integrated circuits, semiconductor manufacturing equipment, telecommunications equipment, scientific instruments, medical equipment, industrial process controls, chemical production machinery, Computer-Aided Design and Computer-Aided Manufacturing, mass transportation equipment and services, power plants, cosmetics and toiletries, and high-value food products. Also, the liberalization of Taiwan's banking, securities, and insurance industries require specialized manpower available from the United States.

Trade with Japan

Japan is Taiwan's second most important trading partner and the largest source of ROC imports. Taiwan is Japan's fourth-largest market and sixth-biggest supplier of imports.

Much of the high technology, machinery, and electronic goods necessary for Taiwan's industrial growth and modernization come from Japan. In 1990 about 60 percent of Japanese imports into Taiwan were industrial components; another 30 percent were machine tools, construction equipment, and other heavy-industrial items. Less than 10 percent of the imports were consumer goods.

In 1991 trade with Japan totalled $28 billion, with Taiwan experiencing a nearly $10 billion deficit, up more than 26 percent over 1990. Loosely speaking, each year Taiwan's trade deficit with Japan cancels the ROC trade surplus with the United States.

In contrast to the generally cooperative trade relationship between the United States and Taiwan, trade between Taipei and Tokyo is often bitter. Taiwan's policy, like that of the United States, is to reduce its trade deficit with Japan through a combination of an appreciation of the yen, more open Japanese markets, fewer purchases of Japanese goods, and increased exports to Japan of high quality products. Also like the United States, Taiwan has great difficulty balancing its trade with Japan. There are several reasons for this, although some are quite different from those influencing U.S.-Japan trade.

In the first place, Taiwan products are not too popular in Japan. Japan can purchase labor-intensive goods more cheaply from other developing countries such as Southeast Asia, and Taiwan's more advanced products are usually not technologically superior to those produced in Japan. Also, Taiwan has few raw materials to export to Japan. Hence, finding a place in Japan's marketplace for Taiwan's products is difficult.

Second, Taiwan's trade liberalization policies, while mostly intended to reduce its trade surplus with the United States, has had the effect of allowing more Japanese products into Taiwan. If Taiwan joins the General Agreement on Tariffs and Trade (GATT), Japan may reap the most benefits because many Japanese products face trade restrictions unilaterally imposed by Taipei.

Third, Tokyo and Taipei do not have official relations, although unofficial liaison was maintained through 1991 by Taiwan's Association of East Asian Relations and Japan's Interchange Association. Japan is very sensitive that its ties with Taiwan do not strain political relations with the PRC. Consequently, Tokyo often does not pay much attention to Taiwan's complaints, despite the fact that trade between Japan and Taiwan is far larger than Japan's trade with mainland China.

Japanese investment on Taiwan has increased significantly in recent years. In 1990 Japanese companies accounted for half of the foreign investments on Taiwan and 65 percent of their dollar value. There were more than 1,200 Japanese companies located on Taiwan, and much of Taiwan's trade with Japan was channelled through these companies. Hence, a great deal of the profit from Taiwan's trade with Japan actually goes to Japanese-owned companies on Taiwan.

In 1991 Japanese investment in Taiwan dropped 36 percent, largely because economic problems in Japan required cut-backs in overseas investments by Japanese bankers and multinationals. With the credit that was available, Japanese investors turned to areas with lower labor costs, such as southern China, Vietnam, and India.

Taiwan's Dollar Diplomacy

As part of its flexible and pragmatic approach to foreign policy since 1987, Taiwan adopted a form of "dollar diplomacy." Simply stated, Taipei used its large volume of trade, rich foreign exchange reserves, and ample opportunities for foreign involvement in the

Six-Year National Development Plan to gain entrance into the world community in ways denied it because of other countries' political concerns about offending the PRC.

Taiwan's brand of dollar diplomacy has been fairly successful. In 1990–1991 improved economic relations were seen with Great Britain, Canada, Finland, Ireland, Italy, Indonesia, Australia, Israel, Peru, Bolivia, Nicaragua, Malaysia, United Arab Emirates, and many other countries. By the end of 1991, all European Community (EC) nations except Portugal had offices in Taipei. The EC itself was represented by the European Council of Commerce and Trade.

One example of the growing success of dollar diplomacy was the effort by France in 1990 and 1991 to upgrade commercial relations with Taipei. Roger Fauroux, Minister of French Industry and Territorial Development, led a 28-member French delegation to Taipei in January 1991. The two sides agreed to open direct flights between Taipei and Paris and to establish several high-tech joint ventures in areas such as nuclear energy, electronics, aerospace, telecommunications, and biochemistry. At the close of his visit, Fauroux said that France would support Taiwan's entrance into GATT and would try to convince other European members to accept the application as well.[6] Significantly, France approved, over strong PRC protests, several advanced arms sales to Taiwan, including sixteen La Fayette-class frigate hulls for $4.8 billion and, reportedly, advanced Mirage fighters.

Since 1987 Taiwan has rapidly expanded its trade with former and existing communist countries, including Russia, Central and Eastern European countries, and Vietnam. Taiwan's decision to trade with communist countries reversed a decades-old policy of strict anti-communism. In part the decision was made to diversify export markets; in part it was Taipei's attempt to follow the examples of Bonn and Seoul in using ties with communist states to gain advantage over rival communist regimes in another portion of their territories—East Germany in the case of Bonn, North Korea in the case of Seoul, and the PRC in the case of Taipei.

The key communist country with which to establish relations from the point of view of all three democratic capitals was the Soviet Union. Therefore, much progress was seen in Taipei when Moscow mayor Gavriil Popov visited Taiwan during late 1990. In January 1991 the governor of Sakhalin Island, Valentin Fyodorov, flew to Taipei to sound out ROC authorities on the possibility of joint exploitation of Sakhalin's rich oil, timber, coal, and fishing resources. In February, still other Soviet officials were in Taipei to facilitate Taiwan's expansion into the Russian market and to establish joint ventures in various parts of the country.

This strategy of diplomatic maneuver lost much of its utility following the August 1991 revolution in the Soviet Union. Nonetheless, Taiwan's commercial interests in the former Soviet bloc remain. In 1991 Taiwan's trade with Eastern Europe amounted to $701 million, while trade with the entire former Soviet bloc totalled $1.1 billion.

International Economic Organizations

In view of its diplomatic isolation, Taipei must rely heavily on economic instruments of foreign policy to protect its interests. Of great importance in this respect is Taipei's role in international economic organizations such as the Asian Development Bank (ADB), the General Agreement on Tariffs and Trade (GATT), and the Organization for Economic Cooperation and Development (OECD).

The ROC was a founding member of the ADB in 1966 and is one of the Bank's seventeen lending countries. In March 1986 the PRC was admitted to ADB membership after the bank's Board of Directors agreed with Beijing that Taipei's participation as the "Republic of China" was unacceptable. Months of negotiation resulted in a compromise whereby the PRC accepted Taiwan's participation under the name "Taipei, China," a formula similar to that used by the international Olympic Committee and other world bodies to enable both the PRC and Taiwan to be members of the same international organization.[7]

The ADB decision created a policy crisis for Taiwan. In the past, the ROC withdrew when the PRC was admitted as the legal representative of China in international governmental organizations. By 1987 Taipei had withdrawn from all but ten such organizations. Fearing that the ROC would disappear entirely from world forums if this policy was carried out further, many in Taiwan urged the government to accept the compromise designation for the ADB. The government countered that to accept the name change would signify in an official organization, as distinct from an unofficial sporting event, that Taiwan was part of the PRC. Under pressure, the government finally announced that it would neither withdraw from the ADB nor participate in it.

This awkward situation ended in April 1988, when Taiwan attended the twenty-first annual ADB conference in Manila as "Taipei, China." This was the first occasion since 1949 where government officials from both the PRC and ROC sat around a conference table. In a good will gesture to Taipei, the PRC and other ADB members allowed Taiwan's delegation to use "Republic of China" in private, unofficial contexts. For its part, Taiwan demonstrated that it would attempt to play a more prominent role in the ADB by donating $1 billion to the Asian Development Fund, thereby securing more ADB voting rights.

In May 1989 Finance Minister Shirley Kuo attended the twenty-second ADB conference held in Beijing. Kuo was the first ROC official to visit mainland China since 1949. The PRC treated the Taiwan delegation with great respect, and Kuo stood with the other delegates when the PRC president entered the conference to welcome the participants.

As Taipei attempts to play a more active role in world affairs, it expects PRC pressure on other countries to deny Taiwan that role to continue. However, Taipei is convinced that, because of its economic strength, other nations will see their interests served by having Taiwan assume larger international responsibilities. One principal test for this reasoning was Taiwan's application for accession into the GATT.

Taiwan applied for admission into GATT on January 1, 1990, under the designation of "Customs Territory of Taiwan, Penghu, Kinmen, and Matsu."[8] The Republic of China was one of the founding members of the GATT in 1946, but it left the organization when it lost the mainland in the Chinese civil war. In 1965 the ROC was given observer status in the international trade forum, but it was asked to leave in 1971 after Taipei lost its seat in the United Nations to the PRC.

In 1990 Taiwan sought to rejoin the GATT on the grounds that it was the world's thirteenth largest trading nation, the second largest investor in Asia, and the holder of the world's largest foreign exchange reserves. In addition, Taiwan wanted to join GATT to resist protectionist pressure from other nations. Since Taiwan was not a member, it had to negotiate separate trade and tariff agreements with many of its 160 trading partners. In these negotiations, Taiwan frequently found itself disadvantaged because other countries could use protectionist threats to gain concessions without Taipei being able to appeal to GATT for restitution.

Under GATT regulations, two-thirds of its members, which total about 100 countries and customs territories, must approve Taiwan's accession as a customs territory. The PRC has applied intense political pressure on other countries to block Taiwan's entrance into GATT. In 1990–1991 Beijing insisted that Taiwan could only join GATT after the PRC itself had been admitted and only then with Beijing's approval.[9] The PRC applied for GATT membership in 1986, but it was not admitted because of the incompatibility of Beijing's centrally planned economy and protectionist trade policies with GATT principles of free markets and fair trade.

Because of strong PRC opposition, the United States and many other countries were reluctant to back Taiwan's entrance into GATT.

But by the end of 1990, important GATT members such as France were beginning to be more supportive of Taiwan's entrance.

The Bush administration shifted its policy toward one of backing Taiwan's accession in July 1991, partly as a trade-off with important Members of Congress to allow unconditional renewal of the U.S. most-favored-nation (MFN) trading status with Beijing. The President made it clear, however, that "U.S. support for Taiwan's accession to GATT as a customs territory should in no way be interpreted as a departure from the long-standing policy of five administrations which acknowledges the Chinese position that there is only one China, and that Taiwan is part of China."[10]

In recognition of its stronger economy, Taiwan was invited by the OECD in January 1989 to take part in discussions about the rights and obligations accruing from developed economic status. Describing Taiwan as one of the "dynamic Asian economies," the OECD issued a highly favorable report in early 1991 on Taiwan's international assistance programs.[11]

Since the mid-1980s Taiwan has actively cooperated with various Asian-Pacific economic groups. In November 1988 President Lee Teng-hui proposed that Asian-Pacific nations eliminate trade barriers between themselves and strengthen technology cooperation to achieve an integrated economic community in Asia.[12]

In May 1989 Taiwan hosted the twenty-second Pacific Basin Economic Council (PBEC) meeting in which sixteen Asian-Pacific countries, including the Soviet Union, sent delegations. Taiwan was admitted into the PBEC in 1984. Taiwan is also a member of the Pacific Economic Cooperation Conference (PEEC). In the PEEC Taiwan participates as "Chinese Taipei." In the PBEC Taiwan is the "Chinese Member Committee in Taipei." In November 1991 the ROC joined the Asian-Pacific Economic Cooperation (APEC) group under the name "Chinese-Taipei." At the same time, APEC admitted the PRC and Hong Kong on equal footing with Taiwan.

In recent years, Taiwan's international economic policy has included providing financial assistance to developing countries. In late 1988 Taiwan established a $1 billion International Economic Cooperation and Development Fund to provide loans and technical assistance to needy nations. By the end of 1990, $143 million in foreign aid grants had been approved. In 1991 an additional $130 million in low-interest loans and technical assistance was sent to ten nations, most of them in Latin America. Taipei also gave $30 million in economic assistance to Jordan, Egypt, and Turkey during the Persian Gulf War in late 1990 and early 1991.

Economic Relations with the PRC

One key reform initiated by President Chiang Ching-kuo before his passing in early 1988 was the October 1987 lifting of some travel bans on ROC citizens wishing to visit mainland China. By the end of 1991 about three million Taiwan visitors had gone to the PRC, spending an estimated $7 billion. Forty million pieces of mail had been exchanged, and ten million phone calls and telegrams had been placed or sent.

At the same time that rules regarding visits were relaxed, Taiwan began to liberalize its regulations governing trade with mainland China. This decision was popular with Taiwan businessmen, who were anxious to open trade with the mainland. Several reasons were involved: the rising cost of raw materials and labor, greater competition for international markets, the threat of protectionism in major trading partners such as the United States, and the need to diversify Taiwan's export markets to avoid overdependency on American consumers.

Another factor was South Korea's strong trading relationship with Beijing. Taiwan businessmen were concerned that Korean imports of cheap Chinese raw materials would give Seoul an export advantage and cut into Taiwan's overseas markets. Taiwan also feared that South Korea would gain an edge in exports to the mainland. Since South Korea was one of the very few substantial nations maintaining diplomatic ties with the Republic of China, there were political factors to be considered as well. In 1991 Sino-Korean trade was $5.5 billion, compared to $3.5 billion in ROK-ROC trade and about $6 billion in Taiwan-mainland trade.

Largely because of pressure from local businessmen, Taipei gradually relaxed the amount of raw material allowed to be imported from the PRC. In August 1988 the import of fifty raw materials were permitted, including pearls, pig iron, coal, aluminum ingots, copper, manganese sulfate, agricultural products, and Chinese medicines. In January 1989 forty more items were added to that list, and it has continued to grow.

In 1991 trade between Taiwan and the PRC, almost all of it indirect through an entrepot, totalled $5.8 billion, a 43.3 percent increase over 1990. This represented only 4 percent of Taiwan's total trade worldwide, but it created 26 percent of Taiwan's trade surplus. Intimately related was Taiwan's trade with Hong Kong, much of which was transshipped to and from the mainland. In 1991 the total value of Taiwan-Hong Kong trade was $12.43 billion, up 45.3 percent from

1990. Taiwan imports from Hong Kong were $1.9 billion, an increase of 34.5 percent. Taiwan's surplus of $10.5 billion was its largest worldwide, accounting for nearly 79 percent of Taiwan's total global surplus in 1991.

Taiwan's exports to China have mainly been in consumer goods such as textiles and dyestuffs, tobacco, motorcycles, shoes and other leather goods, television sets, machines and machine tools, electrical goods, and paper and plastic products. As mentioned earlier, the export of semi-finished goods to Taiwan-owned factories on the mainland for re-export to third countries such as the United States grew significantly in 1991.

Another important component of commercial interaction across the Taiwan Strait is Taiwan investment on the mainland and the establishment of Taiwan-owned businesses. In 1991 the ROC government required Taiwan businessmen with investments on the mainland to register or face penalty. At the end of the year, only 2,500 Taiwan firms had complied, leading to speculation that the actual number of investors and the amount of their investments were not accurately being reported. The PRC, for example, reported in early 1992 there were 3,700 firms on the mainland established with Taiwan investments. One well-informed American scholar estimated in 1990 there were 10,000–13,000 Taiwan firms on mainland China, with investments totalling $4–$5 billion. Most of these investments went to China's coastal and southern provinces, where Taiwan businessmen enjoyed special benefits as "compatriots."[13]

Most Taiwan investments were in light industry, electronic products, garments, toys, footwear, machines, hardware, building materials, and petrochemicals. Land, financial services, and tourist industries were targeted for quick profit. In 1990–1991 a large number of Taiwanese toy, textile, and shoe manufacturers shifted their production facilities across the Taiwan Strait. Labor costs in Taiwan were cited as the main reason. Labor accounted for about 22 percent of total production costs on Taiwan, plus 5 percent for labor benefits.[14] Labor on the mainland represented only 15 percent of production costs.

One famous case involved Formosa Plastics, Taiwan's leading private sector petrochemical conglomerate. Chairman Y.C. Wang said in late 1989 that he wanted to construct a $10 billion naphtha cracking complex in Xiamen rather than on Taiwan because of rising labor costs, environmental costs, a declining work ethnic on Taiwan, and increasing labor-management disputes. Wang said land costs on Taiwan for the project were prohibitive. The costs of the required 300 hectares in Taoyuan County would be $420 million, two hundred times what the land would cost in Texas.

Throughout 1991 both the ROC and PRC governments courted Wang to attract his plants to their territory. The ROC government attempted to persuade Wang not to invest on the mainland because of the bad example it would set for other major Taiwanese investors in high-tech fields. In January 1992 Wang finally announced that he would build Taiwan's sixth naphtha cracking facility, a project costing over $4 billion, in the west coast county of Yunlin.

Since the economies of Taiwan and the mainland are complementary in many ways, there is strong reason to expect that the two sides will draw closer together over time, if political factors do not intervene. However, if Taiwan becomes too dependent upon mainland markets, raw materials, and labor, there is the possibility that Beijing will try to use this dependency to force concessions from Taipei.

To avoid this, the ROC government has cautioned Taiwan businessmen not to become overly dependent on the PRC. In 1991 even indirect trade through Hong Kong was subject to close monitoring. For their part, Taiwan businessmen often believed the government's restrictions were unreasonable. In many ways, the Taiwanese business community has become the most vocal lobby on Taiwan for further liberalization of policies toward the mainland.

Future Economic Policies

In February 1991 the ROC Ministry of Economic Affairs announced mid-term and long-term strategies it would implement on Taiwan. These strategies focused on upgrading industry, expanding trade, improving the investment climate, increasing investments in public construction, stabilizing commodity prices, developing the service sector, and supporting projects in the government's Six-Year National Development Plan.[15]

Problems and Limitations

There are a number of critical problems which must be overcome if Taiwan's economy is to continue to prosper. These problems include the slower expansion of world trade, increased pressure from international competition, resurgence of trade protectionism and proliferation of non-tariff barriers, the growing gap between Taiwan's gross domestic investment and gross savings, a maturing population, lack of balance between social and cultural development and economic development, as well as outdated economic institutions and legislation.

At the same time, there are numerous limitations to Taiwan's economic development. These include excessive dependence on the U.S.

and Japanese economies, difficulties in developing new products because of high unit costs and riskiness of new investment, the need to import most agricultural and industrial materials and energy supplies, the lack of a comprehensive science and technology (S&T) development system, the lack of coordination between S&T and manufacturing needs, reluctance on the part of the private sector to promote research and development, and too heavy dependence on foreign firms for development of technology.

The basic challenge to Taiwan's economy is that local manufacturers must keep pace with international competition. Unless this fundamental challenge is met successfully, Taiwan will export less, import more, and produce less efficiently.

Basic Economic Principles

Taiwan intends to follow certain basic principles in its economic policies through the remainder of this century. Taipei will stress economic liberalization, internationalization, and systematization. Liberalization will allow market and price mechanisms to play a larger role in supply and demand on Taiwan. It will also lead to the reduction of unnecessary government intervention. Liberalization will create a more competitive and equitable economic environment, result in greater efficiency in the utilization of resources, and strengthen economic development.

Through internationalization, Taiwan will seek to expand its economic activities abroad, while at the same time to open wider its domestic market to foreigners. A wider range of foreign companies will be allowed to compete in Taiwan in the expectation that such competition will strengthen local firms for international competition. Moreover, Taiwan will promote a wide range of local and international economic, technological, and cultural exchanges. The strengthening of economic ties with foreign countries will remain a high priority.

Taiwan will systematize its economy by ensuring that rules governing economic activities are rational and streamlined to ensure efficiency. An important ROC goal is to ensure that social harmony is preserved and that the economy serves the national interest of all of China and the people's well-being. This means a more balanced policy between economic growth and improvement in quality of living on Taiwan.

Future Policy Trends

In the future the primary source of Taiwan's economic growth will shift to domestic demand, particularly the service sector. Export expansion will become a secondary, albeit vital source of growth. The expansion of employment, improved labor productivity, and sustained industrial growth will remain top ROC economic policy objectives.

Major efforts will be taken to upgrade the quality of life on Taiwan by promoting social, cultural, and tourist activities. The social welfare system will be improved, and more attention will be paid to environmental issues and improving living conditions.

Manpower and technological development is another important policy trend. Significant efforts will be taken to improve manpower quality, cultivate and recruit high-tech talent, attract additional investment from multinational corporations, expand domestic investment, accelerate the transfer of technology from abroad, improve research and development on Taiwan, and strengthen the application of advanced technology.

One of the most critical steps will be the restructuring of Taiwan's economy. This will be done through the promotion and modernization of the service industry, the automation of industrial production, and the development of technology-intensive industries. At the same time, agricultural production will be expanded and upgraded to ensure a balanced economy.

Economic ties with foreign countries will be strengthened. This will be accomplished through the moderate expansion of exports and imports to achieve a balanced foreign trade, lower import tariff rates and the removal of most non-tariff barriers, the encouragement of foreign investment on Taiwan and Taiwanese investment abroad, the cultivation of substantive economic relations with additional countries, and the strengthening of Taiwan's economy to meet future economic crises.

During the 1990s, the ROC will implement policies in nine key areas to modernize the economy. First, necessary institutions and systems will be established. Policies will be adopted to review and modify economic and social laws and regulations and to streamline legal institutions; to modernize and strengthen the administration, as well as to enhance its efficiency; and to improve the personnel administration of the government, including the recruitment and proper utilization of talented individuals.

Second, manpower planning and manpower quality will be strengthened. Policies to achieve this will include steps to upgrade the quality of the population, maintain its proper distribution and modest growth, and provide greater care to the elderly. Other policies will expand and upgrade the free educational system, especially in technical and vocational schools, strengthen employment services, maintain full employment, improve working conditions, promote harmonious labor-management relations, and enhance labor welfare.

Third, research and development (R&D) in science and technology (S&T) will be promoted. Policies will include the coordination of S&T programs to ensure that the advantages of international cooperation and domestic capabilities are matched with the requirements of national defense and the economy. Other policies will lay the foundation for domestic science and technology by improving the research and development environment on Taiwan and by encouraging private business and individual involvement. Technologies required for ecological conservation, pollution control, medical care, pharmacy, sanitation, and health care will be promoted. Policies will be implemented to cultivate and recruit local talent, exchange technical manpower, and gain technology from advanced nations.

Economic restructuring is a fourth policy area. Policies in three categories will be put into effect: the further development of agriculture, the acceleration of industrial upgrading, and the modernization of services. In terms of agricultural development, the government will adopt policies to increase the efficiency of farming by encouraging professional farmers, expanding the size of farms, and encouraging more advanced farming techniques. Agricultural resources will be better utilized through forest conservation, fishery development, land set aside for agricultural purposes, and specialized regional agricultural production. Self-sufficiency in major crops will be promoted and the production of agricultural products of high economic value will be encouraged.

Policies designed to upgrade industry will improve the domestic investment climate by adopting preferential tax measures, reducing risks to investments in venture-capital firms, and encouraging technology-intensive industries. Other policies will lower protectionist barriers, attract investment from overseas multinationals, speed up the transfer of advanced technologies, and raise productivity. Taiwan will continue to relax restrictions on overseas investments by its companies and encourage the development of Taiwan's own multinational corporations. Assistance will be extended to small and medium-sized companies to ensure their continued contribution to Taiwan's economic growth.

In terms of the modernization of the service sector, Taiwan will establish an integrated transportation and communications network. This will include a mass rapid transit system enabling commuters to travel considerable distances to work in the metropolitan areas. Other policy priorities will improve operating and managerial techniques in commerce and banking, strengthen financial institutions, and upgrade financial services.

Fifth, trade will be liberalized and brought into balance. To promote trade liberalization the ROC will continue to reduce import tariffs and gradually relax regulations on import commodities and areas of origin. The export and import licensing system will be phased out. Moreover, the customs-clearance process will be streamlined to make it faster and more efficient.

To expand export markets Taiwan plans to encourage the export of high value products processed in multiple stages, improve the quality of export commodities, enhance international competitiveness, intensify counter-trade activities, relax restrictions on entrepot trade, assist in the establishment of large trading firms, and expand export markets worldwide.

To reinforce trade ties with foreign nations Taipei will actively participate in international economic affairs and enhance Taiwan's position in the international economic community. Economic cooperation with other countries will be strengthened, the role of ROC commercial representatives abroad will be expanded and better coordinated, and substantive external relations will be expanded. Major efforts will be undertaken to prevent counterfeiting in Taiwan. Steps will be taken to reduce the large trade surplus with the United States and the large trade deficit with Japan.

Sixth, the role of fiscal operations will be strengthened and financial liberalization promoted. Policies will streamline and improve supervision of the budget process, ensure an equitable distribution of public expenditure, establish an equitable tax reform system, deregulate interest rates to allow fuller play of market mechanisms, establish a deposit insurance system, streamline and strengthen the financial market, improve the administrative efficiency of the financial sector, lift unnecessary financial intervention and foreign-exchange controls, help financial institutions offer new services, promote the sound development of financial institutions and upgrade their service quality, promote computerized banking operations, relax restrictions on the operations of foreign banks, allow domestic banks to establish offices overseas, and promote the internationalization of financial operations.

Seventh, public investment and infrastructure development will be strengthened. This will be done through improving transportation and communications systems, ensuring balanced urban and regional development, promoting the development and utilization of water resources, and strengthening tourism development.

Eighth, energy planning will be strengthened. Policies will ensure a more rational energy pricing structure; set energy efficiency standards for industry, housing, and motor vehicles; enforce energy conservation measures; encourage energy-saving facilities and limit expansion of energy-intensive and low value-added industries; expand energy exploration and development; diversify sources of energy and seek to establish stable sources of supply; continue to develop nuclear power, while increasing safeguards for its production and use; and increase research and development in the fields of energy-recycling and energy-saving techniques.

Ninth, the social welfare system will be streamlined and balanced social and economic development promoted. Policies will establish a social insurance scheme and a medical care system, improve the social relief and welfare services system, expand community boundaries and strengthen community organizations, expand cultural activities, and upgrade the national quality of life.

Conclusion

Taiwan's economic success is attributable to sound planning, hard work, U.S. assistance, a favorable international economic environment, and a measure of good luck in choosing policies that proved to be correct. Taiwan has moved to the threshold of a fully developed economy, a status that should be reached by the year 2000. But economic success has also brought domestic and international problems to Taiwan, including social and environment issues at home and more complicated relations with the PRC and other countries.

Because of the ROC's unique diplomatic status, economic prosperity is vital to Taiwan's survival as an international entity. Yet continued prosperity necessitates a massive restructuring of the economy in ways that are both difficult and risky. To meet this challenge, Taipei has mapped out an elaborate, long-term economic strategy that seems to match its resources with goals and opportunity.

The direction of Taiwan's economic strategy is clear. It is moving toward greater liberalization, more balanced trade, increased financial and commercial sophistication, and wider internationalization. The industrial sector, the backbone of the economy, is moving away from labor-intensive products toward the production of high-tech goods. Services are becoming a key growth area of the Taiwan economy. At the same time that this modernization is occurring, greater emphasis is being placed on improving the quality of life on Taiwan, including a cleaner environment and higher levels of consumerism.

Notes

1. Most of the economic data in this chapter has been taken from U.S. Department of Commerce, *Foreign Economic Trends and Their Implications for the United States: Taiwan,* March 1992. Hereafter *FET: Taiwan*. See also various 1992 editions of *Free China Journal,* the ROC's English-language newspaper which reports extensively on Taiwan's economy. The best English source for official ROC statistics is the annual *Taiwan Statistical Data Book,* published by the ROC Council for Economic Planning and Development.

2. *Republic of China Yearbook, 1990–1991* (Taipei, Taiwan: Kwang Hwa Publishing Company, 1990), p. 257.

3. Between September 1985 and December 1988, the New Taiwan Dollar appreciated 43.5 percent against the U.S. Dollar. From December 1988 until April 1989, it rose another 10.4 percent. This was second only to the Japanese yen in terms of appreciation against the U.S. dollar since 1985. In 1991 the New Taiwan Dollar rose 5 percent against the U.S. Dollar from 27.12 to 1 to 25.72 to 1. At the same time, the New Taiwan Dollar appreciated 3 to 11 percent against major European currencies.

4. In 1986 there were 60,000 registered trading companies on Taiwan, of which 40,000 accounted for three-fourths of Taiwan's exports. South Korea, on the other hand, had 7,000 trading companies, of which nine did more than half of the country's export business. See *Asian Wall Street Journal,* April 14, 1989, p. 20.

5. The United States calculates its trade by a different method than Taiwan, resulting in slightly different statistics. The U.S. Commerce Department calculates U.S. imports by value-added/country-of-origin definitions rather than final shipping point. Taiwan calculates the CIF value for imports, which includes customs value, insurance and freight. Moreover, the United States does not consider Taiwan's purchase of gold to be a legitimate purchase of goods and services, while Taipei does. These differences in U.S. and Taiwan accounting procedures make the task of getting consistent trade figures a bit awkward. A further complicating factor is the rapid change in the relative value of the New Taiwan Dollar to the U.S. Dollar.

6. *Free China Journal,* January 14, 1991, p. 1.

7. The Olympic formula for ROC participation in international sporting events is "Chinese Taipei."

8. See "The Accession of the Customs Territory of Taiwan, Penghu, Kinmen and Matsu: GATT" (Taipei, Taiwan: ROC Ministry of Economic Affairs, January 1990).

9. See "Taiwan Can't Independently Join GATT," Letter-to-the-Editor by PRC Embassy Press Counselor, Chen Guoqing, *New York Times,* April 24, 1991, p. A24.

10. Letter of President George Bush to Senator Max S. Baucus, July 19, 1991.

11. Excerpts from the OECD report can be found in *Free China Journal,* February 25, 1991, p. 5.

12. *China Post* (Taiwan), November 29, 1988, p. 6.

13. Jan Prybyla, "The New Taiwan Political Economy," 1990, ms, p. 16.

14. According to a report issued in March 1991, the average monthly wage in Taiwan's manufacturing sector was $781. Wages in the commercial sector averaged $799, and wages in the finance, insurance and realty sectors averaged $1,211. *Free China Journal,* March 7, 1991, p. 7.

15. *Free China Journal,* February 11, 1991, p. 7. The economic goals of Taiwan for the remainder of this century can be found in Council for Economic Planning and Development, *Perspective of the Taiwan Economy Up to the Year of 2000* (Taipei, Taiwan: Executive Yuan, May 1986).

4

Flexible Diplomacy

Accompanying Taiwan's economic and political reforms was a new direction in ROC foreign policy. Adopted in late 1987, Taiwan's new approach to international relations was characterized by a willingness to treat relations both with other countries and with mainland China in a more flexible, pragmatic way. For this reason, Taiwan's new foreign policy was frequently called "flexible," "elastic," or "pragmatic" diplomacy.

This chapter will define "flexible diplomacy" as it was applied toward the international community and toward mainland China through 1991. The impact of flexible diplomacy on U.S. interests in and relations with Taipei during this period will be discussed separately in Chapter 7.

A New Pragmatism

Taiwan's survival as a viable international entity requires at least two conditions: avoiding premature unification with mainland China and gaining acceptance by other states as a legitimate actor in the international community. If Taiwan is not able to establish its international identity, then it will, by default, be viewed as part of the PRC. This has important security implications, because the resolution of Taiwan's status would then be considered by most states to be an internal matter for Beijing to decide.

Prior to 1987 the ROC followed a foreign policy of strict anti-communism. Not even commercial relations were maintained with the communist bloc, especially the Soviet Union and the PRC. Taipei adhered to this ideologically-based foreign policy long after the United States and other Western powers became more pragmatic in their relations with communist states. As a result of this shift in Western strategy, Taipei found itself increasingly isolated as it withdrew from international organizations seating the PRC and severed relations with countries establishing formal ties with Beijing. The fact that the ROC usually lost contests with the PRC for diplomatic recognition contributed to Taipei's growing isolation. The loss of China's seat in the United Nations in 1971 and the withdrawal of U.S. diplomatic recognition in 1979 were symptomatic of this process.

As part of his package of reforms in the months before his death, President Chiang Ching-kuo removed many of the ideological constraints on ROC foreign policy and supported a new diplomatic approach distinguished by its flexibility and pragmatism. As Chiang's successor, President Lee Teng-hui further refined Taiwan's flexible diplomacy.

Flexible diplomacy used the ROC's greatest asset—its considerable economic power, especially trade and foreign exchange reserves—to enhance and expand Taiwan's international presence. Stronger substantive relations, mostly economic, were built with other nations and international organizations, even if these maintained diplomatic ties with the PRC or included Beijing in their membership. One of the goals of flexible diplomacy was to gain a measure of political equality for Taipei with Beijing in the eyes of as many members of the international community as possible. The ROC attempted with its new diplomacy to convey the impression that relations with Taiwan were valuable in themselves and should not be seen as either a variable or obstacle in relations with Beijing.

Conditions Making Flexible Diplomacy Possible

Flexible diplomacy was made possible, even necessary, by a number of developments in Taiwan, the mainland, and the international community in general.

On Taiwan, there was intense pressure during the 1980s to change the nation's foreign policy. The freedom of expression brought by increased democracy led to severe criticism of the KMT's handling of foreign affairs. It was felt that the government adhered too strongly to its anti-communist and anti-PRC principles, resulting in Taiwan's diplomatic isolation and exclusion from most international organizations. The public exerted increasingly strong pressure on the government to adopt a more flexible and pragmatic foreign policy.

Other sources of domestic pressure for greater flexibility, especially in relations with the PRC, came from Taiwan businessmen who wanted to trade with and invest on the mainland and from mainlanders who had come to Taiwan with Chiang Kai-shek after 1945 and who now wanted to visit their homeland.

Accompanying this rise in public pressure were moves within the KMT to reform ROC foreign policy. As younger and more highly educated leaders emerged within the party, the argument was heard that Taiwan was harming its own interests by refusing to participate in international events and organizations when the PRC was present. It was argued that since the United States and other Western countries had adopted a more pragmatic approach to dealing with China and the Soviet Union, Taipei should follow their example or risk complete isolation from the rest of the world.

Another domestic factor was the increased confidence the people and government of Taiwan felt as a result of the ROC's rapid economic growth, successful trade, and large foreign exchange reserves. Having weathered the storm of the U.S. derecognition in 1978–1979, Taipei felt stronger than ever before. This self-confidence enabled Taiwan to attempt a more active, flexible role in international affairs.

Taiwan's self-confidence was enhanced by a sense of greater self-reliance in terms of national security. Taiwan, with some U.S. assistance and with tremendous expenditures of human and financial resources, produced several sophisticated weapons systems. Taiwan's sense of security was strengthened by the belief that the United States, despite the break in diplomatic ties, would support Taiwan in the event of an unprovoked PRC attack. Greater self-confidence in national security provided ROC leaders with a degree of flexibility in their policy toward mainland China and the international community.

Developments on the mainland also contributed to the adoption of Taiwan's flexible diplomacy. The economic and political reforms initiated by Deng Xiaoping in 1978 seemed in the 1986–1987 period unlikely to be reversed in a permanent way. To some in the KMT, this increased the prospects that the mainland would adopt portions of the Taiwan model for China's modernization. To take advantage of these opportunities required the ROC to have increased contact across the Taiwan Strait.

Although generally cautious in their assessments, many on Taiwan believed that Beijing was serious in trying to resolve the reunification issue by peaceful means. This was a necessity given China's priorities of economic modernization and friendly relations with the West. The United States in particular would view PRC hostility toward Taiwan in a negative way. Moreover, any PRC use of force against Taipei would probably entail high costs, but the Four Modernizations required the concentration of most available Chinese resources on economic development. Thus, many held the view that the PRC had to forego its military option to resolve the reunification issue.

Yet another disincentive for a PRC use of force was President Chiang Ching-kuo's decision to allow family visits to the mainland. The increased interaction across the Taiwan Strait and the perception that Beijing saw its interests as being best served by a peaceful policy toward Taiwan convinced the ROC that it was in its interest to adopt a more flexible policy toward the mainland to allow room for maneuverability.

Internationally, there were also developments which contributed to Taipei's adoption of flexible diplomacy. One important factor was the trend in the Asian Pacific region toward increased economic interdependence and political cooperation. In this environment, Taiwan could use its economic strength to great advantage—if its policies were sufficiently flexible and pragmatic.

The changing international environment, especially the discrediting of socialism and communism, gave added credibility to the "Taiwan Experience" in economic and political development, particularly in the Third World where leaders were looking for successful models to emulate. But to deal effectively with these countries, many of which had diplomatic ties with the PRC, required Taiwan to adopt a flexible foreign policy.

After being adopted in the 1987–1988 period, Taiwan's flexible diplomacy had distinct goals. In the short-term, Taipei wanted to use its new foreign policy to break out of diplomatic isolation. In the mid-term, Taiwan wanted to expand both in terms of quantity and quality the level of its relations with other countries. In the long-term, the ROC wanted to use flexible diplomacy as a means to reunify China under a free and democratic system. During the period under consideration in this study, Taipei placed most emphasis on the short-term and mid-term goals of breaking out of diplomatic isolation through actively pursuing a larger international role.

Taiwan's flexible diplomacy achieved several notable successes during the first few years of its implementation. Substantive relations were established or upgraded with most of the European Community, with the newly formed democracies in Central and Eastern Europe, several more countries in Latin America and Africa, Australia, and Pacific island-nations. After the policy was adopted, a much larger number of high level government officials from important countries started to come to Taiwan, including several cabinet-ranking officers from France and other OECD countries. Taiwan officials, including President Lee Teng-hui, were invited on state visits to several countries. All in all, the period between 1987 and 1991 saw a reemergence of Taipei as an international actor of some importance on the world's diplomatic scene.

But several setbacks also occurred, as the PRC mounted something of a counter-offensive to limit the success of Taiwan's flexible diplomacy. The most politically damaging was Saudi Arabia's shift in diplomatic ties from Taipei to Beijing. Singapore established formal relations with the PRC, and Indonesia resumed diplomatic ties with the mainland. The establishment of official relations between the Republic of Korea and the Soviet Union, as well as Seoul's desire to normalize relations with Beijing as part of its "Northern Diplomacy," were also seen as setbacks to Taiwan's diplomatic efforts.

Still, these reversals probably would have occurred regardless of what Taipei did or did not do, so they cannot be attributed to failures on the part of flexible diplomacy. Indeed, flexible diplomacy gave new life and opportunity to Taiwan in the international community. In that sense, the policy was overwhelmingly successful.

The previous chapter discussed Taiwan's use of "dollar diplomacy" as one form of flexible diplomacy to increase its international standing. At the same time that this was occurring, another facet of flexible diplomacy, greater openness with mainland China, was also being implemented. Because of its central role in U.S.-Taiwan-China relations, the remainder of this chapter will examine the ROC-PRC relationship, with special emphasis placed on flexible diplomacy during 1989–1991.

Taiwan's Policy Toward Mainland China

One of the most striking characteristics of flexible diplomacy was Taiwan's willingness to deal more openly with mainland China. For nearly forty years prior to the fall of 1987, ROC policy was to reject all contact with the mainland, although some limited contact did occur through personal visits to the mainland via Hong Kong, scholarly conferences held in third countries, and indirect trade.

After 1987, however, Taipei greatly liberalized its policies toward mainland China, easing restrictions on travel, trade, investment, communications, and many forms of exchange. Joint participation in academic and sporting events became common, and joint membership in international organizations occurred frequently. Taipei even began to accept dual recognition when a state wanted to maintain formal ties with both Beijing and Taipei, although the PRC strongly objected and refused to take part in such an arrangement. The contacts between Taiwan and mainland China grew so rapidly between 1987 and 1991 that both Chinese governments found it difficult to control the exchanges between their respective citizens.

In announcing its new mainland policy in 1987, the ROC insisted that it had not changed its fundamental "three-no" policy of no contacts, no compromise, and no negotiations with Beijing. In effect since 1949, this policy was adjusted in 1987 to mean no "official" contact between high-ranking representatives of the ROC and PRC or the KMT and CCP. In May 1991, however, President Lee Teng-hui abandoned the "three-no" policy altogether, officially ending the civil war with the communists, terminating the "Period of Mobilization for Suppression of the Communist Rebellion," and abolishing the "temporary provisions" giving the president emergency powers to prosecute the war against the communists.

Taiwan's motives in adopting its new policy toward the mainland were varied and will be treated more fully later in this chapter, but officially Taipei explained its policy as an offensive against the PRC to make the mainland people more aware of the superiority of the Taiwan model over that of communism. According to this view, the new policy advanced the ROC goal of reunifying China under the Three Principles of the People. Many in the PRC, however, suspected that Taipei adopted its new policy as a clever tactic to prolong the process of reunification, or, more ominously, to move Taiwan in the direction of independence from the mainland.

This section will summarize Taipei-Beijing relations since 1979, with particular attention paid to developments from 1987–1991. Also of concern will be the likely future of Taiwan's policy toward mainland China.

Relations Since 1979

Relations between the PRC and Taiwan have in some respects been a continuation of the Chinese civil war begun in the 1920s. Many leaders in the Kuomintang (KMT) and the Chinese Communist Party (CCP) continue to hold their intention of replacing the other as ruler of all of China, including Taiwan. Both parties cloak their intentions with other statements. The KMT, for example, says that it will not necessarily have to be the ruling party on the mainland, as long as the ruling party is selected through a democratic process. The CCP claims that it already has been selected "by the will of the people" to be the ruling party of China by virtue of its victory in 1949, but that it is willing to allow the KMT to be the local government of Taiwan for a lengthy period after reunification occurs.

From the outset of its existence in October 1949, the PRC has made the "bringing of Taiwan back to the embrace of the motherland" a national priority. Similarly, the ROC on Taiwan has made reunification its eventual goal as well.[1] The stated goal of national unification is the same, but Beijing and Taipei have considerably different visions of how reunification is to occur and how a united China is to be governed.

At the end of 1991, the PRC model of reunification was "one country, two systems," whereby China would be united politically but Taiwan would retain its capitalist economic system while the mainland would remain socialist. Under this model, the central government would reside in Beijing under the CCP, Taiwan would be considered a province with the status of a special administrative region, and the KMT would head a local government on Taiwan for several decades. After then, Taiwan would become socialist, too. The ROC's model for reunification was found in the "Guidelines for National Unification," a document adopted in 1991 about which more will be said later. The ROC model stressed equality between the PRC and ROC governments but with recognized de facto control over the mainland and Taiwan respectively. Under this model, the future of China would be determined by democratic means. Presumably, the ROC's experience on Taiwan would heavily influence the Chinese people's choice, because the united China envisioned by the ROC was to be politically democratic and economically based on the free market.

Prior to 1978, the PRC's fundamental policy toward reunification was the "liberation" of Taiwan. At various times this was to be accomplished by armed force or by peaceful means. The liberation of Taiwan by armed force became nearly impossible after 1950 when the United States committed itself to the defense of Taiwan as a result of the Korean War.

PRC strategy toward reunification changed significantly in December 1978. During the Third Plenary Session of the Eleventh CCP Central Committee, Deng Xiaoping was confirmed as China's principal leader, the Four Modernizations were accepted as the PRC's economic strategy for the next several decades, normalization of relations with the United States was approved, and "peaceful reunification" was adopted as a new strategy toward Taiwan.

Peaceful Reunification

Just exactly what peaceful reunification meant was fleshed out in subsequent PRC statements. The first major elaboration was National People's Congress Standing Committee Chairman Ye Jianying's "Nine Points Proposal" in September 1981. These remained viable through 1991. They were:

> (1) In order to bring an end to the separation of the Chinese nation as early as possible, talks should be held between the Communist Party of China and the Kuomintang of China on a reciprocal basis so that the two parties will cooperate for the third time to accomplish the great cause of national reunification. The two sides may first send people to meet for an exhaustive exchange of views.

(2) The two sides should make arrangements to facilitate the exchange of mails, trade, air and shipping services, and visits by relatives and tourists as well as academic, cultural and sports exchanges.

(3) After the country is reunited, Taiwan can enjoy a high degree of autonomy as a special administrative region and it can retain its armed forces. The Central Government will not interfere with local affairs on Taiwan.

(4) Taiwan's current socio-economic system will remain unchanged, so will its way of life and its economic and cultural relations with foreign countries. There will be no encroachment on the proprietary rights and lawful right of inheritance over private property, houses, land and enterprises, or on foreign investments.

(5) People in authority and representative personages of various circles in Taiwan may take up posts of leadership in national political bodies and participate in running the state.

(6) When Taiwan's local finance is in difficulty, the Central Government may subsidize it as is fit for the circumstances.

(7) For people of all nationalities and public figures of various circles in Taiwan who wish to come and settle on the mainland, it is guaranteed that proper arrangements will be made for them, that there will be no discrimination against them, and that they will have the freedom of entry and exit.

(8) Industrialists and businessmen in Taiwan are welcome to invest and engage in various economic undertakings on the mainland, and their legal rights, interests and profits are guaranteed.

(9) People of all nationalities, public figures of all circles and mass organizations in Taiwan can make proposals and suggestions regarding affairs of state through various channels and in various ways. . . . China's reunification and prosperity is in the vital interest of the Chinese people of all nationalities—not only those on the mainland, but those in Taiwan as well. The Kuomintang authorities should stick to their one-China position and their opposition to "two Chinas." They should put national interests above everything else, forget previous ill will and join hands with the CCP to accomplish national reunification and to make China prosperous and strong.[2]

Other significant proposals were made by Chinese leaders such as Deng Xiaoping in interviews with visiting Overseas Chinese, particularly scholars from the United States who maintained good relations with Taipei. In one such interview Deng told Seton Hall professor Winston Yang in June 1983:

1. After reunification, Beijing will not dispatch its army to Taiwan, nor will it send officials to take over, to take part in, or to oversee Taiwan's "internal affairs." Beijing will not concern itself with the personnel affairs in Taiwan's administrative structure and will not bother about the troop

movements in Taiwan. . . . Taiwan can maintain its economic system, its way of living, and its party, government, army, and intelligence agency. The mainland and Taiwan will coexist peacefully. He said: "We will never harm even a single blade of grass or a tree on Taiwan." He also said that this arrangement should remain unchanged for at least 100 years. If disputes occur in the course of implementing the reunification terms, both sides can seek solutions through consultation. The most important thing is that neither side will conduct anything causing harm to the other side in its own territory. Taiwan's army will have the right to buy weapons from other countries to consolidate its self-defensive ability.

2. After reunification, Taiwan will enjoy independent legislative rights and can basically maintain its existing laws. On the principle of not violating the Constitution, Taiwan's legislature has the right to enact its own laws which act as the foundation for Taiwan's administration.

3. After reunification, Taiwan will have its independent jurisdiction and judicial organs. The laws and acts on the mainland will not be applied to Taiwan. The court of last instance for Taiwan should be set in Taiwan rather than in Beijing.

4. After reunification, Taiwan will maintain certain rights to handle foreign affairs. It can handle its foreign economic relations independently. The Taiwan authorities can issue special passports to Taiwan people and grant entrance visas to foreigners. It can even have the right to sign some agreements directly with other countries.

5. After reunification, Taiwan can still use its special flag and use the title of "China, Taiwan."[3]

In 1984 during negotiations between London and Beijing over the future of Hong Kong, the PRC started calling its proposal for peaceful reunification "one country, two systems." The new formula was a pragmatic attempt by the PRC to achieve national reunification under the CCP, but to allow Hong Kong, Macao, and Taiwan to retain their way of life under capitalism. Regarding the problem of reunification with Taiwan, Deng Xiaoping said in June 1984:

What is the solution to this problem? Is it for socialism to swallow up Taiwan, or for the "Three Principles of the People" preached by Taiwan to swallow up the mainland? The answer is that neither can swallow up the other. If the problem cannot be solved peacefully then it must be solved by force. This would do neither side any good. Reunification of the country is the aspiration of the whole nation. If it cannot be reunified in 100 years, then it will be reunified in 1,000 years. In my opinion, the only solution to this problem is to practice two systems in one country.[4]

Some indication of what "one country, two systems" might mean for Taiwan came in the Hong Kong Agreement signed by the PRC and the United Kingdom in December 1984. The international agreement transferred the sovereignty of Hong Kong back to the PRC in July 1997. Beijing included in the agreement numerous assurances that the people of Hong Kong would be able to retain their way of life for at least fifty years beyond 1997. Some of the provisions in the 1984 agreement which might be applicable to Taiwan were:

- A high degree of autonomy shall exist, except in foreign and defense affairs, which will be the responsibility of Beijing.

- An executive, legislative, and independent judicial power shall be established with the current laws remaining basically unchanged.

- An executive shall be appointed by Beijing on the basis of local elections or consultations, and held "accountable to the legislature."

- A legislature shall be constituted by elections, which "may on its own authority enact laws in accordance with the provisions of the Basic Law and legal procedures, and report them to the Standing Committee of the National People's Congress for the record."

- The laws of the Hong Kong Special Administrative Region (SAR) shall be from three sources: the Basic Law, the laws previously in force in Hong Kong, and laws enacted by the Hong Kong SAR legislature.

- Judicial power in Hong Kong shall be vested in its own courts. "The courts shall exercise judicial power independently and free from any interference. . . . The power of final judgement . . . shall be vested in the court of final appeals in the Hong Kong SAR."

- "The Hong Kong Special Administrative Region shall maintain the capitalist economic and trade systems previously practiced in Hong Kong." Hong Kong "shall retain the status of a free port and continue a free trade policy, including the free movement of goods and capital." Hong Kong "may on its own maintain and develop economic and trade relations with all states and regions."

- "The current social and economic systems in Hong Kong will remain unchanged, and so will the life-style. Rights and freedoms, including those of the person, of speech, of the press, of assembly, of association, of travel, of movement, of correspondence, of strike, of choice of occupation, of academic research and of religious belief will be ensured by law. . . . Private property, ownership of enterprises, legitimate right of inheritance and foreign investment will be protected by law."

- Hong Kong will remain a separate customs territory. It will remain an international financial center, and its markets for foreign exchange, gold, securities and futures will continue. There will be free flow of capital.

- The Hong Kong dollar will continue to circulate and remain freely convertible. Hong Kong will have independent finances and Beijing will not levy taxes on Hong Kong.

- "Mutually beneficial economic relations" may be established with the United Kingdom "and other countries, whose economic interests in Hong Kong will be given due regard."

- Under the name "Hong Kong, China," the Special Administrative Region "may on its own maintain and develop economic and cultural relations and conclude relevant agreements with states, regions and relevant international organizations."

- Hong Kong may issue its own travel documents and maintain its own public security forces.

- "Apart from displaying the national flag and national emblem of the People's Republic of China," Hong Kong "may use a regional flag and emblem of its own."

- "The Hong Kong Special Administrative Region shall maintain the educational system previously practiced in Hong Kong."[5]

PRC officials recognized that differences existed between Hong Kong and Taiwan and that, therefore, the exact agreement between Beijing and Taipei would have to be negotiated. One primary difference alluded to by Deng and other PRC spokesmen was that, unlike Hong Kong, the PRC will not station troops on Taiwan and Taipei can maintain its own armed forces.

Beijing stressed that the reunification process should begin by establishing the "three links" and "four exchanges." These included links with Taiwan through mail, transport and trade, as well as economic, technological, cultural, and sports exchanges. By the end of 1991 most of these links and exchanges appeared to be gradually permitted by Taipei. At no time since 1978 did the PRC renounce the use of force to solve the Taiwan issue, the implications of which will be discussed in the next chapter.

ROC Response to PRC Reunification Proposals

Whereas the PRC offered fairly specific proposals for China's reunification, until late 1987 Taipei held firmly to its "three-no" policy limiting all contact with the mainland. Beginning in the early 1980s, however, there was some relaxation of the rules as businessmen from Taiwan met more frequently with their counterparts from the mainland in Hong Kong and as scholars from both sides attended conferences in third countries. But the process of widening contacts was slow, with Taipei describing the PRC proposals for peaceful reunification as "united front tactics" and "sugar-coated poison."

The official ROC position during the early 1980s can be seen in Taipei's reaction to Ye Jianying's nine point proposal of September 1981. In a point-by-point rebuttal of Ye's plan, Taiwan said:

1. The problem is not talks but two different ways of life. The ROC wants China to be united under a system which is free, democratic and in the interests of the people. Unification under communism is forever unacceptable. Peaceful unification under conditions of freedom is the common will of the Chinese people everywhere. Moreover, previous talks between the KMT and CPC [Communist Party of China] have resulted in communist treachery; the communists seek to gain through negotiations what they cannot gain on the battlefield.

2. Beijing is proposing the free exchange of mail, trade, visits, and services when these do not exist on the mainland. How can they offer Taiwan—which already enjoys these things—what the communists deny their own people? In essence, there is little that Taiwan would gain from these arrangements.

3. Not only are the communists refusing to acknowledge the legitimacy of the Republic of China, they are proposing that Taiwan retain "a high degree of autonomy as a special administrative region." As shown in the case of Tibet, where Beijing offered similar promises but later brutally imposed communism, the autonomy offered by the PRC is worthless. Besides, Taiwan currently enjoys freedom and has its own armed forces. The proposal gives the ROC nothing but takes away what it already has.

4. A similar argument is made here. Why should Taiwan take the chance that its social-economic structure will be left intact under the communists? To think that Beijing would not eventually impose socialism on the island is naive. When that occurs, the high standard of living enjoyed by the people on Taiwan will be lost. It is far better that Taiwan prosper to demonstrate valid methods of modernization which one day can be applied to development on the mainland.

5. It is unrealistic to expect that leaders of a democratic system such as that which exists on Taiwan could effectively function in a communist state where policy is dominated by those following Marxism-Leninism. Any posts given to current ROC leaders would be ceremonial at best.

6. Taiwan doesn't need Beijing's economic assistance. In truth, the communist leaders would like to share in Taiwan's economic prosperity.

7. Again, it is unrealistic to expect that Beijing will offer the people of Taiwan rights and privileges which are not enjoyed by the people on the mainland. Freedom of movement would have catastrophic results within the system of control on the mainland; it cannot be tolerated, nor promised with true intent.

8. Although it is true that Taiwan's businessmen are similar to fellow tradesmen around the world in looking for investment potential, the fact is that foreign and Overseas Chinese investments on the mainland have not proven to be very profitable. Far more money is to be gained from investments on Taiwan.

9. It is hard to take the communist proposal seriously when the freedom to make suggestions for the direction of government on the mainland is strictly forbidden. Any criticism of communist policy or suggestion for change in leadership is punishable. These inconsistencies lead one to conclude that Ye's proposals were not meant seriously to be considered by Taipei; rather, they were intended to influence opinion in the U.S. and elsewhere in order to further increase pressure on the ROC to accommodate Beijing.[6]

By mid-1982, however, one could begin to see some flexibility in Taiwan's position, although it was conditioned on economic, political, and social reform on the mainland. In June Premier Sun Yun-suan told a conference on Sino-American relations: "If the political, economic, social and cultural gaps between the Chinese mainland and free China continue to narrow, the conditions for peaceful reunification can gradually mature. The obstacles to reunification will be reduced naturally with the passage of time."[7]

The Hong Kong Agreement of December 1984 and the PRC's "one country, two systems" formula required careful response from Taiwan. There were several factors to take into consideration.

First, many KMT leaders believed that Beijing was in an inescapable dilemma. As described by President Chiang Ching-kuo: "If the communist regime does not fundamentally reform itself, it is doomed to growing chaos. However, if the communist regime does make fundamental reform, it is bound for self-destruction."[8]

Second, it was recognized that difficulties would be created for Taipei if it talked with Beijing over the future of China. As one ROC scholar explained:

The ROC . . . cannot afford to enter into any official negotiations with the PRC. Internal politics in Taiwan are delicate and confrontational, and any move by the government to negotiate with the PRC regarding

Taiwan's future would immediately trigger mass opposition. Although the people of Taiwan welcome a united China, this must come about on their terms and not under those imposed by the PRC. It would be suicidal for the Nationalist government to be a party to any negotiations with the PRC so long as the PRC remains an essentially communist state.[9]

Third, despite the political danger of direct talks with Beijing, many on Taiwan saw indirect contact with the PRC to be in the ROC interests. Hong Kong, especially, was "the most important point of contact between mainland China and Taiwan," enabling Taiwan to flood the mainland with "ideas of democracy and freedom, the capitalist system, and even the new Confucianism" which would "have the effect of negating Marxist-Leninist-Stalinist and Mao Tse-tung Thought." One ROC scholar predicted in 1986: "We therefore conclude that the Hong Kong issue of today provides the Republic of China with a turning point in its struggle to bring freedom and democracy to the entire Chinese mainland and to move another step toward the eventual unification of China."[10]

Fourth, a complicating factor in the "one country, two systems" issue was the importance of Hong Kong as Taiwan's third largest trading partner, after the United States and Japan. Most trade through Hong Kong was in fact indirect trade with China. That trade was becoming increasingly important to Taiwan businessmen as they attempted to diversify their markets, find sources of cheap raw materials, and take advantage of low labor costs for labor-intensive industries no longer economical on Taiwan.

Fifth, there was considerable domestic pressure on the ROC government to allow increased contact with the mainland. This pressure came from Taiwan businessmen, elderly Nationalist soldiers wishing to see their homeland, intellectuals tired of the humiliation of diplomatic isolation, and KMT leaders who felt that too little contact across the Taiwan Strait might eventually lead to Taiwan independence. Many officials perceived the need to counter Beijing's well-received proposals for peaceful reunification with forward looking policies from Taipei.

All of these factors contributed to President Chiang Ching-kuo's decision in 1985 to begin to loosen restrictions on contact with the mainland.

Wider Contacts After 1985

Chiang's decision quickly began to have impact on Taiwan-mainland relations. For example, in 1985 about 20,000 Taiwan residents visited the mainland, after first passing through third countries such as Hong Kong, Singapore, and Japan. These individuals were not harassed upon their return to Taiwan.

The next year Taiwan agreed to the designation "Taipei, China" as its name in the Asian Development Bank, the first occasion when Taiwan accepted a name different than the "Republic of China" in an international governmental organization in which the PRC was also seated. In May 1986 representatives from the ROC China Airlines met in Hong Kong with their counterparts from the PRC's Civil Aviation Administration of China to negotiate the return of a Boeing 747 cargo jet diverted to Canton by a defecting Nationalist pilot. In September the ROC announced a policy of allowing Taiwan's participation in international conferences and sporting events held in communist countries, including the PRC.

In October 1987 Taipei announced that all ROC citizens, except government employees and military personnel on active duty, could make one visit each year to relatives on the mainland for a period not to exceed three months. Over 100,000 people on Taiwan immediately inquired into the program administered by the ROC Red Cross.

At the time of the announcement, the government said the visitation policy was adopted on "humanitarian grounds" alone, and that it would "in no way affect the government's policy toward the Chinese communists."[11] Premier Yu Kuo-hwa said that Taipei was launching an "offensive [of] ideas," which would "offer the people of the mainland an alternative more viable and attractive than the communist system that currently rules them, namely freedom, democracy, the prosperity of free enterprise, and stability and security under the rule of law."[12] But it was also clear that Taiwan was hoping its new policy would cast Taipei in a more favorable international light and perhaps benefit Taiwan in its competition with Beijing for the "hearts and minds" of the Chinese people.

For its part, the PRC welcomed Taipei's new visitation policy as a positive step toward eventual reunification. The State Council issued a circular on how visitors from Taiwan were to be received. "Taiwan compatriots" were sincerely welcomed and guaranteed their "freedom to come and go." They were given "lenient treatment" at customs, allowed to visit places "in the same way as their mainland compatriots," and allowed to bring in and exchange any amount of foreign currency.[13]

Taiwan's main opposition party, the Democratic Progressive Party (DPP), was also in favor of the new visitation policy. Kang Ning-hsiang, a leading spokesman for the DPP moderate faction, said that the DPP principle of "self-determination" meant that the people of Taiwan might choose reunification instead of independence. Kang said he personally envisioned three stages for reunification, occurring over a six- to seven-year period: (1) mutual visits and communication to dispel suspicions and doubts on both sides, (2) normalization of trade and investment ties, and (3) "consultations could take place [and] a formula for reunification could be thrashed out." He insisted, however, that the DPP must be consulted in any KMT-CCP talks over the future of Taiwan.[14]

Thus, by the end of 1987 the three principal Chinese parties to a possible reunification of China—KMT, CCP, and DPP—were all in agreement that their mutual interests were served by increased contact between Taiwan and the mainland. This consensus created a new atmosphere in Taiwan-China relations which was still cautious, but more exploratory and conciliatory than in the past.

In 1988 Taipei allowed the level of contact across the Taiwan Strait to continue to grow. For example:

- Private participation in cultural, academic, and scientific events on the mainland was permitted.

- All references to the PRC in official publications were changed from "bandits" to "Mainland China."

- The government announced that some 2,000 Taiwanese soldiers who were stranded in mainland China after 1949 would be allowed to return to Taiwan.

- Beginning in October, mainlanders could visit Taiwan if their relatives were sick or had died and they wished to attend their funeral. In the first month after the new regulation was enacted, over 500 mainlanders were given permission to come to Taiwan.

- In November Taiwan began allowing visits by mainlanders "with outstanding achievements, international prestige and those who have made significant contribution to the development of Chinese culture." These included internationally known academics or famous artists, athletes who had attended the Olympic Games and other formal international competitions, Overseas Chinese scholars who taught in universities or worked in research organizations or who were recommended by leaders of academic institutions, and overseas-based mainland students who were studying in foreign universities for the Masters or PhD degrees.

- Several members of the National Assembly and Legislative Yuan illegally visited the mainland. These included DPP as well as KMT members. None were prosecuted.

- In 1988 more than 200,000 Taiwan citizens booked round-trip flights to visit relatives on the mainland. An average of 10,000 letters went to the mainland each day and some 8,000 letters arrived each day from the mainland to Taiwan.

In July 1988 the thirteenth KMT Party Congress reached a consensus on mainland policy. It was determined that in the future the KMT would continue to base its operations from Taiwan, but would direct its policy toward mainland China. Further, the foreign and domestic policies adopted by the ROC would not be with Taiwan solely in mind, but rather be designed to have an impact on mainland China as well. In effect, the KMT was re-affirming its commitment to "one China" and the eventual democratization of China, even while it adopted new strategies of openness toward the mainland.

The KMT Congress also established certain guidelines for the ROC's mainland policy. First, Taiwan's security had to be protected. Second, the purpose of Taiwan's policy was national reunification. Third, the final goal of ROC policy was to reunify China under a democratic form of government. Fourth, the more relaxed rules governing unofficial contact between the two sides were part of ROC policy to achieve this goal.

President Lee Teng-hui favored more contacts with the mainland and played down ideology in dealing with the PRC. Preferring a concrete approach to unification, he frequently cited the need to increase people-to-people contact across the Taiwan Strait. He stressed the importance of establishing cultural links to bridge differences between the two sides. Lee felt Taiwan's policy toward the PRC should be designed to have an impact on the mainland, but also to reduce Taiwan's isolation in the international community by appearing more reasonable to other countries. Lee's mainland policy was characterized by caution, pragmatism, and political sensitivity. He sought to build a consensus among the different sectors of Taiwan's society before instituting major new initiatives.

Some elements of that consensus began to emerge during 1988 and 1989. First, it was generally agreed that the time was not yet right to discuss reunification with Beijing because of profound differences between the two sides' political systems and standards of living. Second, it was believed that Taiwan's experience in becoming a developed nation could have a powerful influence on economic and political reform on the mainland.

Having laid at least the minimal domestic political framework for expanded relations with mainland China, the ROC began in 1988 and

1989 to place emphasis on the "Taiwan Experience" as a model for China's modernization. Rather than playing an obstructionist role in unification, as was generally the case from 1949–1987, Taiwan now assumed the initiative, arguing for reunification on the basis of Taiwan's own success in economic and political development. Taiwan's planners concentrated on two main issues: (1) how to use the expanding non-official, non-governmental contacts across the Taiwan Strait to affect change on the mainland in a direction favorable to the ROC; and (2) at the same time as these contacts were expanding, how to avoid Taiwan itself being absorbed by the much larger and more powerful mainland China. Finding the proper balance between these two challenges was the essence of Taiwan's flexible diplomacy toward the PRC.

PRC Reaction to Flexible Diplomacy

The PRC's initial reaction to Taiwan's policy of increased contact across the Taiwan Strait was positive. By late 1988, however, Beijing was becoming more apprehensive as Taipei's flexible foreign policy began to have some international impact. The PRC Foreign Ministry claimed in December 1988 that Taiwan's "elastic diplomacy" was trying to create "two Chinas" or "one China, one Taiwan." The Foreign Ministry said that no objection was taken to Taiwan's economic, trade, and cultural exchanges, if these were entirely of an unofficial nature, but official ties and contacts were not permissible with countries having diplomatic relations with the PRC. The Foreign Ministry stated that the Asian Development Bank model of "Taipei, China" was a special case and should not be regarded as a model universally applicable to other intergovernmental and international organizations.[15]

In those few cases where Taiwan was able to establish or reestablish diplomatic relations with countries having official ties with Beijing, the PRC severed its diplomatic relations. Premier Li Peng said Beijing was breaking ties with Belize, for example, because the PRC was sticking to a "one China" policy and would firmly oppose "two Chinas" or "one China, one Taiwan."[16]

The occasions of the ROC establishing diplomatic relations with Grenada in July 1989 and Liberia in October 1989 were greeted with very strong commentaries in *People's Daily*. In the case of Grenada, the commentary said that "dual recognition" of Grenada for both the PRC and ROC would not be tolerated because it would create "two Chinas."[17] A commentary on the occasion of Liberia's shift in diplomatic relations to Taipei was harsher in tone. The commentary said:

The Taiwan authorities have repeatedly claimed there is "only one China," but in recent years they have resorted to "elastic diplomacy" to end their diplomatic isolation. In the name of cultural, economic and trade and scientific and technological exchanges, they attempt to develop official relations with some countries by using their economic buying power. At the same time they have tried to set up representative organs of an official nature in countries that have diplomatic relations with China, violating the principle of "one China" and creating "dual recognition." By so doing the Taiwan authorities not only disregard the wishes of the Chinese people on both sides of the Straits for the peaceful reunification of the motherland, but attempt to seek recognition of Taiwan as a political entity. This leads to the situation of "two Chinas" or "one China, one Taiwan." Taiwan's actions have fractured the sacred unity of China and are held in contempt by the Chinese people at home and abroad. They should recognize that there is no "elasticity" on the issue of "one China" and "the reunification of the motherland." Anybody who violates this is a national criminal and will surely be punished by history.[18]

The strongly worded commentary went on to say: "China ... warns Taiwan authorities that their plan of making use of their economic strength to pursue a flexible diplomacy and their attempt to create 'two Chinas' will not succeed. They will meet with increasingly stronger opposition from the Chinese people, including the compatriots of Taiwan."[19]

PRC scholars such as Li Jiaquan also criticized the various Taiwan proposals for reunification emerging from flexible diplomacy.[20] In one article written in the spring of 1988, Li reviewed Taiwan-inspired models such as "two systems, one country," "two countries, two systems," "one country under separate administrations," "one country, two bodies," and "one country, two seats." These, he said, had four common ideas: (1) that reunification is a matter for the future, (2) that the PRC had to give up its four cardinal principles for reunification to be achieved, (3) that for the time being Beijing and Taipei must be two equal political entities, and (4) that the use of force must be ruled out. Li argued that these proposals were designed to keep "one China, two governments" while not endangering the "legally constituted authority" of the KMT. In Li's view, they were disguised versions of "two Chinas" or "Taiwan independence."[21]

In May 1989 Li Jiaquan published another article in which he criticized Taipei's "one country, two equal governments" formula. According to Li, the proposal was based on three principles differing from the "one country, two systems" proposal of the PRC: (1) Taiwan, as well as the mainland, holds its own sovereignty, instead of Taiwan

being a province of China; (2) the relationship between the governments of mainland China and Taiwan is between equals, instead of
Taiwan being a local government; and (3) the proposal is for a period
of transition toward unification, instead of reunification under two
systems.[22]

In February 1990 Li criticized Taiwan's "elastic diplomacy," arguing
that, under flexible diplomacy, Taiwan claimed to adhere to the
principle of "one China" but only as a guise to promote "two Chinas"
or "one China, one Taiwan." The pursuit of additional diplomatic
relations and official representation in the international community
was following a path of "dual (or double) recognition," which in
essence, Li said, was to pursue "two Chinas." Li warned that the
pursuit of "elastic diplomacy" endangered the peaceful reunification
of China, because it encouraged the spread of the idea of "the
independence of Taiwan."[23]

In November 1990 Li addressed the "one country, two regions"
proposal then being advanced by Premier Hau Pei-tsun. Li Jiaquan said
that the new proposal was more neutral sounding, but it still was
intended to preserve the status quo in the Taiwan Strait until such time
as the socialist system on the mainland had evolved into a capitalist
and democratic system. This, Li said, was an unrealistic and dangerous
expectation on the part of Taiwan authorities and it should be
discarded.[24] A similar article was written by Li in December 1990,
debunking the Taiwan formula of "one country with a good system."[25]

One of the best statements of the PRC position in 1990 was made
by President Yang Shangkun in September.[26] He told reporters from
Taiwan:

> By no means can we recognize that Taiwan and the mainland are two
> governments on an equal footing. That would mean two Chinas. Now,
> some people in Taiwan have racked their brains and come up with the
> slogan "one country, two regions." To realize reunification, however, the
> central government must be located in Beijing and be of the People's
> Republic of China. This is the supreme, non-negotiable principle. In order
> to avoid a situation wherein Taiwan people feel that we are out to annex
> Taiwan, however, we put forward the principle of "one country, two
> systems." This principle was raised before the solution to the Hong Kong
> issue and it has been successful in resolving that and the Macao issues.
> Since Taiwan is different from Hong Kong and Macao, it can have a
> different relationship with the central authorities from that of Hong Kong
> and Macao.

Elaborating on what the "one country, two systems" formula would
mean for Taiwan, Yang said:

"One country, two systems" means Taiwan will not be the same as the other provinces in the mainland, but a special administrative region under the jurisdiction of one China. It will enjoy a higher degree of autonomy than the autonomous regions in the mainland and will be able to carry out a different social system from that of the mainland. You [the Taiwan guests] can carry out your "Three People's Principles" and I can practice my socialism. We will not interfere with each other. In addition, Taiwan can maintain its armed forces. The mainland will not send any person to Taiwan to take part in governmental administration. However, we welcome Taiwan sending some personnel to the mainland to participate in the central government.

As to what the PRC wanted in the immediate future, Yang said the "three exchanges" (the exchange of mail, the exchange of trade, and the exchange of air and shipping services) were essential, along with continued expansion of contacts across the Taiwan Strait. Yang further said that it was necessary for the KMT and CCP to begin discussions to work out the many details leading to reunification. The PRC President said that China refused to rule out the use of force, but that this was "mainly addressed at foreign countries, countries which want to take Taiwan away from China." Yang also said that President Chiang Ching-kuo had "sent some messages which indicated his intent to solve the issue of reunification of the two sides." The PRC was willing not to be too hasty about reunification, Yang said, adding that he did not necessarily expect that he himself would live to see it, but that "those in the room" should live to see it. Yang specifically mentioned, however, Deng Xiaoping's advice that reunification would be easier to resolve if the people involved in the history of the KMT and CCP were still alive. Yang said, "If the issue is further postponed, there are many questions the younger generation of the two parties do not understand. This is the reason behind the anxiety."

Taiwan Systematizes Contact Across the Strait

Taiwan responded to the PRC criticisms of its flexible diplomacy in two ways. First, the ROC threatened to curtail contacts with the mainland if Beijing continued to harm Taiwan's interests. In early 1989, for example, Taipei warned Beijing that if it did not cease its efforts to restrict Taiwan's participation in international organizations, the ROC would find it impossible to continue rapid development of trade and investment on the mainland. One Taiwan official cautioned, if the PRC authorities "do not give us room to maneuver internationally, we're not going to respond positively in terms of the mainland-Taiwan relationship."[27]

Second, Taiwan attempted to refute PRC claims that it was seeking to create "two Chinas." In a Foreign Ministry statement of January 1989, Taipei said that the national task of the ROC "is to reunify China under a free and democratic system that has already taken shape in Taiwan after four decades of effort." The Ministry said that in keeping with a "one China" policy, Taipei would strive to strengthen cooperative ties with friendly countries throughout the world. The Ministry said, "It should never be understood that the ROC is promoting 'two Chinas'."[28]

Lee Teng-hui, Hau Pei-tsun and other KMT leaders made many statements supporting China's reunification. In May 1990 President Lee said in his inauguration speech: "If the Chinese Communist authorities can implement political democracy and a free economic system, renounce the use of military force in the Taiwan Straits, and not interfere with our development of foreign relations on the basis of a one-China policy, we would be willing—on a basis of equality—to establish channels of communication." In the same speech, President Lee announced his intention of terminating the state of civil war between the KMT and the CCP.[29]

ROC leaders also took several steps to institutionalize contact across the Taiwan Strait as an expression of their commitment to the "one China" principle. The attempt to channel more formal contact with the mainland served another purpose as well. The huge volume of unofficial interaction across the Taiwan Strait threatened to get out of Taipei's political control unless effective governing mechanisms were put into place. By the end of 1991, for example, Taiwan residents had made over 2.4 million trips to the mainland and more than 22,000 mainland residents had visited Taiwan. Over forty million letters had been exchanged between 1987 and the end of 1991 and more than twelve million phone calls had been placed.

One of the initial steps to control contact with the mainland was taken in August 1988, when the Mainland Affairs Council was established under the Executive Yuan to coordinate the various ROC government agencies in charge of implementing mainland policy and to control the pace of exchanges across the Taiwan Strait. The Council became a permanent government agency in October 1990, tasked with the responsibility of policy planning and coordination. Also in October 1990 the National Unification Council was established as a non-partisan body under the Office of the President to provide policy guidance and determine consensus for ROC policy toward the mainland.

Another key step was taken in November 1990 with the establishment of the Foundation for Exchanges Across the Taiwan Straits.

Also known as the Straits Exchange Foundation, the private organization was given the following major tasks:

- accepting, ratifying and forwarding on entry and exit documents from the two Chinese sides
- verifying and delivering documents issued on the mainland
- deporting fugitives on both sides of the Taiwan Strait
- arbitrating trade disputes
- promoting cultural and academic exchanges
- providing consultation on general affairs
- helping to protect the legal rights of ROC citizens during their visits to the mainland.

In essence, the Foundation became Taipei's unofficial intermediary between the ROC and the PRC.

In December 1990 President Lee Teng-hui submitted a three-stage blueprint for reunification as a counter offer to Beijing's repeated suggestions that the KMT and CCP engage in high-level dialogue on unification. These "Guidelines for National Unification," formally adopted in March 1991, remained the ROC's principal policy toward the mainland through the end of 1991.[30]

The guidelines committed Taiwan more firmly to unification with the mainland, but they conditioned progress toward unification on Beijing's acceptance of an increased international presence for the ROC and fundamental reform in the PRC. According to the guidelines, the goal of ROC unification policy was "to establish a democratic, free and equitably prosperous China." As fundamental principles, the guidelines specified:

1. Both mainland and Taiwan areas are parts of Chinese territory. Helping to bring about national unification should be the common responsibility of all Chinese people.

2. The unification of China should be for the welfare of all of its people and not be subject to partisan conflict.

3. China's unification should aim at promoting Chinese culture, safeguarding human dignity, guaranteeing fundamental human rights, and practicing democracy and the rule of law.

4. The timing and manner of China's unification should first respect the rights and interests of the people in the Taiwan area, and protect their security and welfare. It should be achieved in gradual phases under the principles of reason, peace, equity, and reciprocity.

A three-stage process of unification was proposed. The short-term first stage focused on building "exchanges and reciprocity." The proposal called for increasing exchanges across the Taiwan Strait, while at the same time "not endangering each other's safety and stability . . . and not denying the other's existence as a political entity." These exchanges would be handled by the respective governments in a controlled fashion through intermediary organizations, such as the Straits Exchange Foundation. During the first phase, "in the mainland area economic reform should be carried out forthrightly . . . and both democracy and the rule of law should be implemented." At the same time, Taiwan would "accelerate constitutional reform and promote national development." In phase one "the two sides of the Straits should end the state of hostility and, under the principle of one China, solve all disputes through peaceful means." At the same time, the two sides should "respect . . . each other in the international community."

The medium-term phase of the guidelines focused on building "mutual trust and cooperation." In this stage, "Direct postal, transport and commerce links should be allowed, and both sides should jointly develop the southeastern coastal area of the Chinese mainland and then gradually extend this development to other areas of the mainland in order to narrow the gap in living standards between the two sides." Both sides should "establish official communication channels on equal footing" and "assist each other . . . in international organizations and activities." Mutual visits by "high-ranking officials on both sides" should be carried out.

The long-term phase was one of "consultation and unification." During this phase,

> A consultative organization for unification should be established through which both sides, in accordance with the will of the people in both the mainland and Taiwan areas, and while adhering to the goals of democracy, economic freedom, social justice and nationalization of the armed forces, jointly discuss the grand task of unification and map out a constitutional system to establish a democratic, free, and equitably prosperous China.

While the guidelines offered much more detail regarding the ROC's plan for unification, they continued to embody the principle of ROC equality with the PRC. Taipei's clear intent in the guidelines was to nudge mainland China in a direction similar to developments on Taiwan. It was in fact calling upon the PRC to surrender its four cardinal principles: adherence to the leadership of the Chinese

Communist Party, to Marxism-Leninism and Mao Zedong thought, to the people's democratic dictatorship, and to the socialist road.

As expected, the PRC criticized the guidelines, noting there was no need for it to treat the Taiwan government as an equal government, nor was there a need for the mainland to change its socialist system. An article written in *Beijing Review* in July 1991 dissected Taipei's description of itself as a "political entity," observing that Taiwan wanted to be treated as an equal to the PRC in the international community. This would lead, according to the article, to dual recognition. Such an approach "provides an opportunity for those who intend to create 'two Chinas,' 'one China, one Taiwan,' 'the independence of Taiwan,' or those who want to perpetuate the division of the country." This was, according to the article, "absolutely unacceptable."[31]

Beijing's concerns about the purpose behind the guidelines were amplified by the ever stronger cries for independence among certain Taiwanese. In June 1991 *Renmin Ribao* commented, "Taiwan independence activities aim to split the country and the nation. This is a very dangerous road. Those who advocate Taiwan independence must stop their activities. Otherwise, their guilt is bound to be condemned by history."[32]

Aware of Beijing's sensitivities to the Taiwan independence movement, the ROC continued to signal its sincerity in desiring eventual reunification. One means was through frequent contact between personnel of the Straits Exchange Foundation and representatives of the PRC government. In late April 1991 delegates from the Foundation met with Chinese officials in Beijing at the invitation of the State Council's Taiwan Affairs Office. The Foundation requested that the PRC create a similar non-governmental organization as a counterpart to itself so that exchanges and dialogue would be more convenient. The Foundation also asked that it be allowed to establish a mainland office to expedite communications.

In greeting the delegation, Tang Shubei, deputy director of the Taiwan Affairs Office, said the PRC insisted on five principles in mainland-Taiwan relations. These were:

> (1) Taiwan is an "indivisible" part of Chinese territory; the unification of China is "a common wish and sacred mission" for Chinese on both sides of the Straits; and the people of both the mainland and Taiwan should work together to promote peaceful unification of the nation.
>
> (2) Beijing firmly adheres to the principle of "one China" and opposes any form of "two Chinas," "one China, one Taiwan," "one country, two governments," or any other such proposal.

(3) Under the principle of "one China," both sides should consider the reality of the different systems on both sides, drop hostility, intensify understanding, seek consensus, protect the rights and interests of the people in both societies, and establish mutual trust to deal reasonably with specific problems arising from contacts.

(4) Both sides should actively promote normal contacts between the people of Taiwan and the mainland; establish direct links of mail, trade, and transport; and encourage and develop bilateral exchanges in regard to economics, culture, athletics, science, technology, and academic research.

(5) Organizations and people on both sides engaged in promoting the "three links and mutual exchanges" should continue the effort, and encourage direct talks between authorities of both sides to solve specific problems in the exchanges.[33]

Taipei's initial reaction to Tang Shubei's statement was that direct mail, trade, and transportation links between Taiwan and the mainland would not be permitted by the ROC government until relations between Beijing and Taipei are "sailing a smooth course."[34] But the cross-Straits dialogue continued at a brisk pace. The Foundation took additional trips to the mainland in July and November 1991. In December the PRC created its counterpart to the Foundation, the Council for Relations Across the Taiwan Straits, closely tied to the State Council's Taiwan Affairs Office.

One of the most revealing explanations of Taiwan's strategy and policy toward the mainland was given in May 1991 by Ma Ying-jeou, vice chairman of the ROC cabinet's Mainland Affairs Council.[35]

Ma warned, "if the Chinese Communists refuse to acknowledge us as a political entity, or refuse continuously to renounce the use of force against us, or refuse to stop interfering with our conduct of external relations under the principle of 'one China,' then we will not go on to the second stage" of the national unification guidelines. Ma emphasized that the ROC was not impatient on unification and did not have in mind a timetable, but rather a *process* of unification. The PRC's "three links," Ma said, will come in the second stage if mutual trust has first been established. Ma commented:

National unification is our unswerving goal, but it is an eventual goal. It is a goal as well as a means. The means is intended to achieve national wealth, national strength and people's welfare. We do not go to unification for the sole purpose of unification. In other words, we want to make sure that unification is for the benefit of not only the people of Taiwan, but also people on the mainland. If we can continue our present strategy, it would always give Chinese Communist authorities the pressure that they should go for democracy and freedom. If we agree to establish the three links, and to accept their "one country, two systems" scheme, I think we will lose our moral justification, and lose whatever we have in Taiwan.

In a more formal presentation, Ma wrote an authoritative article appearing in the February 1992 edition of *Issues and Studies* on the subject of ROC policy toward the mainland.[36] He said Taiwan's position could be summarized in three points:

1. "One China, two areas, two political entities"
2. "Peaceful and democratic unification of China"
3. "The timing and format of China's unification must first respect the rights and interests of the Taiwan people and safeguard their security and welfare. Unification is to be achieved in three phases" as outlined in the Guidelines for National Unification.

Ma specified that Taiwan's approach toward the mainland could be further broken down into several specific policies. These included:

- The ROC will not use force in the process of national unification.
- "Under the one-China principle, Taipei practices 'pragmatic diplomacy,' that is, creating opportunities to resume suspended diplomatic ties or to establish new ones, and to join or rejoin global or regional intergovernmental organizations."
- "Taipei regards itself as the central government of China while Peking is a 'political entity' that controls the mainland area. Taipei proposes the 'one country, two areas, two political entities' scheme, a pragmatic characterization of political reality across the Taiwan Strait, allowing sufficient 'creative ambiguity' for each side to live with."
- Taipei opposes any political negotiations with Beijing until the second stage of the process outlined in the guidelines. At that time the ROC government, not the KMT party, will conduct the negotiations because only the government can represent all of the Taiwan people.
- Direct trade, postal, and transportation links will only occur "when Peking is ready not to deny Taipei's existence as a political entity, not to use force to settle bilateral disputes, and not to interfere with Taipei's conduct of external relations under the one-China principle." Until then, these links will be

indirect. Direct two-way exchanges, however, have rapidly expanded and will continue to do so.

- "Taipei insists that trade with and investment in the mainland must be conducted indirectly. Taipei has, since 1988, permitted the indirect importation of 164 categories of medicinal herbs and industrial raw materials produced on the mainland. Taipei imposes few restrictions on goods shipped to the mainland via a third place. . . . Taiwan companies may invest in 3,679 agricultural and industrial items on the Chinese mainland through their subsidiaries on foreign soil." The ROC government will assist those companies which register their investments according to law and punish those which do not.

- The ROC intends to "build, with Taiwan's security and the welfare of its 20 million people in mind, a national consensus on orderly exchanges with the mainland to foster mutual understanding."

Although outside the time frame of this study, an important clarification of Taiwan's policy toward mainland China was made in August 1992, when the National Unification Council presided over by President Lee Teng-hui defined what was meant by Taipei's "one China principle." According to news reports of the meeting, the term meant "one China, two regions and two political entities." "One China" referred to the Republic of China established in 1912 with sovereignty extending to mainland China, although only Taiwan, Penghu, Kinmen, and Matsu were now under ROC rule. Also, the term signified that China was temporarily split into two political entities as a result of a civil war fought over ideological differences. Further, the National Unification Guidelines were "intended to promote the development of China as a whole and the welfare of all the Chinese people to bring about eventual peaceful unification." The guidelines were also intended "to encourage mainland China to take concrete steps and a pragmatic attitude in handling cross-strait relations and working with Taiwan to build a free, democratic and better China."[37]

Thus, at the beginning of the 1990s, the KMT and the CCP continued to refine their proposals for unification, but remained far apart on the critical issues of how to unify China and the type of political, economic, and social systems to rule China after its unification. Nonetheless, Taiwan's flexible diplomacy and its new pragmatic attitude toward relations with the mainland had opened many avenues of exploration of these complex issues.

Conclusion

Taiwan's flexible diplomacy was a strategy carefully designed to serve many domestic and international purposes. The policy

- accommodated pressure on Taiwan for a larger international role
- allowed Taiwan businessmen to take advantage of commercial opportunities on the mainland and in other socialist countries
- balanced competing pressures on Taiwan from those wishing to promote Taiwan's development as a first priority and those wishing to achieve eventual reunification with the mainland
- provided a practical means to gain wider international recognition as a political entity, thereby making easier commercial relations throughout the world and strengthening Taipei's hand in its complex relationship with the PRC
- provided justification to delay reunification with the mainland until such time as conditions were more favorable to Taipei
- reduced PRC incentives to use force against Taiwan because of its apparent commitment to "one China."

Taiwan's flexible diplomacy used the island's economic strength and the success of its national development to gain higher visibility, greater credibility, and a larger role in the international community. Taipei assumed that its value as a trading partner and source of developmental assistance would be perceived by other countries as being greater than the political costs incurred by offending the PRC if they improved relations with Taiwan. By the end of 1991, Taiwan's flexible foreign policy and its related dollar diplomacy and openness toward the mainland had achieved considerable success, although Beijing had made strong diplomatic advances at Taipei's expense as well.

The prospects for the future of flexible diplomacy look good, even though PRC opposition poses a formidable and constant obstacle. Assuming greater initiative in foreign policy is probably necessary to maintain Taipei's legitimacy at home and abroad. Without a flexible, pragmatic, and somewhat opportunistic foreign policy, Taiwan's international standing will likely weaken, possibly resulting in absorption by the mainland under terms largely dictated by Beijing itself. Hence, for its own interests, Taiwan can be expected to become even more active in promoting itself in international affairs in the future.

Despite the continued political competition between the two Chinese governments, there is a very high probability of increased contact across the Taiwan Strait. Flexible diplomacy permits this, while at the same time allowing the ROC to control the pace of the contact and attempt to moderate PRC policies in directions favorable to ROC interests. At the same time, it is also clear that people-to-people contact is expanding cross-Strait exchange far more swiftly than Taipei expected or might like. Consequently, there is a certain ad hoc sense to many ROC policies and institutions governing Taiwan-mainland China relations as the government tries to "catch-up" to the rapidly changing situation.

There are also important security implications for Taiwan as it uses flexible diplomacy to expand its international presence and to avoid premature reunification with the PRC. These and other security issues will be discussed in the next chapter.

Notes

1. For a detailed discussion of the reunification issue as seen from the perspectives of Beijing, Taipei, and Washington, see Martin L. Lasater, *Policy in Evolution: The U.S. Role in China's Reunification* (Boulder, CO: Westview Press, 1989).

2. *Xinhua,* September 30, 1981, in *Foreign Broadcast Information Service: Daily Report—China* (henceforth *FBIS-China*), September 30, 1981, p. U1.

3. Winston Yang, "Deng Xiaoping's Latest Concept on Peaceful Reunification," *Chishih Nientai,* August 1, 1983, in *FBIS-China,* August 4, 1983, pp. W1-W6.

4. *Xinhua,* June 30, 1984, in *FBIS-China,* July 2, 1984, pp. E1-E2.

5. From *A Draft Agreement between the Government of the United Kingdom of Great Britain and Northern Ireland and the Government of the People's Republic of China on the Future of Hong Kong* (London: Her Majesty's Government, September 26, 1984).

6. Paraphrased from "China's Reunification: Is the 'Nine-Point Proposal' a Yesable Solution" (Taipei, Taiwan: China Mainland Research Center, May 1982).

7. "The China Issue and China's Reunification" (Taipei, Taiwan: Government Information Office, 1982).

8. See Chiang Ching-kuo, "China's Reunification and World Peace," *Free China Review,* May 1986, pp. 61-68.

9. See Shaw Yu-ming, "Taiwan: A View from Taipei," *Foreign Affairs,* 63, 5 (Summer 1985), pp. 1050-1063.

10. Shaw Yu-ming, "An ROC View of the Hong Kong Issue," *Issues and Studies,* 22, 6 (June 1986), p. 30.

11. China News Agency, October 15, 1987, in *FBIS-China*, October 16, 1987, p. 36.

12. *Hong Kong Standard*, October 16, 1987, p. 8.

13. *Xinhua*, October 16, 1987, in *FBIS-China*, October 16, 1987, p. 35.

14. *Asiaweek*, September 6, 1987, p. 26.

15. *Beijing Review*, January 2–8, 1989, pp. 10–11.

16. *Beijing Review*, November 13–19, 1989, pp. 15–16.

17. "'Dual Recognition' Will Get Nowhere," *People's Daily* commentary reprinted in *Beijing Review*, August 14–20, 1989, p. 14.

18. "'Dual Recognition' Not Acceptable," *People's Daily*, October 11, 1989, reprinted in *Beijing Review*, October 23–29, 1989, p. 14.

19. *Ibid.*

20. Li Jiaquan was deputy director and research fellow of the Taiwan Research Institute under the Chinese Academy of Social Sciences in Beijing.

21. Li Jiaquan, "Again on Formula for China's Reunification," *Beijing Review*, March 28–April 3, 1988, pp. 23–27.

22. Li Jiaquan, "Taiwan's New Mainland Policy Raises Concern," *Beijing Review*, May 22–28, 1989, pp. 23–25. For a continuation of his argument, see Li Jiaquan, "More on 'One Country, Two Governments'," *Beijing Review*, July 2–8, 1990, pp. 17–21.

23. Li Jiaquan, "On Taiwan's 'Elastic Diplomacy'," *Beijing Review*, February 26–March 4, 1990, pp. 31–35. See also Zhang Fei, "New Trends in Taiwan," *Beijing Review*, January 9–15, 1989, pp. 7–8; and Jing Wei, "Overstretched: Taiwan's 'Elastic Diplomacy'," *Beijing Review*, April 3–9, 1989, p. 7.

24. Li Jiaquan, "Comment on 'One Country, Two Regions'," *Beijing Review*, November 12–18, 1990, pp. 18–21.

25. Li Jiaquan, "Taiwan: 'One Country with a Good System'?", *Beijing Review*, December 10–16, 1990, pp. 13–17.

26. See speech of "Yang Shangkun on China's Reunification," *Beijing Review*, November 26–December 2, 1990, pp. 11–17.

27. *New York Times*, January 19, 1989, p. A13.

28. *Free China Journal*, January 23, 1989, p. 1.

29. On May 1, 1991, Lee did in fact declare an end to the civil war when he announced the termination of the "Period of Mobilization for Suppression of the Communist Rebellion" and abolished the "Temporary Provisions" which had given the presidency emergency powers to prosecute the war against the communists on the mainland. A few days prior to Lee's announcement, the PLA ceased its nearly 35 years of propaganda broadcasts aimed at Kinmen. *Washington Post*, May 1, 1991, p. A24.

30. See "Guidelines for National Unification" (Taipei, Taiwan: National Unification Council, 1991).

31. Wu Daying, "On Taiwan Authorities' Programme," *Beijing Review*, July 8–14, 1991, pp. 33–35. Wu was director of the Political Science Research Institute under the Chinese Academy of Social Sciences.

32. "'Taiwan Independence' Is a Dangerous Road," *Renmin Ribao*, June 3, 1991, in *Beijing Review*, July 1–7, 1991, pp. 33–34.

33. Cited in *Free China Journal,* May 2, 1991, p. 2.

34. *Ibid.*

35. For the text of Ma's press conference, see *Free China Journal,* May 7, 1991, pp. 2, 7.

36. Ying-jeou Ma, "The Republic of China's Policy Toward the Chinese Mainland," *Issues and Studies,* 28, 2 (February 1992), pp. 1–10.

37. *The China News* (Taipei), August 2, 1992, p. 10.

5

The Security of Taiwan

One of the most crucial determinants of Taiwan's future is the possible use of force by the PRC to bring about reunification. If Beijing were successful in its military efforts, Taiwan would be brought under the control of the PRC. If Beijing failed in its use of force, Taipei would gain a major political victory and tremendously expand its options for the future. There would, for example, be much greater international support for Taiwan becoming an independent state, if its government and citizens so desired. Regardless of the outcome of the conflict, Sino-American relations would be seriously harmed for many years.

U.S. interests in a peaceful settlement of the Taiwan issue have been reaffirmed by successive administrations since that of Harry Truman. From 1954–1979 the United States relied upon a mutual security treaty with the ROC to help deter a PRC attack against Taiwan or the Pescadores. After 1979 U.S. security interests were protected in the Taiwan Relations Act (TRA), which mandated that the United States maintain sufficient forces in the Western Pacific to ensure peace and stability in the Taiwan Strait. The TRA further stipulated that Washington sell Taipei weapons and defense services adequate for Taiwan's self-defense. Taiwan's ability to field such a capability was complicated by the August 17, 1982, U.S.-PRC Joint Communiqué, which placed qualitative and quantitative restrictions on U.S. arms sales to Taiwan. Nonetheless, Taiwan's security remained a matter of concern to the United States, and both the Reagan and Bush administrations took steps to ensure that Taiwan's defense needs were met in the post-communiqué period.

A significant development over the past few years has been Taiwan's ability, with outside technological assistance, to produce many of its own advanced weapons. This has reduced ROC dependence on U.S. arms sales, increased Taipei's self-reliance in security matters, and shorn up Taiwan's self-confidence in its future. Partly as a result, Taiwan has become embolden in both its domestic and foreign policies, including policies toward the mainland.

This chapter will examine Taiwan's security in the early 1990s, noting both the dangers and opportunities which exist for ROC national security as a result of changing domestic and international conditions.

PRC Political Objectives in the Use of Force

In assessing the PRC threat to Taiwan it is important to keep in mind that the issue of war and peace in the Taiwan Strait is far more complex than the Taipei-Beijing military balance of power. The crucial variable is the PRC's perception of the utility of using force against Taiwan. That calculation is heavily influenced by many factors, including Beijing's political objectives in a possible war with Taiwan and a comparison of the costs and benefits to China of pursuing such a policy.

It is widely assumed by both American and Chinese military analysts that Beijing has the military capability to defeat Taiwan in a full-scale war. The vast quantitative differences between the PRC and ROC in terms of armed forces personnel, aircraft, warships, missiles, artillery, tanks, and other weapons, coupled with mainland China's huge military industrial production base, natural resources, and population, mean that in an all-out conflict between the two Chinese sides, the PRC would likely win.[1]

But wars are seldom efforts in which the total resources of two governments are mobilized in a gigantic struggle for total victory or total defeat. There is usually careful calculation of the potential gain versus the potential cost in determining whether force should be used in the first place and whether its use should be continued at various stages of the conflict. For this reason, it is vital to have a clear understanding of the reasons the PRC would initiate a war with Taiwan.

Beijing has said it would consider using force against Taipei under the following conditions: (a) if Taiwan were controlled by a foreign power (interpreted at various times as being the Soviet Union, United States, and Japan); (b) if Taipei developed nuclear weapons; (c) if Taiwan claimed to be an independent state; (d) if the KMT lost internal control of Taiwan; or (e) if Taipei refused to negotiate reunification over an ill-defined "long period of time."[2]

Other possible justifications for a PRC use of force could be: (f) a decision to eliminate the KMT as a political rival to the CCP or to eliminate the "Taiwan Experience" as a model competing with socialism on the mainland; (g) the use of a crisis in the Taiwan Strait by some political faction on the mainland vying for power in a succession

struggle once Deng and other "Long March" leaders have passed from
the scene; or (h) a positive response to calls for PRC military intervention from some faction on Taiwan wanting early unification with
the mainland.

Certain of these justifications for the use of force by the PRC can
be dismissed as highly improbable. These include Taiwan coming
under the control of some other country and Taipei developing
nuclear weapons. Also, the likelihood of the PRC attacking Taiwan
to eliminate the KMT or to destroy the "Taiwan Experience" seems
remote as well.

The PRC might use force to intervene in the event of civil disorder
on the island, but the likelihood of social chaos occurring on Taiwan
is fairly small. Also, Beijing might try to force Taipei to negotiate
reunification after prolonged procrastination, but it seems more probable that Taipei would make sufficient gestures of progress toward
unification to defuse the crisis.

The use of military force in the Taiwan Strait to help some faction
in an internal power struggle in Beijing or Taipei is difficult to assess,
but it probably should not be ruled out. However, there seems little
doubt but that the PRC would use force to stop Taiwan from becoming an independent state.

There are various forms of Taiwan "independence," including what
some describe as Taiwan's current "de facto independence." The form
most intolerable from Beijing's point of view is de jure independence
of Taiwan. The PRC refers to this as "one China, one Taiwan," and it
means that Taiwan would no longer be considered Chinese territory.
Of all the various justifications for a PRC use of force in the Taiwan
Strait, a movement by the government in Taipei toward this form of
Taiwan independence is the most likely to result in war.

PRC Intentions to Use Force Against Taiwan

Since its founding in October 1949, the PRC has set China's unification as a basic national policy objective. Until the late 1970s, the
PRC followed a fundamental strategy of the "liberation" of Taiwan,
usually expressed in military terms. Beginning in late 1978, however,
PRC leaders began to describe their fundamental policy toward Taiwan
as one of "peaceful reunification."

Despite its "peaceful" approach to the Taiwan issue, the PRC refused
to rule out the use of force as a means to draw Taiwan back into the
"embrace of the motherland." Since Taipei does not wish to unify with
the PRC as long as the mainland is under a communist government,
and since the CCP insists that it will never relinquish its leadership

role in Beijing, the possibility exists that the PRC eventually will use force against Taiwan to achieve its goal of national reunification. From Beijing's point of view, this is an historic mission held in common by all Chinese governments. It is extremely unlikely that the PRC will drop unification as a national objective.

Since the Tiananmen Square incident of June 1989, there have been indications that PRC leaders may be reexamining the utility of using force in the Taiwan Strait. According to ROC sources, the following statements on the possible use of force against Taiwan were heard from PRC officials during the August 1989–December 1990 period:[3]

- As far as Taiwan is concerned, we do not renounce a military solution. If they become independent, we will attack them. We will have no choice but to attack them. On this issue of principle we cannot be soft. When I said that we should put the Taiwan issue on our working agenda, I meant to work out a timetable. This timetable should be based upon: first, Taiwan becomes independent; second, Taiwan treats us rudely; and third, Taiwan's dirty hands constantly infiltrate our borders. (Deng Xiaoping, August–September 1989, at a PRC military conference)

- The United States can attack Panama, so we can attack Taiwan, and furthermore, we have better reason for doing so. (Yang Shangkun, March 16, 1990, quoted in *Pai Hsing*, No. 212)

- The adverse current of Taiwan independence set off by some people on the island with ulterior motives has been of particular concern in the recent period. They advocate that Taiwan be split away from the mainland. This must be firmly opposed by all Chinese people, and the Chinese government will definitely not sit idly by and do nothing. (Li Peng, March 20, 1990, from his Report on the Government's Work delivered at the Third Session of the Seventh National People's Congress)

- We are opposed to Taiwan independence, no matter what form it takes. We are firmly opposed to it. If Taiwan becomes independent, we do not eliminate the use of military force to resolve the issue. (Yang Shangkun, May 27, 1990, at a meeting with Overseas Chinese in Argentina)

- The present status of Taiwan is still not stable. The danger of Taiwan being taken over by foreign countries still exists. That is why we are ready to use force to prevent Taiwan's secession.

(Yang Shangkun, September 24, 1990, in a news conference with reporters from Taipei's *China Times*)

- China's decision to use force against Taiwan will be influenced by three factors: first, if Taiwan seeks independence; second, if a foreign nation invades Taiwan; and third, if reunification talks are prolonged for a long period of time. (Chien Weichang, December 9, 1990, at a conference on the Macau Basic Law in Kwangchow)

- Reunification without the backing of a strong military force is pure fantasy. (Jiang Zemin, December 12, 1990, at the National Working Conference on Taiwan)

There was some evidence in the early 1990s of increased PRC military preparation for a possible use of force against Taiwan. In March 1990, for example, it was reported that Beijing had moved about twenty-four of its Jian-8 (or F-8) fighters from the Sino-Soviet border to bases opposite Taiwan. Some additional troop movements into Fujian province were also reported.[4] According to Taiwan news services, a Beijing official said the deployments were partly in response to conflicts within the Kuomintang and increased advocacy of Taiwan independence.[5]

Cheng Ming carried a story in early April 1990 detailing several steps the PRC was taking to prepare for an attack against Taiwan.[6] According to sources said to work in the PRC Office of Taiwan Affairs, it might be necessary to move from a political to a military solution of the Taiwan issue because of the following factors:

1. Taiwan is the largest anti-communist base, it was involved in the [June 1989] rebellion in Beijing, and it is supporting anti-PRC activities among Overseas Chinese. China cannot be stable without recapturing Taiwan.
2. The CCP is researching likely responses to any attack on Taiwan. If one were to occur before 1997, the strongest reactions are expected from Hong Kong and the United States. PRC officials believed that the Taiwan issue should be solved soon, hopefully, within the next five to six years.
3. The tense relations between the PRC and Taiwan are the fault of the KMT, because the Nationalists are not making positive responses to PRC initiatives and are trying to create an independent Taiwan. Both Deng Xiaoping and Yang Shangkun have concluded that Lee Teng-hui is supporting a move toward Taiwan independence.

The *Cheng Ming* article referred to additional preparations taken by the PRC to suggest that consideration was being given to a military solution to the Taiwan issue. These included increased numbers of PRC agents being sent to Taiwan, simulations of airborne and amphibious attacks against Taiwan, and the development of new strategic and tactical studies of how to defeat Taiwan through combined military and political means.

Cheng Ming also carried a report of a secret Beijing meeting in July 1990 to formulate general principles for PRC policy toward Taiwan.[7] According to the article, CCP leaders were deeply divided. A "dove faction," comprised of Jiang Zemin, Li Ruihuan, and Ding Guangen, stressed a peaceful political solution but did not oppose the use of force if necessary. A "hawk faction," comprised of Yang Shangkun, Wang Zhen, and some senior military cadre wanted to rely on the military option and to make no concessions to Taiwan. Reportedly, Deng Xiaoping endorsed Jiang Zemin's suggestions to establish more communication links with Taiwan, adopt more favorable policies toward Taiwan investors, and state that the CCP will only use force to prevent the independence movement from dominating Taiwan. According to the report, all Taiwan affairs offices on the mainland were given increased financial allocations to expand and upgrade the timeliness and quality of their work.

The *South China Morning Post* reported in September 1990 that Ding Guangen, head of the PRC's Taiwan Affairs Office, said that between 1992 and 1994 the KMT and CCP should hold talks, while reunification should be achieved by 1995. Ding said that if Taiwan resists unification after 1995, military force should be considered.[8]

In March 1991, *Cheng Ming* reported that the PRC was stepping up a "war of nerves" against Taiwan, including movement of additional airborne, artillery, radar, and guided missile forces into Fujian. Several fishing boats were reportedly armed, and PRC fishermen were passing along false documents to confuse ROC officials and spread fears among the Taiwan population.[9]

One of the most forceful warnings from the PRC was heard from Yang Shangkun in October 1991. Yang said that Taiwan independence activities had multiplied in recent years, but that the reunification of China was in the fundamental interest of the Chinese people. Yang warned the separatists not to miscalculate, saying, "Those who play with fire will perish by fire."[10]

To a certain extent, these statements and activities can be dismissed as psychological pressure being exerted on Taipei to convince ROC leaders to move more quickly to formalize links with the mainland.

They also warn both the ROC government and separatists on Taiwan not to push the Taiwan independence issue too far. However, it probably would be a mistake to dismiss these warnings as mere rhetoric or symbolic gestures. There are several factors in the early 1990s which suggest that the PRC may indeed be considering the use of force against Taiwan as a viable option.

First, the advanced age of Deng Xiaoping, Chen Yun, Yang Shangkun, and other senior CCP leaders necessitates that, if reunification is to be achieved in their lifetimes, some dramatic movement on the issue must take place in the near future. Despite increased contact across the Taiwan Strait, there is no indication that Taipei is willing to accept the "one country, two systems" proposal. Indeed, Taipei is now advancing its own formulas which are attracting favorable world attention.

Second, the pending leadership transition and possible power struggle in Beijing mean that various factions are looking toward unresolved issues to find advantage against their opponents. One such issue is Taiwan, which is gaining in policy importance now that the Hong Kong and Macau issues have been settled in principle and PRC security has been enhanced through the collapse of the Soviet threat.

Third, the domestic and international repercussions of Tiananmen have made peaceful reunification less attractive to the people of Taiwan and the international community in general. The domestic political situation within the PRC makes a return to major economic, social, and political reform difficult and uncertain. This puts the CCP in an uncomfortable dilemma: it needs to reform to attract Taiwan, but the reforms might lead to the loss of CCP power. Under such circumstances, progress toward unification through peaceful means may not be possible.

Fourth, the PRC has lost considerable influence in world affairs because of Tiananmen and the collapse of the Soviet Union. Beijing no longer enjoys a favorable international image or the ability to play the "strategic triangle" to its advantage. Not being "special" any longer in the eyes of the United States and other countries has weakened the PRC's ability to mount international pressure on Taipei. At the same time, Taiwan's prestige in the international community is growing steadily because of its economic strength, rapid democratization, and flexible diplomacy.

Fifth, the United States is reducing its military presence in the Western Pacific. The possibility of U.S. intervention in the Taiwan Strait has been an important deterrent to war in the region since June 1950. There are several current trends in U.S. policy which might convince the PRC that Washington's intervention is becoming less likely.

For example, U.S. forces in the Asian Pacific region are being reduced by 10–15 percent.[11] The Philippine government has refused to allow continued U.S. access to Clark and Subic air and naval bases. Although U.S. naval and air units remain substantial in the Western Pacific, and at least some of the missions performed by Clark and Subic can be duplicated by facilities elsewhere, trends toward U.S. military reductions worldwide could be read by Beijing as an indication that Washington would not likely intervene on a major scale in the Taiwan Strait should the PRC attack Taiwan.

Also, many PRC analysts believe the United States is becoming weaker because of its domestic economic and political problems. As one report noted, "Although the end of the Cold War has left the United States as the only superpower, its real power and position has very clearly been weakened."[12] Moreover, many in Beijing believe that it is more important for the PRC to gain control of Taiwan than to have a few years of sour relations with the United States.

Sixth, the reduction of the Soviet, Vietnamese, and Indian threats along China's borders has freed the PLA to concentrate on unresolved territorial issues in the Taiwan Strait and South China Sea. In many ways, these are similar operational environments, so preparations to defend PRC interests in the South China Sea can also be applied to some extent to the Taiwan situation. The PRC is acquiring power projection forces, thus becoming more able to fill the power vacuum left in the region by the withdrawal of U.S. and Soviet forces.

Seventh, certain developments on Taiwan are very troublesome to many PRC leaders. In the first place, the so-called "Taiwan Experience" has made an adverse impact on the attitudes of the Chinese people, especially the young and educated, toward the Chinese Communist Party. The crisis of CCP credibility on the mainland is reaching epic proportions. Many Chinese leaders feel uncomfortable with comparisons with developments on Taiwan.

Second, democratization and Taiwanization have dramatically increased the possibility that the people of Taiwan will elect to move further in the direction of de jure separation from mainland China. Whether this will be the eventual outcome of the democratic process on Taiwan is uncertain, but PRC leaders are uncomfortable with open discussion of the independence issue. Many in Beijing believe they cannot take a chance that Taiwan will decide in a democratic fashion to unify with the mainland.

Third, the growing economic strength of the ROC is being translated through flexible diplomacy into an increased international role for

Taipei. This is seen not only in trade and commercial contacts, but also in participation in international organizations and even in some diplomatic gains. From Beijing's point of view, Taiwan's recent success in these areas are at least partial defeat of the PRC strategy to isolate Taipei internationally. The failure of this strategy may lead to a reexamination of other options to see if they might be more effective in achieving reunification.

All of these factors suggest that the PRC is keeping open its military option as a possible way to solve the Taiwan issue. For this reason, it is important to examine the PLA's capabilities to take military action in the Taiwan Strait and to consider the effectiveness of Taipei's deterrent posture.

Comparison of Military Capabilities

In terms of total military capabilities in 1990–1991, the PRC enjoyed clear superiority over Taiwan in most categories. Only in destroyers did Taiwan have a small advantage over the mainland (24 versus 18).[13] Fairly close numbers were found for frigates (10 for Taipei and 37 for Beijing), missile patrol craft (52 versus 215), mine warfare vessels (8 versus 52), amphibious ships (26 versus 58), and fighters that could operate in a ground attack mode (444 versus 500). In all other areas Taiwan was vastly outnumbered, frequently by a ratio of 10 to 1 (for example, total armed forces, total troops, infantry divisions, total naval personnel, submarines, fast attack craft, air force personnel, total combat aircraft, and fighter interceptors). Beijing enjoyed a monopoly on certain weapons systems, such as strategic nuclear forces, naval bombers and fighters, air force bombers, and medium- and long-ranged ballistic missiles.

In an all-out military confrontation between the two Chinese sides, Taiwan would face almost certain defeat without major U.S. intervention on its behalf or the collapse of political will to continue the war on the part of Beijing. However, Taiwan has certain advantages over the PRC, one of which is the fact that the ROC has only one potential enemy on which to concentrate its forces, whereas the PRC must maintain an adequate military presence against Russia, India, and Vietnam, as well as keep a wary eye on Japan, the Korean peninsula, and developments in Tibet. The PLA also has extensive domestic duties as the military arm of the CCP ultimately responsible for maintaining political control over the mainland's one billion people.

In terms of forces readily available to both sides in the Taiwan Strait region during 1990–1991, the PLA deployed three Integrated Group Armies comprised of eleven infantry divisions and one armored division (roughly 130,000 men) in the Nanjing Military Region, facing Taiwan's army of some 270,000 troops, 30,000 Marines, and 1.5 million army reserves. The ROC deployed about 55,000 army personnel on Kinmen and 18,000 on Matsu. The PLA, however, could mobilize almost unlimited numbers of army personnel and deploy them to the Fujian front within a few months.

The PRC East Sea Fleet had two submarine, two escort, one mine warfare, and one amphibious squadrons assigned to its headquarters in Shanghai. Some 270 patrol and coastal combatants, many of which were missile-equipped, were also deployed with the East Sea Fleet. In a crisis, the East Sea Fleet could easily be reinforced with ships from the North Sea Fleet headquartered in Qingdao or the South Sea Fleet headquartered in Zhanjiang.

Facing the PLA navy were four Taiwan submarines, including two recently built and delivered by The Netherlands. Taiwan's navy included twenty-four destroyers, but these were outdated (some commissioned in 1946) and in the process of being replaced. Taiwan's ten frigates and eight coastal minesweepers were similarly outdated. The surface fleet included fourteen Gearing DD-710 destroyers, most of which were updated with Hsiung Feng surface-to-surface missiles, surface-to-air missiles, and antisubmarine rockets. Six Allen M. Sumner DD-692 and four Fletcher DD-992 class destroyers were similarly upgraded.

Modern guided missile patrol craft of various sizes were being acquired by Taiwan. The ROC built two Lung Chiang guided missile patrol boats and fifty Hai Ou small missile patrol boats. Several large missile patrol boats were reportedly on order from The Netherlands and South Korea. In addition, Taiwan possessed thirty-two S-2 Tracker antisubmarine warfare (ASW) aircraft, being refitted by Grumman, and had started building at least six modern FFG-7 Oliver Hazard Perry-class frigates from blueprints purchased from the United States.

At least seven major PLA air bases were within 250 nautical miles of Taiwan, placing aircraft stationed there within five to seven minutes of their targets on the island. Because of the relative ease of redeploying air units, the entire PLA air force should be considered. In 1990–1991 the PRC had some 5,894 naval and air force combat aircraft, including 150 medium H-6 bombers, 480 light H-5 bombers, 550 Q-5 ground attack fighters, and some 4,600 fighters. Of the latter, the J-6, a obsolescent derivative of the Soviet MiG-19 Farmer, was the most numerous interceptor, totalling more than 3,000 aircraft.

Taiwan had 504 combat aircraft, of which 220 were F-5E. Other combat aircraft included fifty-five F-5F, eight F-5B, eight F-104D/DJ, 120 F-104G, thirty-three TF-104G, and three reconnaissance RF-104G.

Taiwan also possessed a fairly effective air-defense system. It included two surface-to-air (SAM) systems, the Sky Bow I, which was a combination of U.S. Patriot and Improved Hawk systems, and Sky Bow II, a high altitude system with a 100 kilometer range. Taiwan also acquired from the United States considerable numbers of Improved Chaparral and Improved Sea Chaparral air defense missiles. Improved-Hawk SAMs and Standard shipborne SAMs were also deployed.

PRC Military Options Against Taiwan

Beijing faces a dilemma in selecting a military option to use against Taiwan. If too little force is used, then the military option is ineffective. Taipei would gain considerable international sympathy and there is a chance that the international community might support Taiwan if it chose to become an independent country. In other words, too little force could create political difficulties for Beijing without achieving its primary objective of reunification.

On the other hand, if too much force is used, Taiwan's economic infrastructure might be badly damaged and the probability of the United States directly intervening on Taiwan's behalf increases substantially. Too much force could destroy Taiwan's potential contribution to China's modernization or result in a war with the United States with unpredictable consequences.

What the PRC needs is a plan that minimizes the damage to Taiwan's infrastructure, limits the possibility of U.S. intervention, and convinces Taipei to accept reunification. Under such a plan, the PRC might not have to use massive amounts of force, but that force would have to be available in case it was needed.

This being said, there are several ways in which force could be used against Taiwan, including

- fifth column" or special operations forces to support a coup within Taiwan
- bombardment of Kinmen and Matsu
- invasion of Kinmen and Matsu
- deployment of large numbers of armed fishing boats around Taiwan for a show of force
- surprise missile attack on key facilities
- use of chemical, biological, bacteriological, or nuclear weapons
- blockade of Taiwan

- destruction of ROC air and naval forces
- amphibious invasion of Taiwan.

Each of these possible options merit closer analysis to determine their viability.

"Fifth Column" or Special Operations Forces to Support a Coup within Taiwan. Most analysts believe the PRC would have to risk an all-out war with Taiwan and the United States to use force to reunify China. However, this objective could be achieved with lower levels of force in conjunction with efforts inside Taiwan itself to bring about early reunification. Those within Taiwan who might participate in such a conspiracy would include mainlanders who would prefer re-unification rather than Taiwan independence, as well as Taiwanese who might be attracted by promises of a prominent role in a future Taiwan administration or favorable economic concessions.

Under this scenario, the PRC would use special operations forces (SOF) inserted into Taiwan through covert means or through illegal immigration to stir up trouble, while the co-conspirators on Taiwan would declare martial law or take other action to seize policy direction in Taipei. Once in power, the co-conspirators would agree to reunify with the mainland, probably under terms very favorable to Taiwan so that negative reaction on the island and from the international community would be minimal. Some sort of deal might also be cut with the KMT and the DPP to give them face-saving roles in mainland politics and Taiwan affairs.

Unlike the direct military options discussed below, this approach would be a classic indirect strategy designed to minimize violence and harm to Taiwanese. The possibility of U.S. intervention would also be greatly reduced, if only because of the unclear nature of the PRC aggression and uncertainty in Washington as to whom to support on Taiwan.

The PRC does have the capability to insert SOF forces and probably already has some "fifth column" elements in place in Taiwan. This type of operation would not require massive PLA mobilization, al-though it might occur in conjunction with such an effort to cause a crisis in Taipei or to distract attention from true PRC intentions.

Bombardment of Kinmen and Matsu. Other than signalling an im-patience on the part of Beijing and perhaps a warning to Taipei not to proceed further in some objectionable policy, a bombardment of the offshore islands would not seem likely.

In the first place, if the bombardment was interpreted as a prelude to an attack against the Pescadores or Taiwan (as was the case in

1955 and 1958), then the action against the offshore islands would immediately precipitate a major crisis in Sino-American relations. The United States might negate the August 17 communiqué and substantially increase its sale of advanced military equipment to the ROC.

Second, it is improbable that such a bombardment would have the effect of forcing Taipei to negotiate reunification on Beijing's terms. It would threaten military personnel and civilians on the offshore islands, but it would not achieve the main PRC political objective. Indeed, such a limited use of force would give Taipei an opportunity and justification to argue for greater international recognition of its independence from the mainland, if it chose to do so.

The PLA has the capability with its forces currently deployed in the Taiwan Strait region to carry out this option.

Invasion of Kinmen and Matsu. Whereas a successful invasion of the offshore islands could result in the loss of a substantial number of ROC troops, the costs to the PRC would be high because the islands are heavily fortified.

No doubt, the islands would be resupplied by Taiwan. This would create the possibility of a repeat of the earlier Quemoy crises in which U.S. ships escorted ROC vessels to within a few miles of the offshore islands. It makes little sense for the PRC to risk military confrontation with the United States over the islands. Even if Kinmen and Matsu were captured by the PLA, it would not achieve PRC political objectives. In fact, the loss of the offshore islands would make it easier for Taipei to declare itself an independent nation with no claim of representing mainland China.

The PLA has most of the forces necessary for such an endeavor already deployed in the Taiwan Strait region, but it would probably move additional divisions into the area in preparation for an amphibious invasion of the offshore islands. Additional movement of air and naval units could also be expected because of the need to counter ROC efforts to resupply and reinforce the offshore islands. Due to the possible rapid escalation of the conflict, the PLA must prepare for a major confrontation with ROC forces even if the initial PRC objective is limited to the offshore islands.

Deployment of Armed Fishing Boats Around Taiwan. It is doubtful this method of coercion would be effective in bending Taipei to Beijing's will. Instead, it would alert the international community of the PRC threat and probably result in increased U.S. arms sales to Taiwan. Thus, the probability of Beijing actually using this tactic is small, unless it would be part of a larger military campaign or solely for harassment.

The PLA has the capability to conduct this operation, although additional fishing boats would probably have to be sent to the Taiwan Strait region if large numbers were to be deployed around the islands controlled by the ROC. The PRC would have to make an important decision whether it intended to protect these fishing vessels if they came under attack or seizure by the ROC navy. If such a commitment were made beforehand, then the PLA would have to reinforce its air and naval units in the Taiwan Strait in preparation for a possible wider conflict with Taipei.

Surprise Missile Attack. This is an area of growing concern to Taiwan, because of the accuracy and destructive potential of conventionally armed, precision-guided munitions, particularly ground attack missiles fired from ground, sea, or air platforms. That China possesses such weapons is demonstrated by its sale of Hai Ying Silkworm missiles to Iran, CSS-2 Dong Feng intermediate range ballistic missiles to Saudi Arabia, and short-ranged M-11 missiles to Pakistan and M-9 missiles to Syria.[14] PRC capabilities in this regard are also seen in its successful ICBM and satellite launching programs.

Although not much information is available to properly assess this threat to Taiwan, one would suspect, based on the Iraqi use of Scud missiles in the Persian Gulf War, that the missiles themselves would not be sufficient to force Taipei to the negotiating table. The threat from this type of attack is not too serious, because the accuracy of PRC missiles is such that damage would probably be light to high-priority targets but heavy to the surrounding civilian population.

Nonetheless, as the accuracy of PRC missiles improve and their numbers increase, they could pose a greater threat to Taiwan. Certainly, their psychological impact on the people of Taiwan would be great. This form of state terrorism, however, would result in widespread international condemnation of the PRC.

To help deter the PRC missile threat, Taipei may purchase or develop a tactical anti-ballistic missile defense system, similar to the U.S. Patriot system used in the Persian Gulf War, or deploy limited numbers of its own surface-to-surface missiles. It is not believed that the PRC currently has enough missiles in range of Taiwan to carry out this sort of attack, but the missiles could be brought into the region fairly quickly if Beijing so desired.

Weapons of Mass Destruction. The PRC has the capability of using chemical, biological, bacteriological, or nuclear weapons against Taiwan. The use of these weapons of mass destruction is highly improbable, however, because of international condemnation and the historical judgment levied by the Chinese people on any government using such weapons against fellow Chinese. It should be noted, moreover, that Taipei's own nuclear weapons research may be continuing. During a December 1988 interpellation in the Legislative Yuan, Yen Chen-hsing, chairman of Taiwan's Atomic Energy Commission, said Taiwan "absolutely" has the capability to produce nuclear weapons. Yen said that Taiwan had never stopped research on nuclear arms development. Nonetheless, the government did not produce nuclear weapons because it was a signatory of the Nuclear Arms Non-proliferation Treaty.[15]

Blockade of Taiwan. Careful attention must be paid to this military option because it could, under some circumstances, result in the capitulation of Taipei.[16] A limited blockade, one simply declared or lightly enforced, probably would not be sufficient to cause Taipei to negotiate. It would, however, create significant problems for Taipei in terms of anxiety on the part of the Taiwan population and unwillingness on the part of many foreign owned ships to call on Taiwan's ports due to high insurance rates and potential harm.

A greater threat to Taiwan would come from a fully enforced blockade of the island. Such an approach might be adopted by Beijing because the political costs of not succeeding in bringing Taipei to the negotiating table once force was employed would be too high.

To achieve Beijing's political objective of reunification, three military objectives would be sought: (a) close Taiwan's ports and preclude any shipping from entering or leaving Taiwan; (b) degrade the logistical support and morale of ROC military forces so they would be unable to offer an effective resistance to a full-scale invasion; and (c) if necessary, invade Taiwan and destroy all military resistance to the PRC.

Most experts believe that a blockade is the greatest military threat to Taiwan, but assessments vary as to whether a blockade would be successful in forcing Taipei to the negotiating table. Without question, a blockade could severely damage Taiwan's economy given its heavy dependence on trade. On the other hand, Taiwan is largely self-sufficient in food production, and critical resources such as petroleum are held in at least two months' reserves. In all likelihood, a blockade's outcome, as in other forms of attrition warfare, would hinge on the political will of Beijing and Taipei respectively. Generally speaking, blockades have not often resulted in capitulation in war, and there is little reason to expect that it would succeed in the case of Taiwan.

A blockade would be relatively easy for Beijing to declare, and the deployment of submarines to demonstrate a determination to enforce the blockade would be within PRC capabilities. However, a successful sustained blockade might be very difficult to execute without enormous expenditure of PRC resources. For one thing,

Taiwan plans to respond to a high intensity blockade—the only type likely to be effective—with an immediate escalation of the conflict. This would include the use of Taiwan's air force against mainland shipping and port targets, as well as the mining of PRC ports such as Shanghai.

Yet another factor escalating the cost of a PRC blockade would be the adverse reaction of the United States, Japan, Western Europe, and perhaps even Russia. The Taiwan Strait and Bashi Channel are international sea lanes of great importance in ship-borne traffic between Northeast and Southeast Asia, as well as between the Indian and Pacific Oceans. A blockade of Taiwan would interfere with this trade. Moreover, given the growing interdependence of world trade—which increasingly includes the PRC—a blockade of Taiwan would hurt the interests of far more countries than Taiwan. Under modern conditions, a PRC blockade of Taiwan would in effect be a blockade of the PRC itself.

Nor would it easy for Beijing to stop ships calling on Taiwan. In 1984, for instance, more than 34,000 ships carrying cargoes from more than 100 nations went in and out of Taiwan's ports. The total tonnage of these ships was nearly 350 million tons. The difficulty of strangling Taiwan economically becomes obvious when one considers that in all of World War II, the United States sank only eight million tons of Japanese ships.[17]

There are several critical variables which would heavily influence the outcome of a PRC blockade: (a) the intervention of the United States; (b) the effectiveness of ROC stockpiling; (c) the ability to resupply the island through east coast ports and facilities; (d) the ability of the PLA to project air superiority over the east coast of Taiwan; (e) the effectiveness of PRC nuclear submarines to interdict ROC escort vessels on the eastern side of the island and, conversely, the effectiveness of ROC antisubmarine warfare (ASW) efforts in this area; (f) Taipei's will to resist and the morale of the Taiwanese people; and (g) the determination on the part of the PRC to enforce the blockade and, if necessary, to escalate the conflict.

If the blockade and the other aspects of the military campaign against Taiwan were successful, then the PRC would achieve its political objective of forcing Taipei to reunify under Beijing's terms. If the military campaign failed, then the opportunity of the PRC to control Taiwan any time in the foreseeable future would be lost. Defeat in such a major military campaign might have serious internal repercussions within the PRC leadership and certainly would have profound international repercussions on China's foreign relations.

An effective blockade against Taiwan must include surface ships and aircraft as well, because the ROC would attempt to break the blockade through the location and destruction of PRC submarines. If the PRC did deploy surface ships and aircraft, the ROC would attack these, as well as their bases. Hence, even a limited blockade has the high probability of rapid escalation. The PRC must be prepared for that. Therefore, the PLA would have to heavily reinforce its naval and air units in the Taiwan Strait region before a blockade could be enforced.

Destruction of ROC Air and Naval Forces. The destruction of the ROC air and naval forces would be required if the PRC were to carry out a successful blockade of Taiwan or invade and occupy the island. These are very difficult missions for the PLA to accomplish.

It has long been thought that the single most important key to Taiwan's military deterrence is the maintenance of qualitative air superiority over the Taiwan Strait. Air superiority would enable Taipei to exact prohibitively high costs on PRC aircraft, ships, and amphibious forces in case of an assault on Taiwan. Under optimum conditions, air superiority might enable Taiwan to defeat attacking mainland forces.

Taipei strategists believe that Taiwan's security depends on an ability to thwart a limited PRC air-sea-land attack on the island. This can be achieved through both offensive and defensive tactical air operations, until the loss of essential material and bases halt the PRC offensive. This strategy is based on three key assumptions. First, competing pressures on Beijing would prevent the PRC from concentrating all of its offensive power against Taiwan. Second, as the time and costs of the operation escalated, PRC planners would find the military option less and less attractive. Third, the United States and other powers would aid Taiwan diplomatically and perhaps militarily in a limited way.

Most Western analysts assume that the PRC would lose at least 500 aircraft in a battle for air superiority over the Taiwan Strait. Some estimates range much higher. As to the outcome of such an air battle, in the late 1970s several U.S. experts predicted that within two or three weeks Taiwan's air force "would be neutralized."[18] Military planners from Taiwan are now far less pessimistic, believing that the PRC would have to commit around 4,000 aircraft to overwhelm the island's air defenses, and that each aircraft would last for only about four missions—far too high a cost for the PRC to bear given its long-term security concerns vis-a-vis Russia, Japan, Vietnam, and India and the costs involved in replacing these aircraft.[19]

It is beyond the capability of the PLA to destroy Taiwan's air force on the ground. This will be especially true toward the end of the 1990s, when the ROC's Chia-Shan project is completed. This project is located on the southeastern side of the island and is comprised of an elaborate underground system of tunnels and interconnecting aircraft hangers, fuel lines, and storage depots designed to ensure that Taiwan's fighters have survivable bases. Approximately 200 of the projected fleet of 250 domestically produced fighters (the IDF) reportedly will be housed in the protective facilities.

One critical factor in determining the air threat to Taiwan is the race between the two Chinese governments to modernize their respective air forces. In the past, largely through purchases of U.S. aircraft and technology, Taiwan maintained a high degree of technological advantage over the PRC air force. However, with the steady modernization and growing professionalism of the PLA since 1978 and the restrictions placed on U.S. arms sales to Taiwan by the August 17 communiqué, Taipei's qualitative advantage is at risk. Of deep concern to Taiwan is the transfer of advanced defense technology to the PRC from other countries.

The most serious recent example arose in 1990, when it was announced that the PRC was prepared to buy from the Soviet Union at least a dozen SU-24 Fencers, a Mach-2 light bomber with a combat radius of about 1,000 kilometers. The Chinese and Soviets were also discussing the possible sale of a squadron of SU-27 Flanker and MiG-29 Fulcrum fighters. The SU-27 is a fighter-interceptor which entered production in the mid-1980s and is equipped with lookdown/shoot-down radar and advanced air-to-air missiles effective against low-flying aircraft and cruise missiles. The MiG-29 is also a sophisticated fighter-interceptor, which entered production in the 1980s and incorporates technology roughly equivalent to front-line NATO aircraft.[20]

PLA leaders were anxious to purchase Soviet equipment to update their weapons technology following the quick defeat of Iraq in the Gulf War. One of the main lessons of the conflict was the decisive role played by superior weapons. It was announced shortly after the war that the PRC would increase its 1991 defense budget nearly 12 percent to modernize weapons and equipment.[21]

Although many Western analysts were skeptical at first of the reported PRC-Soviet deal, it was publicly revealed in 1992 that China had indeed purchased at least twenty-four SU-27s from Russia. These were to be based in Shanghai or Hainan, close enough for the 4,000 kilometer range SU-27 to pose a threat to Taiwan. Talks with Moscow were ongoing regarding the purchase of MiG-29s, Mig-31s, and technical assistance to help the PLA develop its indigenous F-10 fighter.[22] The MiG-31 reportedly would be manufactured in China.[23]

These purchases and technology transfers are of concern to Taipei, because the mainstay of Taiwan's air deterrent is the F-5E and F-104, both built with 1950s–1960s technology and clearly outclassed by the modern Soviet fighters being acquired by Beijing. The SU-27 is comparable to the U.S. F-15 Eagle; neither the F-5E nor the IDF are any match for the aircraft.

Given the importance of air superiority to its defense, Taipei places high priority on the acquisition of a replacement fighter. Until the January 1982 decision by the Reagan administration not to sell Taiwan the FX fighter and the subsequent August 17 communiqué, Taiwan had assumed that such an aircraft could eventually be purchased from the United States. But the 1982 decisions and the difficulty of acquiring aircraft from other countries convinced Taipei to build its own indigenous fighter, the IDF.[24] Dubbed the "Ching-kuo" after former President Chiang Ching-kuo, the IDF was rolled out in December 1988 and the first test flights took place the following year. If all goes well, about 250 of the aircraft will be produced to meet Taiwan's air defense needs for the 1990s.

Developed by Taiwan's Aero Industry Development Center (AIDC), the IDF program cost several billion dollars and involved commercial assistance from General Dynamics for the airframe, Garrett for engine development, and Lear Siegler for the plane's avionics package. Washington stressed that there was no U.S. government involvement in the program.[25]

The plane is designed for close-in air superiority. The IDF is a fairly sophisticated fighter, with some antiship capability. A rapid take-off ability is one of the aircraft's major strengths. The time from runway to intercept is said to be faster than that of the F-16. Later models will achieve speeds of at least Mach 1.8.

The IDF has a low radar profile and is capable of firing several kinds of air-to-air missiles, including those similar to the AIM 9-L and Phoenix. It missile carrying capacity is greater than that of the F-5E or F-104. It is armed with a General Electric Vulcan M-61A cannon and carries various missiles, such as four Sky Sword I air-to-air missiles, or three Hsiung Feng II antiship missiles and two Sky Sword I missiles. Its pulse Doppler fire control radar provides air and sea search modes with a range of about 150km and a look-down/shoot-down capability. The fighter has day-night fighting capabilities and the ability to attack from low or high altitudes. According to Taiwan's military, the IDF is comparable to the F-16 in terms of its defensive capability.[26] The IDF's speed and flight distance is not equal to that of the PRC's F-8, but the IDF is said to be superior because of its quicker reaction time and better weapons. The problem with the IDF is that it is still an experimental aircraft and Taiwan has had little experience building fighters. Also, most experts consider the IDF to be underpowered. One of the prototypes of the fighter crashed in 1991, resulting in the death of its pilot. Potential new engines for the IDF include a scaled-down version of the General Dynamics F404 or an upgraded version of the Garrett engine now in the plane, but as of mid-1992 the engine problem had not been solved.

Because of the PRC's purchase of SU-27s, there was considerable speculation in mid-1992 about the possibility of Taiwan acquiring either F-16s from the United States or more than one hundred Mirage 2000-5 fighters from France. The sale of both types of planes became deeply enmeshed with domestic politics, since huge layoffs at General Dynamics and Dassault Aviation were expected unless the sales to Taiwan went forward. The possibility of landing a sizeable chunk of Taiwan's $303 billion national development plan were also major contributing factors to American and French calculations of whether to sell a new fighter to Taiwan and risk downgrading relations with Beijing.[27] In the case of the United States, such a sale would call into question the relevancy of the August 17 communiqué. (Despite PRC objections, the Bush administration decided to approve a sale to Taiwan of 150 F-16A/B fighters in September 1992. France reportedly also agreed to sell Taiwan 60 Mirage fighters.)

If Taiwan is able to maintain a qualitative edge in air superiority over the PRC in the Taiwan Strait, then the PRC costs in attempting to resolve the Taiwan issue by force will likely remain prohibitively high. However, if Beijing can neutralize Taiwan's air force, then Taipei's deterrence will be seriously weakened. For this reason, the race between the PRC and ROC to acquire new fighters is closely watched by military experts worldwide.

Still, even the destruction of Taiwan's air force might not be sufficient to force Taipei to surrender to Beijing. PLA air force bombers do not have the pinpoint accuracy of U.S. air forces, which played such a major role in the 1991 Gulf War. As such, the outcome still might have to be decided on the ground.

A similar conclusion can be reached regarding the PRC ability to destroy the ROC navy. Taiwan naval officers are concerned about the PRC surface fleet, particularly the many small missile attack craft which could pose a formidable challenge to the larger, slower destroyers and frigates carrying the ROC flag. Neither side possesses advanced electronic countermeasures. A missile exchange between the two sides would likely be determined by the number of ships and missiles brought into play. Existing ratios point to a PRC advantage. Both sides are making major efforts to upgrade their antiship missiles. The two ROC submarines purchased from The Netherlands, for example, are equipped with tubes enabling them to launch subsurface-to-surface missiles such as the Hsiung Feng II.

PRC submarines, of which 92 are the tactical attack variety, pose an even greater threat to Taiwan than PLA surface ships. The fourteen Gearing destroyers in the Taiwan navy have been equipped with antisubmarine rockets. The remaining destroyers and some of the frigates are armed with antisubmarine torpedoes of approximately the same range as the torpedoes carried by PRC submarines. Without significant upgrading of Taiwan's antisubmarine warfare capabilities, the fleet's ability to deter or defeat PRC submarine attack remains questionable.

Because of this recognized deficiency, ASW modernization is a high ROC priority, of which the 3,585-ton FFG-7 program is one example. Under the commercial transaction, the warships will be built in Taiwan to replace the destroyers and frigates now comprising the backbone of Taipei's fleet. Six of the frigates will be built initially, with a possible option of six more. The United States said the $40 million sale was for defensive purposes only and that the technology transfer did not violate the terms of the August 17 communiqué.[28]

Another area of priority has been ship air-defense systems. Taiwan has received substantial numbers of sophisticated American missiles in this area, such as Improved Sea Chaparral and Standard shipborne SAMs, but much remains to be upgraded on Taiwan's surface ships for air defense purposes.

At the end of 1991, the PRC did not have sufficient numbers of aircraft or ships in the Taiwan Strait region to destroy Taiwan's air and naval forces. Indeed, it would meet such heavy resistance from the ROC that a massive redeployment of air and naval units from PLA bases throughout China would have to occur before this option could be implemented. A surprise attack to accomplish this objective is not within PLA capabilities. Whether, after such redeployment, the PRC could destroy ROC air and naval forces is subject to continuing debate, although most analysts believed the PLA could eventually do so in view of its vastly superior numbers. If the United States quickly responded to a PRC attack with replacement missiles and aircraft, and certainly if American-piloted aircraft were brought into action, then it is improbable that the PRC could succeed with this force option.

Amphibious Invasion of Taiwan. Barring the collapse of will on the part of Taipei, a successful amphibious invasion of Taiwan may be the only military option available to Beijing to accomplish its political objective of reunification. At the same time, this option is the most difficult for Beijing to put into operation. It certainly is the most costly. Because of the great difficulty and costs involved, most American analysts have dismissed the PRC threat to invade Taiwan as being highly improbable.

Indeed, from available evidence—such as construction of landing vessels, concentration of amphibious forces in the Taiwan Strait area, large-scale amphibious exercises and training—there is little to suggest that Beijing is seriously planning this military option. If the PRC did decide to pursue this course, the United States and ROC would have several years of warning time in which to formulate a response.

Estimates of the number of PLA divisions required to successfully invade Taiwan range upward of forty or more. During World War II, the United States estimated that it would take 300,000 American troops to defeat 32,000 Japanese ground forces then occupying Taiwan—a ten to one ratio.[29] Assuming a very low three to one numerical advantage needed by the PLA to successfully invade Taiwan today, a minimum of 800,000–900,000 troops would be required to defeat Taiwan's standing army of 270,000 soldiers and 30,000 Marines. The PLA figure would grow to astronomical levels if ROC army reserves were added to its defense, which of course they would be.

A significant factor contributing to the low probability of a PRC invasion of Taiwan is the lack of Chinese amphibious capabilities. It was estimated in 1979 that PRC naval vessels, including motorized junks, would be able to transport 100,000–150,000 troops to Taiwan.[30] Somewhat troubling to Taipei, however, is the PRC's new emphasis on combined service operations and construction of landing vehicles. The PRC now has about 58 fairly large amphibious vessels and some 400 smaller amphibious craft. Most U.S. analysts believe these to be intended for use in the South China Sea, where Beijing has territorial disputes in the Paracel and Spratly islands with Vietnam and other countries, but they could also be used in the Taiwan Strait. Nonetheless, a major construction program to build large amphibious landing ships would be required before the PRC could invade Taiwan. Such a program would last several years and would no doubt be detected far in advance of any actual threat to Taiwan.

Another factor reducing the credibility of a PRC amphibious invasion of Taiwan is the low performance level of the PLA, as seen in its relatively unsophisticated punitive expedition against Vietnam in 1979. The PLA is known to suffer major internal weaknesses, including lack of mobility and mechanization, poor logistics, limited power projection capability, obsolescent weapons, and weak command and control capabilities. Although training in combined forces operations is proceeding, the scale of coordinated operations required to invade Taiwan is beyond current PLA capability.

The probability of a successful PRC amphibious invasion of Taiwan is very low throughout the 1990s, although the implied *threat* of an invasion of Taiwan or the offshore islands is certainly within the capabilities of the PRC. This threat places a degree of psychological pressure on the people of Taiwan, even though actual PLA capabilities lag far behind.

Taiwan has responded to this threat by taking steps to make an invasion as prohibitively expensive as possible. This includes, in addition to sea and air defenses discussed above, the mass production of M48H tanks which would form a succession of armored barriers to invading PLA troops.

All in all, the PRC does not have the capability to mount this kind of operation, even with a redeployment of personnel and equipment to the Taiwan Strait region. The PRC lacks the amphibious lift capability to move sufficient forces, even lightly armed, across the Strait. Since these forces would face a series of deeply entrenched and heavily armored ROC defenses, the ability of the PRC to successfully invade Taiwan with its existing force structure is virtually non-existent. If the PRC dedicated its shipbuilding facilities to amphibious lift over the next eight to ten years, then such a capability could be acquired. Hence, even if the PRC could overwhelm ROC air and naval units, and even if the United States did not provide massive support for Taipei, an amphibious invasion of Taiwan is not now within PRC capabilities. A limited insertion of PLA units by air or naval vessels is possible, however, but their numbers would be too small to be effective except under circumstances mentioned in the first scenario.

Need for Updated Analysis

In the past, there was a tendency for analysts to consider the qualitative superiority of ROC forces to be sufficient to discourage PRC military action in the Taiwan Strait. There now is some question about the relative technological superiority of the ROC. The PLA is steadily modernizing in critical areas required against Taiwan, such as command and control, stand-off and precision guided munitions, and combined forces tactics.

The intention of ROC military planners is that Taiwan's new generation of aircraft, naval vessels, missiles, radars, command and control centers, tanks, and other weapons systems will be operational toward the end of the 1990s—before the PLA modernization program reaches threatening levels. These systems are designed to be sufficient to discourage future PRC military adventurism in the Taiwan Strait.

Some Western analysts are no longer confident that Taipei will be able to maintain its qualitative advantage. They point to the limitations inherent in the August 17 communiqué and constant PRC pressure on other foreign suppliers of arms and defense technology not to sell to Taiwan.

An analysis of the comparative capabilities of new PRC and ROC weapons and defense systems is needed, especially in the key areas of air defense, naval surface warfare, and antisubmarine warfare. This examination should include the potential impact of the SU-27 and other proposed Russian aircraft sales to the PRC, and the acquisition of advanced fighters by Taiwan from the United States and France. Until a more detailed analysis of these systems is made, an accurate evaluation of mid- and long-term PRC air and naval capabilities against ROC defenses is difficult.

Taiwan's Strategy of Deterrence

Given the progress Taiwan has made in its defense modernization over the past few years, including the anticipated success of the IDF and the FFG-7 frigate programs, Taiwan's military officers generally have a high degree of confidence in their ability to deter the PRC from attacking Taiwan over the next ten years.

In an interview with *Jane's Defence Weekly* in January 1991, ROC Defense Minister Chen Li-an said that Taiwan does not rely upon the United States for its defense, but rather on its own military. He said the ROC strategy would be to mobilize its active and reserve military force to prevent the PLA from landing on the island. The ROC strategy would be to gain an upper hand in the air and sea, and then to carry the attack to the enemy. Chen said the Chinese Communists would most likely try to blockade Taiwan. Alternatively, the PRC would land on one or more outlying islands for staging amphibious and other types of attack against Taiwan and to try to force Taipei to negotiate. Chen said it is no longer possible for the PLA to neutralize Taiwan's air force within two or three weeks. Instead, the Defense Minister said, "once enemy planes are in our radar range, we should be able to maintain the upper hand."[31]

Despite this confidence, there is also the perception in Taipei that the long-term PRC threat will continue to exist. As such, Taiwan's deterrent strategy has several dimensions, only one of which is military. The interaction of these dimensions weaves a sophisticated web of deterrence that is quite formidable. One aspect of Taiwan's deterrent strategy is to make Beijing's costs in attacking Taipei prohibitively expensive.

Maximizing PRC Costs in Attacking Taiwan

Since the PRC's political objectives are less than the total annihilation of Taiwan and its people, Beijing must calculate the estimated military, political, and economic costs involved in attacking Taiwan and weigh those costs against the potential benefits of successfully using military force. Taipei aims to make PRC costs as high as possible in as many ways as possible.

As noted earlier, ROC military strategy in the case of a high-intensity blockade is to escalate the conflict quickly and to prolong it indefinitely in order to maximize PLA costs. It would be enormously expensive for the PRC to initiate an attack against Taiwan and militarily to defeat it. Even if conservative estimates of PRC loses are used, the PLA might sustain over 50,000 casualties and lose some 500 aircraft, dozens of submarines and surface ships, and great quantities of various missiles. The loss of military equipment would take years to replace, resulting in a deterioration of China's ability to protect its interests elsewhere in Asia.

There is also the possibility of American military intervention on behalf of Taiwan. The use of Airborne Warning and Control Systems (AWACS) to help coordinate Taiwan's air defense and even modest antisubmarine warfare (ASW) support to the north, east, and south of Taiwan would greatly increase PRC loses with little threat to American lives. In addition, there is high probability that the United States would abrogate the August 17 communiqué and sell Taiwan advanced weapons such as more modern aircraft and antiair and antiship missiles.

Even if the PRC were able to gain air superiority over Taiwan and to control the sea around the island, this in itself might not be sufficient to force the ROC government to surrender. Taiwan is a mountainous island, honeycombed with defensive barriers, and well stocked with supplies for a prolonged ground or even guerrilla war. If the PLA were able to gain an amphibious foothold on Taiwan's west coast, they likely would meet stiff resistance throughout the island from the ROC military and Taiwanese people.

The military cost to attack and invade Taiwan would be horrendous, but there are significant political costs as well. In the event of a PRC use of force in the Taiwan Strait, there would be a period of at least several years during which Beijing would lose friendly relations with the United States, Japan, much of Southeast Asia, and Europe.

International reaction would be far more critical and long-lasting than that experienced in the aftermath of Tiananmen Square. China's international prestige would be adversely affected, and its access to international lending institutions would be severely curtailed.

Another potential political cost would be the impact of the war on the PRC's political and military leadership. A decision to attack Taiwan would be hotly debated in Beijing, if only because of timing and alternative methods of coercing Taipei. If the war proved too costly or inconclusive, then certain leaders might be disgraced and a major change in leadership might occur.

Economically, a PRC attack against Taiwan would be an enormous drain on Beijing's limited resources. Many merchant ships would be sunk; coastal infrastructure would be damaged, including ports like Shanghai; severe economic dislocation would occur as transportation systems and scarce resources were diverted to military use rather than to the civilian sector; foreign exchange might be depleted; and foreign trade and investment would be severely disrupted.

Moreover, if Taiwan were conquered, then Beijing would be strapped with a massive rebuilding and assistance program to help the island recover as a productive province of China. This would take years and further delay the modernization of the Chinese mainland.

Another essential element in Taipei's deterrent strategy is to involve the United States to the greatest extent possible on the ROC side.

The U.S. Role in Taiwan's Deterrence

The United States plays a crucial role in Taiwan's security. That role includes both military and nonmilitary contributions to Taiwan's deterrence against a PRC attack. Militarily, the United States has sold substantial amounts of both government-to-government foreign military sales (FMS) and commercial munitions sales to Taiwan. The United States contributes in a nonmilitary way to Taiwan's deterrence through many of its political and economic policies toward both Taipei and Beijing and by maintaining a large forward deployed military force in the Western Pacific.

U.S. Arms Sales in Post-Communiqué Period. The United States sought to minimize the damage done to Taiwan's security by the August 17 communiqué by interpreting the agreement as narrowly as possible. Thus, for example, the U.S. position was that the communiqué lacked precedence over the Taiwan Relations Act and that the communiqué linked U.S. promises to reduce future arms sales to Taiwan to the continuation of Beijing's policy of peaceful reunification. The United States also interpreted the communiqué to allow a fairly

high level of arms sales to Taiwan and even higher levels of
defense-related technology. The United States did this because, while
it sought strategic cooperation with Beijing against the common Soviet
threat, it did not want to harm Taiwan's security interests. Moreover,
as the PRC moved to normalize relations with the Soviet Union, the
incentives to defer to Beijing on arms sales to Taiwan dissipated as
well.

The fundamental American perception in this matter was that peace
and stability in East Asia could best be maintained by continued peace
in the Taiwan Strait. Until a peaceful resolution of the Taiwan issue
could be found, U.S. interests would be served by helping Taiwan
field a minimal but effective deterrence against the PRC. A practical
demonstration of this interest was the high level of military equipment
sold to Taiwan immediately after the signing of the August 17
communiqué.

Two days after the communiqué's release to the public, the United
States announced that it would permit Taiwan to co-produce with
Northrop Corporation an additional thirty F-5Es and thirty F-5Fs over
the next two and a half years, a package worth $622 million. Two
additional sales were announced for 500 Maverick air-to-ground
missiles and $97 million worth of various armored vehicles. In
February 1983 the United States sold Taiwan sixty-six F-104G fighters,
previously owned by West Germany, for $31 million. And in July the
administration sold Taipei $530 million in military equipment,
including land- and sea-based Chaparral missiles for air defense, SM-1
Standard missiles for shipborne air defense, AIM-7F Sparrow radar-
homing air-to-air missiles, conversion kits for M-4 tanks, tank-recovery
vehicles, and aircraft spare parts.

A key decision was announced in March 1983, when the State
Department released figures setting ceilings for arms sales to Taiwan
at $800 million for fiscal year 1983 and $760 million for fiscal year
1984. The figures for authorized sales in 1979, 1980, and 1981—the
base years referred to in the communiqué—were $598 million, $601
million, and $295 million, respectively. To reconcile the 1983 and
1984 figures with these base years, the State Department explained
that an "inflationary index" had been applied. Thus, the $598 million
of 1979 would be equivalent to $830 million in current, inflated
dollars.[32]

In early July 1985 the United States sold Taiwan 262 Chaparral
ground-to-air missiles for $94 million to replace obsolete M42
anti-aircraft guns. This sale, plus the previous year's sale of 12 C-130
transport aircraft to replace obsolete Taiwan planes, demonstrated that,
because of the difficulty in finding operational equipment of old

vintage, the United States had decided limited upgraded sales could be made within the framework of the communiqué.

In early 1986 the United States sold Taiwan 200 MGM-71 TOW anti-tank missiles worth $15.6 million. And in August Washington announced another arms sale to Taiwan, a $260 million avionics package to modernize thirty S-2 maritime-surveillance and ASW aircraft.

The trend since 1986 has been for the United States to sell Taiwan more advanced technology to upgrade its armed forces. For example, the U.S. government permitted American companies to help Taiwan develop its indigenous IDF fighter and to build FFG-7 frigates for ASW activities.

FMS sales do continue, however, In May 1989, for example, the United States sold Taiwan $108 million in spare parts for the ROC fleet of F-5s, F-100s, F-104s, T-33s, T-28s, and C-130 aircraft. In late 1990 Taiwan began negotiations with Bell to purchase up to forty AH-1 Cobra attack helicopters, a deal reportedly worth several billion dollars. Also in late 1990 Hughes was preparing to sell Taiwan about 500 imaging infrared Maverick air-to-surface missiles specially de-signed for antiship missions. Hughes also was deeply involved in upgrading Taiwan's air defense system, including a $100 million project to improve Taiwan's Tien Wang (Sky Net) system, similar to the North American Aerospace Defense Command linking together all air defense operations from ground radar to air squadrons and missile units. Hughes was also negotiating, along with Litton Industries, for another $100 million deal to establish a secure, jam resistant digital data link between bases and aircraft.[33]

When information about the U.S. commercial role in the IDF pro-gram became known, PRC General Secretary Hu Yaobang warned that the United States could be violating the terms of the August 17 communiqué by supplying Taiwan with advanced technology it did not already possess.[34] As a result of this and other technology trans-fers, China in 1986 attempted to persuade the United States to redefine the August 17 communiqué to include limitations on the sale of advanced technology to Taiwan. China was told that U.S. government-licensed transfers of technology to Taipei were permitted under the August 17 agreement, since the communiqué did not explicitly limit technology transfers but only arms sales.[35] Sentiment existed in the U.S. government to sell Taiwan even more sophisticated weapons if the communiqué's restrictions were not in place. One administration official said, if China "wants to declare the 17 August Communiqué dead, Reagan would like nothing better."[36]

To clarify its policy on arms sales to Taiwan once and for all, the United States sent a note to Beijing in mid-August 1986 stating that the communiqué stood on its own and there was no need to reinterpret or renegotiate it. One American source said, "We don't want to reopen negotiations with the Chinese on this score. The text is very clear. It talks of arms sales and not technology."[37]

Trends Toward Commercial Sales. Since 1986 the U.S.-Taiwan military relationship has been characterized by greater sophistication but less publicity. An increasingly large percentage of military sales are licensed commercial sales instead of Foreign Military Sales (FMS).[38] In 1990 the estimated U.S. FMS to Taiwan was $480 million, whereas commercial sales were $160 million. In 1992 these figures were $485 million and $135 million, respectively.

For its part, Taiwan would prefer more FMS and less commercial sales, but it is relatively satisfied because much of its needs can be purchased off-the-shelf without inclusion in the government-reported figures cited above. These off-the-shelf component purchases are rumored to be at least equivalent in value to those reported by the U.S. government.

The combination of foreign commercial sales and technology transfers, coupled with Taiwan's own massive investments in defense related research, development, and production, are enabling Taiwan to modernize its fighter aircraft, guided missile frigates, tanks, and a wide range of missiles without creating a major diplomatic crisis in Sino-American relations. For example, Taiwan's Tien Chien (Sky Sword) air-to-air missile resembles the U.S. AIM-9 Sidewinder. And the Hsiung Feng II (Male Bee) antiship missile resembles the U.S. RGM-84 Harpoon. Taiwan's M48H tank is a hybrid combination of the chassis of the M60A3, the turret of the M48 with a 105 millimeter main gun, and an advanced fire control system from the M1.

A great many of Taiwan's weapons are upgraded, developed, or reversed engineered in the Chung-Shan Institute of Science and Technology and the Aero Industry Development Center. In addition to the IDF, in late 1990 the Institute and Center were working on such projects as:

- three versions of the Tien Kung (Sky Bow) air defense system, the second of which is comparable to the U.S. Patriot system and the third of which is specifically designed to intercept incoming tactical ballistic missiles

- the Chang Bai air defense system which is similar to the U.S. Aegis system

- at least two versions of the Tien Chien air-to-air missile, the latest of which will be comparable to the U.S. AIM-120
- at last two versions of the Hsiung Feng (Male Bee) antiship system, the first similar to an enhanced version of Israel's Gabriel 2 system and the second similar to the U.S. Harpoon.

The Reagan administration encouraged Taiwan to make more commercial purchases and to develop its own defense industry. The Bush administration continued this policy, facilitating technology transfers and commercial sales, and in many areas increasing their level of sophistication. In addition, during the late 1980s the United States reopened its professional military schools to Taiwan officers, in some cases at a higher level than existed prior to 1979.

U.S. Non-military Role in Taiwan's Deterrence. In addition to its military-related activities, the United States contributes to Taiwan's deterrence in several other important ways. These include public and private statements that a peaceful resolution of the Taiwan issue is in the U.S. interest. These statements are made fairly frequently, particularly in times of tension in the Taiwan Strait. Periodically, the United States reminds Beijing that the future level of U.S. arms sales to Taiwan is linked to the PRC's continuation of a peaceful policy. These reaffirmations of U.S. interest are backed by a substantial forward deployed U.S. military force in the Western Pacific.

Another U.S. contribution to deterring a PRC use of force against Taiwan is friendly Sino-American relations. Although it has come at some cost to Taipei in terms of national pride and diplomatic recognition, the fact that Washington and Beijing seek to maintain friendly relations enables each side to frankly discuss their concerns over the Taiwan issue. The United States is aware of PRC sensitivities and has taken many steps to assure China that Washington is not attempting to create an independent Taiwan. Beijing, too, is aware of U.S. concerns about a peaceful resolution of the Taiwan issue and has been careful to avoid reckless military posturing in the Taiwan Strait.

The close commercial and people-to-people contact Americans maintain with the people of Taiwan is yet another U.S. contribution to Taiwan's security. The PRC is aware of this friendship and understands its implications should force be used against Taiwan. The fact that many Americans like Taiwan enhances the self-esteem and confidence of the Taiwan people and government, contributing to stable and peaceful progress on the island. These feelings are further strengthened by Washington's support for Taiwan's participation in international organizations, when this can be done within the framework of U.S.-PRC diplomatic relations.

Other Elements of Taiwan's Deterrence

In addition to the United States, Taipei seeks to involve as many other international entities as possible with its fate. This adds to the political, economic, and psychological costs the PRC must weigh as it contemplates the use of force in the Taiwan Strait. Of particular importance in this regard are the attitudes and actions of Japan, South Korea, Russia, the ASEAN states, the United Nations, and other major international organizations. None of these are as important in Taiwan's strategy of deterrence as the United States, but they do contribute to that strategy. This dimension of Taiwan's strategy is growing stronger with the success of flexible diplomacy and ROC economic policies of internationalization, liberalization, and overseas investment.

There are several domestic steps Taiwan has taken to help deter a PRC attack. Democratization and Taiwanization have strengthened national unity and made Taiwan politically more unpalatable to Beijing's leaders. ROC statements and actions reaffirming a "one China" policy give incentives to the PRC not to attack Taiwan. The huge financial investment on the mainland by Taiwanese adds to this incentive, as does the rapidly growing trade between the two sides.

Taiwan's economic performance plays several crucial roles in deterring a PRC attack. Domestically, a strong economy helps to maintain social stability on Taiwan and provides the funds, technology, and industrial base necessary for modernizing Taiwan's armed forces. Taiwan's economic success has unified its population, so that virtually no one wants to give up his current standard of living for an uncertain life under the PRC.

Internationally, deterrence is enhanced by Taiwan's highly visible role in trade and large foreign exchange reserves. This strengthens perceptions in the United States and other major countries that Taiwan's future is too important to ignore. These perceptions complicate Beijing's planning for a possible use of force, because of the high price it must pay in terms of negative international response.

Ideology also plays a role in Taiwan's deterrence strategy. Taipei's pro-Western, anti-communist ideology tends to strengthen Taiwan's internal unity, secure Overseas Chinese support, and appeal to sympathetic audiences in the United States, Western Europe, and other non-communist countries. Although ideology plays a less central role in domestic and international politics than it did in the past, the "Taiwan Experience" under the *San Min Chu-I* stands in stark contrast to the failure of communism throughout the world. This ideological difference helps to distinguish in the minds of Chinese and foreigners alike the distinctive characteristics of the two Chinese systems. If the contrast between the two systems did not exist, then Taiwanese support for the KMT would erode, the commitment of Overseas Chinese to Taiwan might fade, and foreign—particularly American— support for Taipei would be greatly reduced.

Conclusion

Most analysts concerned with Taiwan's security conclude that the probability of Beijing using force in the Taiwan Strait is small. The determining factors usually cited are: (1) the PRC lacks the amphibious capability to invade Taiwan; (2) Beijing is deterred by the prospects of U.S. military intervention; and (3) CCP leaders lack incentive to attack Taiwan because they believe peaceful reunification is possible and that such an attack would harm China's modernization. Such analysis suggests that the probable costs to the PRC in attacking Taiwan far outweigh the probabilities of success, and thus the possibility of Beijing's using force is remote.

If this argument is valid, then the policy guidelines for Taiwan's security are straightforward: (1) do nothing to assist the PRC to develop its amphibious capability or to acquire superiority in military systems of high value in the Taiwan Strait operational environment; (2) assist Taiwan to maintain a sufficient self-defense capability to keep PLA costs prohibitively high and chances for PRC military success uncertain; (3) make clear to PRC leaders that the United States would likely intervene militarily on Taiwan's behalf if the island were attacked by the mainland; (4) maintain an adequate U.S. military presence in the Western Pacific to intervene in the Taiwan Strait if necessary; (5) take steps to convince Beijing that China's unification will eventually occur through peaceful means; (6) do not allow the Taiwan independence movement to gain control of public policy on Taiwan; and (7) encourage China's modernization along pragmatic lines.[39]

With few exceptions, the policies followed by Washington and Taipei in recent years reflect these guiding principles. But what of the future? Do current trends suggest that these principles of deterrence will remain viable, or does there appear to be some weakening of Taiwan's deterrent formula? A brief examination of these trends implies that some are strengthening Taiwan's deterrence while other trends seem to be weakening its elements. The effects of other trends have yet to be clearly established. These various trends and their influence on Taiwan's deterrence can be summarized as follows:

Trends Strengthening Deterrence:

- Taiwan is placing a new generation of advanced weapons into operation.

- The United States no longer defers to the PRC on the Taiwan issue because of the Soviet threat.

- U.S. forces available for intervention in the Taiwan Strait are vastly superior to those of the PRC, and Washington has a wide range of military options to make the cost of attack prohibitively high to Beijing.

- The increased interaction across the Taiwan Strait decreases the incentives for Beijing to attack Taiwan.

- Recent elections in Taiwan suggest that the KMT will remain in power and that independence is not preferred by the vast majority of the Taiwan people.

- PRC leaders seem committed to a policy of moderate and pragmatic reform on the mainland.

Trends Weakening Deterrence:

- The PLA is modernizing in areas of utility in the Taiwan Strait, and it is no longer preoccupied with the Soviet, Vietnamese, or Indian threats to China's borders.

- Taiwan is currently weak in certain critical military areas, especially air defense fighters.

- Political will on the part of the American people to sustain overseas commitments is weakening due to concerns over the domestic economy and lack of clearly defined threats to U.S. security interests.

- U.S. forward deployed forces in the Western Pacific are being reduced as part of an overall military restructuring.

- Beijing is very concerned that Taiwan's international position is becoming stronger through flexible diplomacy; at the same time, the PRC continues to be subject to harsh international criticism.

- Beijing's policies of peaceful reunification and "one country, two systems" have failed to attract Taiwan.

- The DPP and other advocates of Taiwan independence have forced the issue of Taiwan's future to the policy forefront of

PRC decision-makers, reducing their flexibility to be patient on the issue.

Trends Creating Uncertainties for Deterrence:

- The qualitative superiority of ROC armed forces over those of the PLA is open to question.
- The U.S. response to a PRC use of force is difficult to predict.
- Uncertainty exists as to whether Taiwan's foreign policy and policies toward the mainland are advancing or obstructing China's unification.
- The actual level of support for Taiwan independence is uncertain, and it may increase under certain circumstances.

Overall, these trends suggest that the threat environment in the Taiwan Strait during the 1990s will be characterized by a degree of uncertainty and differences of perception in Washington, Taipei, and Beijing. Certainly, the PRC threat will remain, and it will be perceived by some as growing. On the other hand, the threat appears manageable. In any case, an actual use of force against Taiwan before the year 2000 seems very unlikely without severe provocation. The need for a smooth transfer of Hong Kong to PRC sovereignty in 1997 greatly increases this probability.

With these considerations in mind, the United States can help maintain deterrence in the Taiwan Strait in the 1990s by:

1. selling Taiwan advanced defensive equipment and technology within the framework of the Taiwan Relations Act and the August 17 communiqué
2. making clear to the PRC that the United States is committed to defend Taiwan if it is attacked
3. maintaining a strong military presence in the Western Pacific to intervene in the Taiwan Strait if necessary.

Taipei, for its part, can enhance deterrence by:

1. continuing to modernize its armed forces on a priority basis
2. expanding friendly contact with the PRC
3. adhering to the "one China" principle in its public policy statements
4. keeping the Taiwan independence movement under control within the context of democracy

5. expanding international contacts through flexible diplomacy.

Other members of the international community can contribute to peace in the Taiwan Strait by:

1. informing Beijing of their interests in a peaceful settlement of the Taiwan issue
2. controlling arms sales to ensure a balance of power in the Taiwan Strait
3. allowing Taipei to play a meaningful role in international affairs within the context of the "one China" principle.

The latter point is especially important because moderate policies on Taiwan—as on the mainland—are more likely to prevail if the government and people on the island do not feel isolated. Beijing should not be made to feel that a larger international role for Taiwan is a "zero-sum" game leading to Taiwan independence or the ROC replacing the PRC in the world community.

If the PRC did use force against Taiwan, it would likely be a sophisticated and carefully timed approach combining military, economic, political, and international pressures. Former CCP General Secretary Hu Yaobang indicated this would be the case in his well-known interview with *Pai Hsing* in May 1985 outlining a possible blockade against Taiwan.[40] It might not be a "one-shot" effort of high intensity conflict. It might be subtly staged to send clear signals of warning to Taipei, yet not of sufficient intensity to draw American intervention. One example of low intensity conflict is the use of PRC special operation forces in coordination with pro-unification groups on Taiwan. Such a scenario might make an appropriate U.S. response difficult to formulate.

Regardless of the type of analysis used, the probability of a PRC use of force against Taiwan before the end of the century seems low. On the other hand, the probability of force never being used in the Taiwan Strait also seems low as long as Taiwan is separated from the mainland and the KMT, CCP, and DPP hold mutually incompatible views.

Because of this lingering, if ill-defined, threat to Taiwan's security, it is important to maintain the viability of the basic principles of deterrence in the Taiwan Strait. As one or more of these principles is weakened, compensation should be found by strengthening other principles. Deterring the PRC is far more preferable than defeating Beijing once hostilities have begun.

Notes

1. For a discussion of various PRC military options against Taiwan, see Martin L. Lasater, *Taiwan: Facing Mounting Threats* (Washington, D.C: Heritage Foundation, 1987). Also see the author's chapter on the ROC-PRC military balance in Steven W. Mosher, ed., *The United States and the Republic of China: Democratic Friends, Strategic Allies and Economic Partners* (New Brunswick, NJ: Transaction Publishers, 1990). For a more political analysis, see Parris H. Chang and Martin L. Lasater, eds., *If the PRC Crosses the Taiwan Strait: The International Response* (Lanham, MD: University Press of America, 1993). Much of the material in this chapter is summarized from these earlier extensive studies of Taiwan's security situation.

2. See Guo-cang Huan, "Taiwan: A View from Beijing," *Foreign Affairs*, 63, 5 (summer 1985), p. 1068.

3. See "A Study of a Possible Communist Attack on Taiwan" (Taipei, Taiwan: Government Information Office, June 1991).

4. *China Post*, March 14, 1990, in *Foreign Broadcast Information Service: China* (hereafter *FBIS–China*), March 22, 1990, p. 53.

5. Taipei Domestic Service, March 18, 1990, in *FBIS–China*, March 22, 1990, pp. 53–54.

6. "Mainland Said to be Preparing to Attack Taiwan," *Cheng Ming*, April 1, 1990, in *FBIS–China*, April 2, 1990, pp. 46–48.

7. "Secret Meeting on New Taiwan Policy Described," *Cheng Ming*, August 1, 1990, in *FBIS–China*, August 9, 1990, pp. 23–35.

8. "Deng Attacks Li Teng-hui's Independence Stance," *South China Morning Post*, September 19, 1990, in *FBIS–China*, September 19, 1990, p. 11.

9. *Cheng Ming*, in *FBIS–China*, March 12, 1991, pp. 23–25.

10. Reported in *Beijing Review*, October 21–27, 1991, p. 10.

11. See *A Strategic Framework for the Asian Pacific Rim: Looking Toward the 21st Century* (Washington, D.C.: Department of Defense, May 1990).

12. Huang Yong in New China News Agency analysis carried in various official PRC newspapers. Quoted in *China News*, August 17, 1992, p. 1.

13. The comparison between PRC and Taiwan military forces is taken from *The Military Balance: 1990–1991* (London: International Institute for Strategic Studies, 1990), pp. 148–152; 177–179.

14. See Gary Milhollin and Gerald White, "A New China Syndrome: Beijing's Atomic Bazaar," *Washington Post*, May 12, 1991, p. C1.

15. *China Post*, December 8, 1988, p. 12.

16. For a discussion of this scenario, see Martin L. Lasater, ed., *Beijing's Blockade Threat to Taiwan* (Washington, D.C.: Heritage Foundation, 1986). See also Paul H.B. Godwin, "The Use of Military Force Against Taiwan: Potential PRC Scenarios," in Chang and Lasater, eds., *If the PRC Crosses the Taiwan Strait*, pp. 15–33.

17. *Beijing's Blockade Threat to Taiwan*, p. 13.

18. Admiral Edwin K. Snyder in U.S. Senate Foreign Relations Committee, *Taiwan* (Washington, D.C.: Government Printing Office, 1979), p. 586.

19. See *Beijing's Blockade Threat to Taiwan*, pp. 8–9.

20. See "Cannon for Fodder," *Far Eastern Economic Review*, March 28, 1991, p. 11. Also see *New York Times*, May 16, 1991, p. A11. For a comparison of these Soviet aircraft and existing PRC fighters, see Harlan W. Jencks, *Some Political and Military Implications of Soviet Warplane Sales to the PRC*, SCPS Papers No. 6 (Kaohsiung, Taiwan: National Sun Yat-sen University, April 1991).

21. See *Washington Post*, March 27, 1991, p. A28. The PRC defense budget had also received a major increase in 1990, possibly as a reward for the PLA's help in suppressing the June 1989 crisis in Beijing.

22. *Far Eastern Economic Review*, June 4, 1992, pp. 18–19.

23. *Free China Journal*, August 4, 1992, p. 2.

24. For background on the IDF program, see *Aviation Week and Space Technology*, April 21, 1986, p. 77.

25. *Jane's Defence Weekly*, January 7, 1989, p. 4.

26. *Central Daily News*, August 25, 1988, p. 2.

27. *Los Angeles Times*, July 5, 1992, p. 1.

28. *Navy News and Undersea Technology*, 4, 13 (June 19, 1987), p. 1.

29. "Legislative History, P.L. 96-8 (Taiwan Relations Act)," *U.S. Code Congressional and Administrative News*, 4 (June 1979), 96th Cong., 1st sess., p. 661.

30. *Ibid.*

31. The interview was reported in *Free China Journal*, January 24, 1991, p. 2.

32. *Washington Post*, March 22, 1983, p. A12.

33. A notable exception to the trend toward commercial transfers was the September 1992 sale of 150 F-16s to Taiwan for $6 billion. This sale, along with the expected French sale of 60 Mirage 2000-5 fighters valued at $2.6 billion, occurred beyond the time-frame of this study. A series of well-informed articles about Taiwan's defense and the role of U.S. technical assistance written by Barbara Amouyal can be found in *Defense News*, October 8, October 15, October 29, and November 5, 1990.

34. *Far Eastern Economic Review*, July 24, 1986, p. 27. See also Zhang Jingxu, "A Preliminary Analysis of the 'Taiwan Straits Military Power Balance' Theory," *Liaowang*, July 28, 1986, in *FBIS–China*, August 1, 1986, pp. B2–B4.

35. *Washington Post*, April 25, 1986, p. A32.

36. *Far Eastern Economic Review*, July 3, 1986, p. 11.

37. *Far Eastern Economic Review*, August 28, 1986, pp. 26–27.

38. See Robert Karniol, "Notable Shift in Taiwan's Arms Trade with USA," *Jane's Defence Weekly*, July 11, 1987, p. 13; and Robert Karniol, "U.S. Arms Sales to Taiwan Continue at a High Level," *Jane's Defence Weekly*, November 28, 1987, p. 1243.

39. Further elaboration of these principles can be found in Martin L. Lasater, "Principles of Deterrence in the Taiwan Strait," in Chang and Lasater, eds., *If the PRC Crosses the Taiwan Strait*, pp. 155–164.

40. For a transcript of the interview, see *Pai Hsing*, June 1, 1985, in *FBIS–China*, June 3, 1985, pp. W1–W35.

PART TWO

Policy Implications
for the United States

6

Beyond Containment in Asia: U.S. Strategy and Policy in the 1990s

Part One discussed the political, economic, foreign policy, and security developments in the Republic of China since 1987 which have created a "new" Taiwan. Part Two will examine the implications of these developments for U.S. interests, especially in the wider context of U.S. strategy and policy in Asia over the next decade. The current Chapter 6 will discuss U.S. strategy and policy toward Asia in the post-containment period. Chapter 7 will examine U.S. interests in Taiwan in the early 1990s, while Chapter 8 will conclude with suggested policy changes that might better serve U.S. interests in Taiwan over the next several years.

Strategic Background

One of the basic national security interests of the United States since the late 1800s has been to prevent the domination of East Asia by a single country. Not wishing to be a dominant power itself, the United States since 1900 pursued a strategy of balancing interests between various powers in Asia so that no one could dominate the region. In the early 1900s this strategy was expressed through the "open door policy" toward China, but it has been applied to other Asian nations as well.

From the late 1800s until the end of World War II, the nation most aggressively attempting to dominate East Asia was Japan. The conflict in interests between Japan seeking regional hegemony and the United States seeking to preserve a balance of power led inevitably to World War II, a war strategists on both sides had been rehearsing for twenty years. Following the war, the most powerful threat to a regional balance of power came from the Soviet Union, which allied with the newly formed People's Republic of China (PRC) after 1949. To prevent the expansion of Soviet and Chinese influence in Asia, the United States extended its national security strategy of containment to the rimland of Asia.

One advantage of containment as a national security strategy was the word's innate flexibility, allowing for various operational strategies, interpretations, and doctrines. Another advantage of containment was its descriptive power in articulating fundamental American goals in the Cold War era. These goals centered around the necessity of the United States to shoulder "the responsibility to lead and help defend the world's free nations."[1]

During the late 1950s and early 1960s, a development of immense strategic importance to the United States occurred: the breakup of the Sino-Soviet alliance. The Sino-Soviet dispute led to armed confrontation between Beijing and Moscow in 1969, and throughout the 1970s the Soviet Union built its own military ring of containment around China. Eventually, Moscow deployed about one-third of its armed forces around PRC borders.

The Sino-Soviet dispute made communist domination of Asia an impossibility. As China asserted its independence and resisted Soviet incursions into Asia, the United States began to include the PRC as a key element in its containment strategy against the Soviet Union. This became firm policy following the U.S. opening to China by President Richard Nixon in 1969–1972.

There were three broad levels of U.S. strategic interests served by the Sino-Soviet split. First, China's defection from the Soviet bloc prevented the Eurasian landmass from coming under the control of the Soviet Union. Second, hostility between Moscow and Beijing contributed to the PRC decision to normalize relations with the United States in 1979. This served important U.S. diplomatic, political, and economic interests, and enhanced regional stability in East Asia. And third, Chinese fear of a Soviet attack resulted in Beijing perceiving Moscow, not Washington, as China's principal enemy. Both the United States and China reduced their military assets targeted on each other and began, especially after 1978, to pursue parallel policies on important regional issues such as Afghanistan, Cambodia, and the prevention of war on the Korean peninsula.

Largely as a result of the Sino-Soviet confrontation, the United States reversed its policy of containing China and adopted a policy of supporting PRC efforts to build a strong, secure, and modernizing China. This shift in policy developed gradually over the decade of the 1970s and became firmly anchored in U.S. strategy during the early 1980s. The cost of this strategy was Washington's severance of diplomatic relations with the ROC, the abrogation of the U.S.-ROC Mutual Defense Treaty, the withdrawal of American military personnel from Taiwan, and qualitative and quantitative restrictions placed on future U.S. arms sales to Taipei.

Another major shift in the Asian strategic equation came in the late 1980s, as both Moscow and Hanoi took steps to improve relations with Beijing. The Soviet Union began to withdraw its troops from Afghanistan and Mongolia, while the Vietnamese started to withdraw from Cambodia. China responded in a positive way by indicating that normalization of relations with the Soviet Union and Vietnam were indeed possible. Normalized Sino-Soviet relations were symbolized by the summit meeting between Mikhail Gorbachev and Deng Xiaoping in Beijing in May 1989.

Warming relations between the Soviet Union, China, and Vietnam created a new strategic environment for the United States in Asia. Whereas the decade of the 1980s was characterized by Sino-Soviet and Sino-Vietnamese hostility, the 1990s emerged as a period of normalized and increasingly cooperative relations between these states. Because each was introducing market mechanisms to stimulate a decaying economy, there was also recognition that openness to the West was necessary for their economic development.

By 1989 it also became apparent that the Soviet threat to the United States had been reduced dramatically. The reduction of this threat made containment outdated as a U.S. national security strategy. One of the early goals of President George Bush, who entered office in January 1989, was to find a new U.S. strategy "beyond containment."

According to the Bush administration, U.S. objectives in the post-containment period would center on the creation of a "new world order" of justice, peace, prosperity, and harmony. The President described his vision of the new world order in the following way:

> What is it that we want to see? It is a growing community of democracies anchoring international peace and stability, and a dynamic free-market system generating prosperity and progress on a global scale. The economic foundation of this new era is the proven success of the free market—and nurturing that foundation are the values rooted in freedom and democracy.[2]

A major test of the new world order came in August 1990, when Iraq invaded Kuwait, sending shock waves throughout the world which had been basking in peace following the end of the Cold War. After being assured of both international and domestic support for his actions, President Bush ordered massive American military forces into the Persian Gulf. In explaining his actions before the Congress, Bush listed as one of his main reasons the need to protect the new world order.[3]

Bush demonstrated in the Persian Gulf War that he believed the United States should play a leading role in the creation and protection of the new world order. At the same time, it was also clear that he did not envision the United States playing this role unilaterally. In the Kuwaiti crisis, for example, Bush chose to work through the United Nations and to have other countries pay a substantial share of the costs involved in deploying U.S. military forces to the Middle East. Also, in a major shift from Cold War politics, the Bush administration was willing to cooperate closely with countries formerly hostile to U.S. interests, including the Soviet Union, Iran, and Syria.

In August 1991 yet another development of major strategic importance occurred: the demise of the Soviet Communist Party and the breakup of the Union of Soviet Socialist Republics (USSR). These events were precipitated by a failed coup attempt between August 19–21 against President Mikhail Gorbachev and his replacement by a State Committee for the State of Emergency. The Committee, dominated by senior military, KGB, and Interior Ministry officials, was comprised of communist hardliners opposed to Gorbachev's sweeping reforms.

Instead of recognizing the legitimacy of the coup, the United States and other Western nations froze economic assistance to the USSR, held emergency meetings of NATO, and refused to have anything to do with the new government. In the Soviet Union itself, Boris N. Yeltsin, president of the Russian federated republic, called on the people to oppose the Committee through civil disobedience. His defiance was supported by hundreds of thousands of Soviet citizens around the country, who formed a human wall in front of troops and tanks called in by the Committee to support the coup. Many key military and security units refused to go along with the plotters, resulting in their inability to arrest Yeltsin and secure control of the country. By August 21 the coup attempt had failed.

The results of the coup failure were far more revolutionary than the coup itself. Boris Yeltsin emerged as a dominant leader, surpassing Gorbachev in political power. Gorbachev himself resigned from the Communist Party and called for the seizure of its property. With ten of the Soviet Union's fifteen republics moving toward full independence, the USSR itself collapsed. In desperation, the leaders of the republics of Armenia, Azerbaijan, Byelorussia, Kazakhstan, Kirghizia, Russia, Tadzhikistan, Turkmenia, Ukraine, and Uzbekistan worked to form a new union. Georgia participated as an observer. Estonia, Latvia, and Lithuania were granted their complete independence, were promptly recognized by the West, and shortly thereafter were admitted into the United Nations. Moldavia also declared its independence, seeking to become part of Romania. In 1991–1992 the new CIS Commonwealth was attempting to head in the direction of democracy and free enterprise, although most of its republics faced enormous political, economic, and social difficulties, including ethnic strife which threatened the very existence of some.

The collapse of the Soviet Union, Russia's adoption of political democracy and the free market, the rapid withdrawal of the Soviet military into the Russian heartland, extensive new arms control agreements, and the Commonwealth's appeals for closer cooperation and even economic assistance from the West reduced the remaining threat to U.S. interests from Moscow to nil proportions. Indeed, the Department of Defense told Congress in early September 1991 that it was prepared to distribute food and other vital necessities in the former Soviet Union during the winter to prevent famine and social chaos.

The remainder of this chapter will focus on U.S. strategy and policy toward the Asian Pacific region since the end of the Cold War. Of special concern will be the evolving status of Sino-American relations since 1989. This discussion lays the foundation for an examination of U.S. interests in the "new" Taiwan in the next chapter.

U.S. Policy Toward Asia Under President Bush

From the outset of the Bush administration, it was clear that containment was no longer a viable strategy for the United States in Asia. As early as June 1989 Secretary of State James Baker defined the four pillars of U.S. policy toward Asia under President Bush as being: (1) continued U.S. commitment to the Asian Pacific region, (2) nurturing a global relationship with Japan, (3) maintaining constructive relations with China, and (4) support for Asian Pacific economic cooperation.

In attempting to define more precisely a new U.S. strategy toward Asia, the administration emphasized the unique and crucial role played by the United States in sustaining the dynamic balance in the region.[4] U.S. strategy and policy under President Bush sought to ensure that the United States would continue to play that role.

There were several elements to Bush's policy toward Asia, centering around the themes of economic integration and diversity in security arrangements. The keystone of U.S. policy was U.S. relations with Japan. Those relations were based on several principles: economic balance on both sides of the Pacific, a deepening security relationship, and a growing global partnership.

Relations with China were also key to U.S. strategy and policy. The Bush administration believed that China should not be isolated or permitted to become a spoiler in Asian politics. Washington wanted to engage Beijing in meaningful dialogue, not because it approved of

PRC human rights or other policies, but because China played a major role in the emerging multipolar world. A fundamental assumption of the administration was that a modernizing China at peace with itself and its neighbors was essential to stability in East Asia. A second major assumption was that engagement with the PRC on a broad range of global and regional issues would encourage China's modernization along liberal lines. More will be said about Bush's China policy later in this chapter.

Other major elements of U.S. foreign policy in Asia were: constructive relations with ASEAN, including bilateral treaties with Thailand and the Philippines; consolidating democracy in countries such as the Philippines and voicing U.S. concerns about violent repression in Burma; enhancing regional economic cooperation through such forums as the Asia Pacific Economic Cooperation process (APEC); maintaining close relations with Australia and (assuming changes in its ban on U.S. ships carrying nuclear weapons) with New Zealand; resolving regional trouble spots, particularly in Indochina and on the Korean peninsula, as a means of enhancing regional cooperation and security; and achieving a consensus on proper security relationships in Asia.

In formulating its policy toward Asia, the Bush administration recognized that fundamental shifts were taking place in global politics. These included the bankruptcy of communism, worldwide integration heightened by technological change, and global movements toward market-oriented economies and political pluralism. These trends were welcomed by Washington, because they were considered to be the realization of American goals held since the end of World War II.

But there were problems as well. Of special concern to the Bush administration were a reemergence of ethno-nationalism, regional antagonisms, and ambitions held in abeyance because of the Cold War. These local antagonisms were fueled by access to modern weaponry. There were basic contradictions in the international environment which complicated U.S. national security policy. Power was becoming more diffuse between nations, even as they were becoming more interdependent. The technological and information revolutions were eroding national boundaries, yet nationalism was becoming a more powerful force in the world. Technological and commercial capabilities were becoming more important than military capabilities in determining the power of nations; but at the same time, advanced weapons, including weapons of mass destruction, were proliferating.

In terms of security, the Bush administration viewed East Asia in three sub-regional zones: Northeast Asia, Southeast Asia, and the South Pacific. Because of the multi-dimensional security environment in Asia and the multipolar pattern of power relationships in the region, the administration rejected a comprehensive regional security arrangement in favor of a series of security arrangements. This diversity in the sphere of security was in sharp contrast with the integration occurring in the economic sphere. Hence, one description of Bush policy in Asia in the early 1990s was "integration in economics, diversity in defense."[5]

The structure of U.S. security policy toward Asia was a continuation of what existed in the Reagan administration: an overlapping system of defense alliances and political alignments. This system included U.S. bilateral security treaties with Japan, South Korea, the Philippines, and Thailand; the ANZUS (Australia, New Zealand, and the United States) security treaty; and the South Pacific Forum. Anchoring U.S. security in Asia was Japan, with U.S. forward deployed forces reinforced by bilateral treaties with other Asian security partners.

In terms of its arms control policies in Asia, the Bush administration preferred to see unilateral reductions in the forces of the major countries, rather than a regional arms control agreement. The main reason for this was that the United States was a trading nation dependent on the forward deployment of its navy. There were, in addition, technical difficulties in finding similarities in the force structures of the United States, the Soviet Union and later Russia, and other major Asian powers because of the different missions each played in the region.

Another problem with arms control agreements in Asia was that U.S. forward deployed forces played a much broader role in the Pacific than simply countering the remnants of the Soviet threat. From the point of view of the Bush administration, even if the Soviet (or Russian) threat disappeared entirely, the U.S. forward deployed presence would continue to play a vital role in maintaining the balance of power in the region. If the balance wheel of U.S. forces was removed, the region could become much more unstable and the interests of the United States and other friendly Pacific Rim countries would be adversely affected.

The perception of the role of the United States as a balancing wheel in Asia was a key concept of the Bush administration in the early 1990s. It became the catch-phrase of U.S. strategy in the Asian Pacific region, replacing containment as the justification for continued forward deployed U.S. military forces. The balancing role of the United States in Asian Pacific security affairs was explained in a document entitled *A Strategic Framework for the Asian Pacific Rim: Looking Toward the 21st Century,* submitted to the Congress in April 1990 by the Office for International Security Affairs (ISA) in the Department of Defense.[6]

The Strategic Framework Report

The ISA report was written in recognition of the need to redefine the U.S. role and strategy in Asia. The study argued that, in spite of the reduced Soviet threat in Asia, U.S. interests in the region will remain similar to those of the past. The report identified these interests as being:

- protecting the United States from attack
- supporting U.S. global deterrence policy
- preserving U.S. political and economic access to the region
- maintaining the balance of power to prevent the rise of any regional hegemony
- strengthening the Western orientation of Asian nations
- fostering the growth of democracy and human rights
- deterring nuclear proliferation
- ensuring freedom of navigation.

The report further stated that the basic elements of U.S. Asian strategy will remain valid for the near future. These basic elements were "forward deployed forces, overseas bases, and bilateral security arrangements." According to the report, these elements of U.S. Asian strategy were "essential to maintaining regional stability, deterring aggression, and preserving U.S. interests."[7]

Given these considerations, and the need to preserve both peacetime and wartime deterrent and warfighting capabilities in the Pacific, the Pentagon report concluded that the existing U.S. military presence in the East Asia and Pacific (EAP) region should remain largely intact. The study recommended, however, that some reductions (mostly in ground forces) take place to reflect the improved international climate and to help reduce the U.S. budget deficit.

The report suggested that U.S. military adjustments occur in three phases through the end of the 1990s. In Phase I (1990–1993) an initial reduction of 14,000–15,000 personnel out of some 135,000 U.S. troops forward deployed in the Pacific would take place. Some 7,000 personnel would be removed from Korea (5,000 Army and 2,000 Air Force); between 5,000 and 6,000 Air Force and Army personnel would be withdrawn from Japan; and approximately 2,000 personnel would be withdrawn from the Philippines.

Phase II (1993–1995) and Phase III (1995–2000) adjustments would depend on the international situation prevailing at the time.

According to the plan, the United States would have a sustainable (but not defined) presence in the region by the end of Phase III. U.S. forward deployed forces in Japan would remain over the long-term with few changes. U.S. air forces would remain at Misawa, for example, and a carrier task force would be home ported at Yokosuka. Facilities on Okinawa would also be retained. U.S. forces in Korea would be at a minimum level necessary to maintain deterrence, with Republic of Korea forces taking a leading role in Korean defense. The report stated that the United States would like to retain its facilities in the Philippines, but the Defense Department was prepared to find alternative facilities if necessary. (This point became moot when the Philippine Senate refused to ratify a new treaty negotiated in mid-July 1991 extending continued basing rights to the United States.)

In an important strategic formulation, the ISA report and ranking Defense Department officials described the future role of the U.S. military in the Western Pacific as that of "regional balancer, honest broker, and ultimate security guarantor."[8] Another phrase used to describe the role of the U.S. military in the Asian Pacific Rim was an "irreplaceable balance wheel."

In attempting to explain what this meant, Department of Defense officials involved with the report said a "balance wheel" had no specific function other than to keep the other "gears"—Asian nations—in place. In other words, the U.S. military would have no specific function other than to play a "unique and central stabilizing role" in the region. According to these officials, the key phrase describing the mission of the U.S. military in Asia was a "central stabilizing role."[9] One high-ranking State Department official used the term "arbiter" to describe the U.S. role.[10]

By defining the U.S. role as an "irreplaceable balance wheel," the Bush administration implicitly changed the fundamental U.S. strategy in the Asian Pacific region from one of "containment" to one of maintaining a regional "balance of power."

As noted earlier, U.S. strategy in Asia has traditionally included a strong element of balance of power. In fact, as cited in the *Strategic Framework* study, one of the enduring U.S. interests in Asia has been "maintaining the balance of power to prevent the rise of any regional hegemony."[11] Elsewhere in the study, this aspect of U.S. strategy was described in this way: "In broader terms, our presence has contributed to regional peace, stability, and prosperity by providing the balance necessary to ensure that no single state assumed a hegemonic position."[12]

Under the strategic plan outlined by the Office of International Security Affairs, the United States would seek to maintain the balance of power in Asia through several means. These would include:

1. maintaining a strong forward deployed military force in the region for the purposes of deterrence and, if need be, early military response to a crisis
2. coordinating policies with other Asian Pacific nations through bilateral and multilateral channels to minimize conflict and to maximize regional stability and prosperity
3. attempting to play the role of "honest broker" to help resolve problems between the Asian nations themselves.

The retention of the U.S. force posture in Asia at essentially the same level as that maintained during the Cold War was justified on the grounds that the Soviet Union (now Russia) continued to maintain very credible forces in Northeast Asia. More importantly, such a forward based U.S. posture was necessary because of the proliferation of advanced weapons among regional powers. This required sophisticated U.S. systems, including aircraft carrier battle groups, to be available in case of international crisis on the Korean peninsula or elsewhere in the region.[13]

The Persian Gulf War

In January 1991 the United States achieved a total victory in its military confrontation with Iraq. The minor role played by Moscow in the Persian Gulf crisis and the overwhelming power projection capabilities displayed by the United States in the war confirmed that in the 1990s the world's only superpower was the United States. These developments caused military analysts and politicians to reconsider the role of the United States in world politics, including basic assumptions about American strategy and the type of armed forces necessary to implement that strategy.

President George Bush said the victory over Iraq had "kicked the Vietnam syndrome once and for all." In a news conference on March 1, 1991, the President said the U.S. victory would convince others in the world that the United States would use force to protect its interests, thus enhancing deterrence to aggression worldwide.[14] Former Secretary of State George P. Shultz said the war dramatically proved that "we're the only...ones really able to project power on a large scale." And Volker Ruehe, general secretary of Germany's ruling Christian

Democratic Union, said, "The United States is the only one who could play such a role."[15]

Factors Contributing to U.S. Victory

There is no question but that the United States gained enormous political capital by its victory in the Persian Gulf War. But an analysis of the reasons behind this victory suggest that there were at least three contributing factors which have direct relevance to a future U.S. strategy in Asia.

First, there was the key role played by the U.S. military, including its sophisticated weapons systems and unique power projection capabilities. Second, there was the substantial international political support given the U.S. effort, including a large coalition of nations supporting United Nations' resolutions against Iraq. This international backing gave the United States the political, moral, and allied military (including host nation) support necessary to prosecute a successful war in the difficult political environment of the Middle East. And third, there was the enormous financial contribution made to the war effort by other nations. While the United States made up 70 percent of the armed forces fighting the Iraqis, other nations—principally Saudi Arabia, Kuwait, Japan, and Germany—financed most of its expenses. According to the Office of Management and Budget, the total U.S. cost of the Persian Gulf War was $61 billion. The total pledges from coalition partners was about $54 billion, of which $48.2 billion was in cash and $5.4 billion was in kind, mostly fuel. As of August 15, 1991, some $46.6 billion of pledged funds had been received by Washington.[16]

All of these factors—the unique role of U.S. power projection capabilities, the political necessity of strong international backing before engaging in a major conflict, and the necessity of foreign economic assistance to help finance such large-scale military operations—will have important influence on a future U.S. strategy in Asia. The United States is the world's only superpower, but it is not the world's dominant power. Increasingly, Washington must take action in concert with other nations, although its leadership potential is widely recognized in most capitals of the world.

Effect of the Gulf War on Asia

The reaction of most Asian nations to the U.S. war effort in the Gulf was cautious at first, although the public in many countries—including the PRC—applauded the U.S. intervention. Both the PRC and Malaysia provided important political support in the U.N. which made the passage of U.S. backed resolutions possible. Also, many East Asian countries were among the first to adhere to the full U.N. sanctions against Iraq. South Korea offered transport services to the United States and to the multilateral Arab forces opposing Iraq. The Koreans also assisted financially. Australia sent military forces to help the coalition and provided financial assistance. New Zealand provided airlift and other transportation assistance to coalition partners. Indonesia and Malaysia increased their oil production to make up for oil lost to Asian nations because of the war. Singapore and Brunei helped to ease the economic burden on front-line states and developing nations adversely affected by the war, such as the Philippines. Taiwan contributed financially to aid Arab nations hurt by the conflict.[17]

After some prodding by the United States, Japan played a major role in helping to finance the coalition effort. Tokyo pledged over $13 billion out of the total $54 billion promised by coalition partners. Japan's contribution included $9 billion to Operation Desert Storm to support military operations against Iraq, $2 billion to Operation Desert Shield to support the international forces deployed to the Gulf, $2.1 billion in highly concessional loans to the front-line states, and some $60 million in refugee relief.

There were a number of important results of the Gulf War. East Asian and Pacific (EAP) nations became more firmly part of the global network of nations. In addition to becoming more aware of the international repercussions of crises far from their shores, Asian nations found that they had an important political role in the U.N. and other international forums, as well as important financial and logistics roles in coalition defense efforts. The Persian Gulf conflict thus was an important precedent in which Asian countries became deeply involved in crises beyond the EAP region.

A second result of the Persian Gulf War was the increased sense of global partnership between the United States and Japan. The United States became the world's only superpower, but it was heavily dependent upon Japan's support. This backing was not only financial; it included extending political support on regional and global issues and hosting American base facilities for forward deployed forces in Asia.[18] The growing partnership means that Japan will have a larger role, more responsibility, and increased influence in U.S. strategy and policy toward the Asian Pacific region in the future.

The New World Order

The U.S. victory in the Persian Gulf War breathed new life into the President's earlier vision of a "new world order." In his State of the

Union address on January 29, 1991, the President said that the United States was in the Persian Gulf to defend the new world order in which diverse nations would work together for the universal aspirations of "peace and security, freedom, and the rule of law."[19]

In a major speech on the new world order at the Air University at Maxwell Air Force Base on April 13, 1991, the President contrasted the new world with the past four decades, which were characterized by a world locked in a conflict of arms and ideas between two systems.[20] He compared the ending of the Cold War to the ending of the First and Second World Wars. In all three instances, he said, the ending of the confrontation gave birth to a dream of a world in which major powers worked together to ensure peace. Bush said that he did not have a specific "blueprint" in mind that would govern the conduct of nations or some supernational structure or institution which would manage the new world order. Nor, he said, did the new world order mean surrendering national sovereignty or forfeiting national interests. The President said the concept referred to "new ways of working with other nations to deter aggression and to achieve stability, to achieve prosperity and, above all, to achieve peace."

According to Bush, the new world order was based on a shared commitment between nations to a common set of principles. These principles included "peaceful settlements of disputes, solidarity against aggression, reduced and controlled arsenals, and just treatment of all peoples." The President also said that the quest for a new world order was, in part, "a challenge to keep the dangers of disorder at bay." Regarding U.S. and other developed nations participation in the new order, Bush said, "In a world as interdependent as ours, no industrialized nation can maintain membership in good standing in the global community without assuming its fair share of responsibility for peace and security."

Bush described the new world order as "a tool for addressing a new world of possibilities." The new world order, he said, "gains its mission and shape not just from shared interests, but from shared ideals." Bush observed that the United States is the home for these ideals. He said, "the ideals that have spawned new freedoms throughout the world have received their boldest and clearest expression in...the United States." Bush said, "what makes us American is our allegiance to an idea that all people everywhere must be free."

Bush's comments on the new world order reflected his vision of what he would like to see the world become. From his actions in the Persian Gulf War and his statements on the new world order, certain operating principles underlying Bush's foreign policy might be extrapolated. These operating principles can be surmised as follows:

1. The United States is committed to greater economic and perhaps even political integration, but it does not have a specific framework of organization in mind. The process of integration is what is important at this stage, not a specific outcome.

2. The process of integration should occur naturally and through consensus, not through the dictates of the United States or other major powers.

3. The United States wants to work with like-minded nations to solve specific problems through peaceful means. The elimination of problems such as Cambodia and Korea will contribute to the process of integration.

4. If necessary, the United States is willing to use force to resist hegemony and to restore balance and stability. Under most circumstances, these military operations should be widely backed by the international community. Other nations should contribute their own resources to see that the operations are successful and concluded quickly.

5. The United States is firmly committed to the expansion of democracy and free enterprise. It will encourage a peaceful process of change along these lines in authoritarian states.

6. The key values which the United States seeks to promote and may defend with military force include: peace, security, and the rule of law; promotion of mutual prosperity; deterrence of aggression; preservation of stability; peaceful settlement of disputes; reduced arsenals around the world, especially weapons of mass destruction and their delivery systems; just treatment of all peoples, even minorities within sovereign states; political and economic freedom; and the encouragement of reforms through dialogue and negotiations.

7. The U.S. goal is to create a growing community of democratic nations anchoring international peace and stability, and an international economic system based on the free market system which generates prosperity and progress on a global scale.

8. The economic foundation of the new world order is the proven success of the free market. The philosophical foundations of the new world order are values rooted in freedom and democracy.

9. The United States will maintain a strong commitment to the principle that all men everywhere deserve to be free.

10. The United States is willing to play a leadership role in bringing about the new world order, but it seeks to do this through consensus building and through the contributions of all states. The United States believes in the shared responsibility of industrialized nations to help preserve international peace and security.

11. In a non-ideological, pragmatic way, the United States is willing to work with all countries toward these goals, regardless of the nature of past relationships.

The role of these implicit foreign policy operating principles on U.S. interests toward Taiwan in the 1990s will be discussed in the next chapter.

Sino-American Relations
Under the Bush Administration, 1989–1991

The most important event in Sino-American relations during the early months of the Bush administration was the June 1989 Tiananmen Square incident in which the People's Liberation Army (PLA) killed several hundred demonstrators. The fact that this was seen on television by millions of Americans had a profound and perhaps lasting effect on American attitudes toward the communist government in Beijing. Despite efforts by President Bush to maintain cordial relations with the PRC, the incident poisoned U.S.-China relations in the eyes of many Americans. This sentiment was reflected strongly in the mass media, among American intellectuals, and in the Congress.

The PRC did little to improve its negative image in the United States through 1991, falling back instead into a xenophobic arrogance that heightened rather than defused the growing sense of alienation between Beijing and the American people. Human rights abuses continued, many of them directed against students, workers, and intellectuals involved in the May–June 1989 demonstrations in Beijing. Statements by CCP leaders suggested that the preservation of the party's hold on power was more important than improvement in the lives of the Chinese people. Throughout 1990 and 1991 there was a marked return to ideological work among the masses, wide repression of political opposition, and a slowdown of both political and economic liberalization.

PRC policies contrasted sharply with major changes occurring in Eastern Europe, the Soviet Union, and many other socialist countries. The impression left in the minds of the American people, and reinforced by statements from PRC leaders themselves, was that China had become the last major bastion of communism, a system proven ineffective and outdated by virtually every other government and people in the world.

The American public thus came to view the PRC government as oppressive and out-of-touch with reality. The return to orthodox Marxist-Leninist approaches to political and economic policies seemed hopelessly out of date with global liberalizing trends. Added to this negative perception of the PRC were Chinese policies at sharp variance with U.S. interests. These included a rapidly growing Sino-American trade imbalance in China's favor and the sale of both advanced missiles and nuclear technology to countries in the Middle East and South Asia.

In 1990 China enjoyed a $10.4 billion trade surplus with the United States. In 1991 China's trade surplus with the United States was $12.7 billion, the world's second highest after Japan. The size of the surplus was a matter of concern to many in the United States, but of greater political importance was the perception that it was achieved through unfair trading practices. These practices included failure to honor U.S. intellectual property rights, refusal to remove protectionist barriers against imports from the United States, illegal PRC textile shipments through third countries, and Chinese exports made by political prisoners.

PRC missile sales to the Third World were even more troubling to the U.S. government. Beijing was reported by U.S. intelligence as being ready to sell M-9 short-ranged ballistic missiles to Syria and M-11 short-range ballistic missiles to Pakistan. The M-9 has a range of 360–370 miles and would give Syria the ability to hit military targets in Israel with great accuracy and reliability. The M-11 could carry an 800-kilogram warhead more than 180 miles to targets in India.[21] Because of the volatile nature of politics in the Middle East and South Asia, the missiles sales were seen by Washington as destabilizing to international peace. In mid-1991 the United States began pressuring China to adhere to the Missile Technology Control Regime, participated in by sixteen nations to halt the spread of long-range missiles.

The United States was also concerned by Chinese shipments of nuclear materials and technology to Pakistan and certain other countries. According to one report, in 1983 the PRC gave Pakistan the design of a tested nuclear weapon with a yield of about 25 kilotons; Beijing also provide Pakistan with enough weapons-grade uranium for at least two nuclear weapons.[22] Chinese scientists worked in Pakistan's Kahuta complex, where nuclear weapons research took place. Between 1982 and 1987 Beijing sold India about 150 tons of heavy water, which is used to make plutonium. In addition, China sold uranium to South Africa, uranium and heavy water to Argentina, enriched uranium to Brazil, and a heavy water reactor to Algeria. After much international pressure, China finally agreed in late 1991 to join the Nuclear Nonproliferation Treaty.

These and other divisive issues in Sino-American relations became highly politicized during the spring and summer of 1991, when debate arose over whether the United States should grant China most-favored-nation (MFN) trading status for one more year. The Democratic-controlled Congress used the MFN issue to sharply criticize the President for his support of China.

Bush's policy toward China was based on his perceptions of how best to change the PRC in a direction favorable to U.S. interests. In fact, despite the setback to U.S. interests as a result of Tiananmen and subsequent internal developments in China, the Bush administration assigned a high priority to the maintenance of friendly relations with Beijing. Assistant Secretary of State Richard Solomon described the administration's China policy in testimony before the Senate Foreign Relations Committee in June 1990: "Our approach is to try to preserve a key relationship that serves important national interests, while at the same time sending a clear message that Beijing's human rights performance has been—and remains—unacceptable, precluding a fully normal relationship."[23]

The President personally explained his China policy in a commencement address at Yale University on May 27, 1991.[24] In his speech, the President said the United States needed to remain engaged with China in order to try to change Chinese behavior in ways closer to U.S. ideals. These ideals included freedom, democracy, human rights, and freer trade.

According to Bush, it was in U.S. interests to find opportunities to cooperate with the PRC because of China's size, enormous population, and ability to affect the stability of East Asia. The Chinese also played central roles in Cambodia, Korea, and in many multinational organizations such as the U.N. Its cooperation in the U.N., said the President, was essential to pass resolutions against Iraq's invasion of Kuwait.

The President emphasized, however, that the United States did not hesitate to take appropriate action against the Chinese government when problems arose in its behavior. For example, the United States was the first nation to condemn the use of violence against the peaceful demonstrations in Tiananmen, and it was the first to guarantee the rights of Chinese students to remain in the United States. The United States was also the first nation to impose sanctions against the PRC, and it was one of the last among the Western democracies to keep the original sanctions in place.

The President noted that the United States also cited China under the trade rules of a Special 301 for pirating U.S. copyrights and patents. Moreover, his administration took strong issue with the Chinese government on its exports of missiles and nuclear technology.

The President said he was in favor of unconditional extension of MFN to China because it was the ordinary basis of world trade and because ending MFN would hurt those in China whom the United States wanted most to encourage: individuals and provinces seeking to expand the free market, trade, and contact with the West. Also, the President argued, continuing MFN would enable the United States to remain engaged with China, and thus to export U.S. ideals of freedom and democracy.

The President said the power of the ideal of democracy was capable of transforming China. That democratic ideal was best transferred to China through trade and other normal commercial contacts with the Chinese people. The President remarked: "If we pursue a policy that cultivates contacts with the Chinese people, promotes commerce to our benefit, we can help create a climate for democratic change. No nation on Earth has discovered a way to import the world's goods and services—while stopping foreign ideas at the border. Just as the democratic idea has transformed nations on every continent—so, too, change will inevitably come to China."

The Role of Congress

Although the President strongly supported continued cordial relations with the PRC, the U.S. Congress was in a different mood. The annual congressional debate surrounding the granting of MFN to China after 1990 became the chief forum for Members of Congress to seek to play a role in U.S. policy toward the PRC. This level of congressional activism was an indication of public doubt about Bush's China policy, a concern in marked contrast to the high ratings given Bush for his handling of other areas of foreign policy. As noted earlier, it was congressional opposition over unconditional MFN to China that forced the administration to change its policy of opposing Taiwan's entrance into GATT.

There were several reasons why China policy had again become an issue of contention between the Congress and the White House. One factor was the reemergence in the Congress of a strong ideological commitment to democracy and freedom after the collapse of communism. Another factor was China's negative image as one of the few remaining communist countries, and a nation which routinely violated the human rights of its citizens. A third factor was that many Members of Congress were angry with Bush's attempts to maintain normal relations with the PRC after Tiananmen, going so far as to send his National Security Advisor to Beijing on a secret mission shortly after the incident while publicly saying that high-level exchanges between the two governments had been stopped. A fourth factor was that China policy was one of the few foreign policy issues on which

Democrats in Congress could safely criticize the Republican President. A fifth factor was that the end of the Cold War removed the President's ability to dominate foreign policy issues on the grounds of national security. Thus, Congress as a whole was less inclined to defer to Bush on the controversial issue of China policy.

Effect of the Persian Gulf War on China

The Iraqi War had mixed effects on Sino-American relations. On the one hand, the United States was grateful for China's cooperation in the U.N. Beijing thus reinforced the U.S. perception of China's importance as a powerful country with which the United States had to deal carefully. The generally cooperative PRC actions in the U.N. also contributed to the decision by Western nations that most of the post-Tiananmen sanctions had outlived their usefulness and should gradually be lifted.

On the other hand, the war had troubling implications for leaders in Beijing. It proved that the United States was the only remaining superpower, and it demonstrated that Washington would use military force to protect its interests. After its victory in the Cold War and in the Gulf, Washington experienced a rebirth of ideological commitment to the promotion and defense of freedom. Most Americans clearly did not like Beijing's communist leadership, considering the aging cadre to be outdated and reactionary. From the point of view of many senior leaders in Beijing, the most threatening nation to China in the 1990s was not the Soviet Union or Russia, but rather the United States—and not primarily for military reasons but for ideological reasons.

This PRC concern over a new level of American activism in world affairs was heightened by the vulnerability of the PLA to modern U.S. weapons, strategy, and tactics. This problem could not be remedied quickly and would require massive infusions of capital over a period of time to purchase advanced military equipment and defense technology. The sharp increase in the PRC defense budget since the Gulf War reflects Beijing's decision to modernize the PLA much more quickly than previously envisioned.

The difficulties facing Sino-American relations in the 1990s become apparent when comparing the respective views of the United States and the PRC on the new world order, or the "new international order," as China likes to refer to it.

PRC View of the New World Order

In contrast to the Bush administration's vision of the new world order based on democratic values and the free market system, China's vision of the new international order was based on the Five Principles of Peaceful Coexistence (mutual respect for sovereignty and territorial integrity, mutual non-aggression, non-interference in each other's internal affairs, equality and mutual benefit, and peaceful co-existence).[25]

The PRC faulted the Bush plan for a new world order on several grounds. These may be summarized as:

1. The United States does not have the strength to fulfill its ambition of leading the new world order.
2. The American people do not support such an activist role for the United States in world affairs.
3. U.S. allies hold different visions of the new world order, specifically objecting to the leading role of the United States.
4. Future U.S.-Russian relations are unpredictable, and thus to base a great deal of the new world order on that relationship may not be realistic.
5. The new world order stresses U.S. values too much; the rest of the world will not accept U.S. values as universal standards.
6. Democracy, freedom, and human rights are fundamentally domestic issues—not universal standards to be imposed by the United States.
7. Since Bush's new world order is based on these values, but the rest of the world is not willing to accept these standards, the new world order proposed by President Bush cannot be realized.

China proposed instead that a new international order be established. It would be based on the fundamental right of all countries to choose their own social system, ideology, political and economic model, and path of development in view of their unique national characteristics. Differences in these areas, which are inevitable given the world's diversity, should not impede normal relations and cooperation between states. Those relations should be based solely on mutual interests. All countries—big and small, rich and poor—should have equal rights in discussing and handling world affairs. The PRC stressed that international disputes should be solved through peaceful negotiations. No country should impose its will upon others nor use or threaten the use of force in a unilateral way.

According to the PRC, the new international order must include not only a new political order but also a new economic order. This is because the core of most international problems in the post-Cold War period have their roots in the economic differences between the North (developed countries) and the South (developing countries). The principles of the new economic order should include the right of every

country to choose its own economic system, to control its own resources, and to participate in international economic affairs on an equal
basis. No political strings should be attached to economic assistance
from the developed world to the developing world.

The core of China's new international order was the principle that
the affairs of a given country should be handled by the government
and people of that country without interference from other nations.
The PRC pointed out that this principle was embodied in the U.N.
Charter. If the principle was carried out in practice, the United Nations
could play a larger role in the future.

The significant differences between the U.S. and Chinese visions of
the new world order have profound policy implications. Although it
is beyond the scope of this book to explore these in detail, a few
should be mentioned because they demonstrate the contrast between
Taipei's policies, which are in basic harmony with the new world
order envisioned by the United States, and Beijing's policies, which
in many ways oppose what the United States is trying to accomplish
in the post-Cold War era. For example:

- In the Asian Pacific Rim the United States is attempting to
  build a new Pacific partnership based on an "enduring sense
  of community" centered around common security, political,
  and economic interests and common values of prosperity,
  democracy, and freedom. The PRC, on the other hand, accepts
  multipolarity but cannot support a new world order led by
  the United States. Instead, China supports a multipolar world
  characterized by non-interference in internal affairs. China
  opposes what it sees as an increased tendency for ideological
  intervention by the West in the affairs of sovereign states.

- The United States believes that its forward deployed forces play
  an essential role in maintaining a regional balance of power in
  Asia. China, on the other hand, thinks that Washington greatly
  overestimates its own importance in this regard and that the
  U.S. military presence should be reduced much more than that
  outlined in the *Strategic Framework* study.

- The United States believes that authoritarianism, especially the
  variety found in communist states, is collapsing worldwide.
  Political pluralism has won the ideological battle for the hearts
  and minds of people everywhere. The United States will use
  its commercial strength and its technology, especially in mass
  communications, to promote the cause of freedom. The CCP,
  on the other hand, insists that it will not allow a multiparty

system in China, but rather will adhere to a system of multiparty cooperation under the leadership of the Communist Party. PRC leaders see "bourgeois liberalization" and "peaceful evolution" as evidence of a continued class struggle. In essence, this is a struggle for power against the CCP, involving outside interference and anti-socialist forces on the mainland. Beijing considers "peaceful evolution" to be a long-term U.S. strategy to undermine socialism through a "soft attack" or a "peace strategy" against the CCP. Communist leaders believe that individualism is incompatible with socialism and the Chinese spirit of collectivism.

- The United States considers itself to be a leading free nation with special responsibilities to promote and protect human rights, including political and economic freedom. Beijing, on the other hand, while believing in human rights, considers these to be matters for each individual country to decide in accordance with its internal conditions. The PRC views Western attempts to impose human rights standards on China as interference in Chinese internal affairs.

More examples could be provided, but the point is that the United States is home to the ideas which many senior PRC leaders most fear. Moreover, since Washington is very open about its strategy to change Chinese society through increased contact, there can be no doubt but that the CCP views the United States as its principal enemy in the immediate post-Cold War period. The PRC has a point. As seen in the case of Eastern Europe and the Soviet Union, once the foundations of socialism and communist party control are eroded, then the foundations of the communist state quickly crumble. PRC leaders have carefully studied the lessons of the Soviet bloc, and it is reasonable to expect that Beijing will do all in its power to prevent the collapse of communism in China.

As will be seen in the next chapter, the Taiwan issue brings to the forefront many of the contradictions that exist between the United States and the People's Republic of China, despite the intentions of both Washington and Beijing to preserve their mutually beneficial relationship.

Conclusion

One of the foreign policy problems faced by the Bush administration was its inability to clearly define a national strategy "beyond containment." The *Strategic Framework* report contributed to this process in terms of U.S. strategy toward Asia by implicitly suggesting that the United States move from containment to a balance of power strategy. Although the United States has a strong, traditional interest in maintaining a balance of power in Asia, such a strategy may not be adequate to replace containment in the 1990s and beyond. There are several reasons:

1. It is enormously difficult to define what is meant by an acceptable balance of power in the EAP region, which is one of the most dynamic regions of the world politically, economically, and militarily.

2. As power evolves in the region, who will decide when the new distribution of power becomes a threat and to whom? Will Tokyo accept Beijing's judgment, or will Beijing accept that of Washington?

3. Congress and the American public might not support a sufficiently large forward deployed U.S. military presence in the Western Pacific to maintain a balance of power, even if one could be defined.

4. A balance of power system will succeed only under certain conditions: (a) if one or more powers are so dominant that they can compel the other nations to accept a given distribution of power, or (b) most of the major countries in the region agree to maintain the status quo. These conditions are not found in the Asian Pacific Rim.

5. A balance of power strategy focuses too much attention on the military aspects of national security and not enough on the lowering of incentives for conflict through political and economic means. In the Asian Pacific region the importance of economic and political instruments of national power are increasing, while the relative importance of military instruments of national power are decreasing.

6. If the United States failed in its attempt to maintain a balance of power in the EAP region, Asian perceptions of declining U.S. power and influence would increase. The reduction of U.S. influence in the region would occur precisely at the time when the importance of the Asian Pacific Rim to the United States is growing.

These difficulties suggest that a shift in U.S. national security strategy in the Asian Pacific region from containment to balance of power may prove to be very troublesome to Washington. However, it is also true that the United States cannot afford "strategic drift" in its policies toward Asia. Simply preserving the elements of containment in the region without a coordinating strategy will not withstand congressional and public criticism in an era of sharp reductions in defense expenditures.

One possible replacement for containment as an overarching U.S. strategy for the Asian Pacific region is "integration." Indeed, integration has become an increasingly important U.S. objective in the post-containment period. President Bush referred to the integration of the Soviet Union in this way:

> The grand strategy of the West during the postwar period has been based on the concept of containment: checking the Soviet Union's expansionist aims, in the hope that the Soviet system itself would one day be forced to confront its internal contradictions. The ferment in the Soviet Union today affirms the wisdom of this strategy. And now we have a precious opportunity to move beyond containment...
>
> Our goal—integrating the Soviet Union into the community of nations—is every bit as ambitious as containment was at its time. And it holds tremendous promise for international stability.[26]

In terms of U.S. strategic objectives in Asia, President Bush's goal of integrating the Soviet Union into the international community could be expanded to include the remaining socialist states of Asia: the PRC, North Korea, Vietnam, Cambodia, Laos, and Burma.

A basic assumption behind an integration strategy is that joining the international community helps to moderate the policies of communist states and reduces even further their ideological, political, economic, and military threats to U.S. interests. The purpose of integration is to stabilize the international system and thus contribute to international peace.

There is some evidence that integration may achieve these goals. A correlation seems to exist between efforts by socialist states to enter the global economic and political system and the setting aside of their intentions to destroy that system. Moreover, the initial efforts of some communist countries to integrate with the world community have increased their cooperation in seeking a peaceful resolution of regional issues such as Afghanistan, Cambodia, and the reunification of Germany and Korea. It is also important to note that, with few exceptions, most socialist governments in Asia are interested in becoming more fully integrated into the international community.

The significant reduction of the Soviet (now Russian) threat and the desire of most socialist states to be integrated into the global economic and political community create a unique opportunity to shift U.S. strategic emphasis away from a primarily defensive national security strategy (such as "containment" and "balance of power") to one more constructive in nature.

A strategy of integration would have three fundamental objectives in Asia:

1. To maintain adequate regional security and deterrence at both nuclear and conventional levels.
2. To expedite the integration of Asian socialist countries into the world economic and political system.
3. To position the United States to take full economic and political advantage of the forthcoming "Pacific Century."

Like the maintenance of a balance of power, integration was in recent years a part of U.S. containment strategy in Asia. But unlike U.S. interests in a balance of power, U.S. interests in integration were deliberately understated. Implicitness was necessary because the articulation of wanting to integrate socialist countries into the international system might well have caused socialist governments to reject integration on nationalist or ideological grounds. But with the fading of the Cold War and the willingness of socialist countries to seek integration with the global system as a means of salvaging their economies, a strategy of explicit integration could be adopted by the United States.

The strategic goal of integration over the next decade would be to integrate peacefully the Asian socialist countries into the global economic and political system. This would be an historic accomplishment, concluding the final chapter of the Cold War.

A strategy of integration is based on the assumption that the post-Cold War era will be one of closer cooperation and coordination between most Asian countries. Integration in this sense is not the elimination of national boundaries, national sovereignty, or national identity. It is growing interdependence and increased cooperation between governments to serve mutual interests. Integration thus recognizes and respects national diversity in Asia.

A strategy of integration would place high premium on political and economic instruments of national power, while not neglecting the utility of U.S. forward deployed military forces in the Western Pacific. To play a leadership role in the Asian Pacific region under a strategy of integration, the United States must become stronger economically and more competitive in international trade in Asia.

To be successful, a strategy of integration would require considerable international cooperation. Alliances such as those presently existing between the United States and Japan and the United States and Australia would be preserved, although their main purpose would change from a primarily defensive mission to one of promoting regional peace and stability. Broadly based cooperative arrangements, such as the several organizations and conferences promoting Pacific

Basin economic cooperation, would be needed to facilitate the process of integration at various levels. International cooperation would also include special arrangements involving selected countries to help resolve "hot spots" such as Cambodia and Korea. To the extent consistent with its own interests, the United States would need to be more supportive of such cooperative endeavors and assume more of a leadership role in their formation and sustainment.

A strategy of integration would be ideally suited to promote U.S. ideological and human rights interests. This is because the world economic system depends on the free market, and there is a strong trend toward democratization in most countries of the world. Because of the close connection between economic growth, a liberal political system, and greater importance attached to individual performance—hence, personal value—a strategy of integration would strongly promote the cause of liberalism in Asia.

A successful strategy of integration would also require a flexible, forward deployed U.S. military presence in Asia with strong power projection and deterrent capabilities. This would be necessary for several reasons. First, the transition from the Cold War to a new historical era may well be a time of instability in certain Asian countries. Second, there remains the remnants of the Soviet nuclear and conventional threat in Northeast Asia. Third, several other threats to U.S. interests in Asia continue to exist. And fourth, the U.S. military presence tends to reduce regional arms races and to promote resolution of international disputes by peaceful means.

The level of U.S. forces deployed in the Western Pacific would be tied to several factors, including (a) the level of threat to U.S. interests; (b) the level of stabilizing influence played by U.S. forward deployed forces; (c) the cost-effectiveness of basing U.S. forces in Asia as opposed to the continental United States; (d) the utility of forward-based forces as perceived by host countries; and (e) budget constraints in Washington. For the short-term, the U.S. force posture in the region under a strategy of integration would remain largely as recommended by the Pentagon in its *Strategic Framework* report.

A strategy of integration would also fit well with the major factors contributing to the U.S. success in the Persian Gulf War. These included the unique role of U.S. power projection capabilities, strong international political backing for the U.S. war effort, and substantial foreign economic assistance to help pay the costs of the war and its aftermath.

A strategy of integration would require a powerful forward deployed military force to protect U.S. interests in Asia. No other country can provide these forces. A strategy of integration recognizes the necessity of these U.S. forces and provides a justification for their continued presence to both host countries and to Americans.

A strategy of integration would be based on international cooperation. It would seek to strengthen and broaden areas of international cooperation and coordination. At the same time, however, a strategy of integration would be flexible in its timetable and framework. No country in Asia would be forced into an unwanted role or relationship. The fundamental purpose of a strategy of integration would be to serve mutual interests in national prosperity and international peace.

A strategy of integration would give the United States not only the moral justification but also the political muscle to request a more equitable contribution to mutual defense in the EAP region. Such a strategy would probably aid in the consensus definition of Japan's defensive role. Likewise, the various roles played by other Asian countries could be discussed and hopefully rationalized to meet legitimate self-defense needs.

Although the Bush administration did not call its post-containment strategy in Asia one of "integration," there was strong evidence that such a strategy was in fact being adopted—at least in part. As mentioned previously, Assistant Secretary of State Richard Solomon described the Bush security policy toward Asia as "integration in economics" and "diversity in defense." These terms and the arguments found in the *Strategic Framework* study suggested that, while the Bush administration had not found an appropriate name for its new strategy in Asia, it would be characterized by integration in the area of economics (and to some extent in politics) and balance of power in the area of security. Both are essential to protect U.S. interests in the Asian Pacific Rim over the next decade. Maintaining a balance of power in Asia is a traditional U.S. strategy that should be continued. Integration is an emerging U.S. strategy that needs to be more fully explored and developed.

Notes

1. President George Bush in Preface to "National Security Strategy of the United States" (Washington, D.C.: The White House, March 1990).

2. George Bush, "Security Strategy for the 1990s," *Department of State Current Policy*, No. 1178 (May 1989). The President's remarks were presented at the graduation ceremony of the Coast Guard Academy in New London, Connecticut, May 24, 1989.

3. The text of Bush's statement to the Joint Session of Congress can be found in *New York Times*, September 12, 1990, p. A20. In his March 6, 1991, address to a Joint Session of Congress at the conclusion of the Persian Gulf

War, Bush said he saw the war as the first test for the "new world order...in which freedom and respect for human rights find a home among all nations." See his speech in the *Washington Post,* March 7, 1991, p. A32.

4. The following discussion is taken from Richard H. Solomon, "Sustaining the Dynamic Balance in East Asia and the Pacific," *Department of State Current Policy,* No. 1255 (February 1990). Solomon was Assistant Secretary of State for East Asian and Pacific Affairs.

5. Richard H. Solomon, "Asian Security in the 1990s: Integration in Economics, Diversity in Defense," *Department of State Dispatch,* 1, 10 (November 5, 1990).

6. *A Strategic Framework for the Asian Pacific Rim: Looking Toward the 21st Century* (Washington, D.C.: Office of the Assistant Secretary of Defense for International Security Affairs, April 1990). The report was a requirement contained in the FY 1990 Defense Authorization Act. Henceforth referred to as *A Strategic Framework.*

7. *A Strategic Framework,* p. 5.

8. See "Statement of Paul Wolfowitz, Under Secretary of Defense for Policy before the Senate Armed Services Committee," April 19, 1990, pp. 8–9, ms.

9. *A Strategic Framework,* p. 5.

10. Assistant Secretary of State Richard Solomon said, "a real or perceived U.S. reluctance to play the role of regional balancer, honest broker, and arbiter would be inherently destabilizing." See Solomon, "Asian Security in the 1990s: Integration in Economics, Diversity in Defense," p. 4.

11. *A Strategic Framework,* p. 5.

12. *Ibid.,* p. 2 .

13. In February 1991 the Department of Defense sent a follow-up report to the Congress stating that the *Strategic Framework* study had been well-received by Asian nations and was being implemented according to schedule. See *A Strategic Framework for the Asian Pacific Rim: Looking Toward the 21st Century: A Report to Congress* (Washington, D.C.: Department of Defense, February 28, 1991).

14. CNN live coverage of a press conference at the White House in Washington, D.C., March 1, 1991.

15. *Washington Post,* March 3, 1991, p. A31.

16. *New York Times,* August 16, 1991, p. D2.

17. See Richard H. Solomon, "The Persian Gulf Crisis: East Asian Efforts and Effects," *Department of State Dispatch,* 1, 5 (October 1, 1990).

18. In January 1991 the United States and Japan signed a new five-year host-nation-support agreement whereby Tokyo will pay $17 billion to support U.S. troops stationed in Japan. That is the most generous of any nation. By 1995 Japan will pay 53 percent of the total cost of U.S. forces in that country.

19. George Bush, "Address by the President on the State of the Union," The White House Office of the Press Secretary, January 29, 1991.

20. George Bush, "Address by the President to the Air University," The White House Office of the Press Secretary, April 13, 1991.

21. *Washington Post,* June 11, 1991, p. A14; *ibid.,* June 13, 1991, p. A36.

22. See Gary Milhollin and Gerald White, "A New China Syndrome: Beijing's Atomic Bazaar," *Washington Post,* May 12, 1991, p. C1.

23. Richard H. Solomon, "China and MFN: Engagement, Not Isolation, Is Catalyst for Change," *Department of State Current Policy,* No. 1282 (June 1990).

24. "Remarks by the President in Commencement Address to Yale University," The White House, Office of the Press Secretary (Kennebunkport, Maine), May 27, 1991.

25. Chinese scholars have written fairly extensively on Beijing's view of the new international order. See, for example, Han Xu, "New World Order: A Chinese Perspective," *Beijing Review,* September 9–15, 1991, pp. 31–34; Qian Qichen, "Establishing a Just and Equitable New International Order," *Beijing Review,* October 7–13, 1991, pp. 11–16; and Pan Tongwen, "New World Order—According to Mr. Bush," *Beijing Review,* October 28–November 3, 1991, pp. 12–14.

26. George Bush, "Security Strategy for the 1990s," p. 2.

7

U.S. Interests in the Republic of China

U.S. interests in the Republic of China have evolved considerably over the past few decades. In the 1920s, when the United States first recognized the Republic of China, Washington hoped that the ROC would be able to unify mainland China and stabilize the country. The territorial integrity and stability of China were in U.S. interests from a balance of power perspective to counter Japanese hegemony and from the perspective of trade.

In the late 1930s and early 1940s the ROC became important to the United States in its military confrontation with Japan. China's role in absorbing the attention of vast numbers of Japanese soldiers and equipment eased the Allied war effort in both Europe and Asia. In the process, the ROC suffered nearly twelve million civilian and military casualties.

Following World War II until the collapse of the Nationalist effort on the mainland, the United States hoped that the ROC would be able to resolve its differences with the Chinese Communist Party (CCP) in order to unify China and repair the devastated Chinese economy. For a brief period between 1948 and June 1950, the Truman administration concluded that few U.S. interests would be harmed by the elimination of the Nationalist government. From the outbreak of the Korean War until the late 1960s, however, the United States considered the ROC on Taiwan to be an important link in the strategy of containment in Asia.

The relative importance of the ROC to U.S. interests declined throughout the 1970s and 1980s, as Washington attached higher priority to its relations with the PRC to counter the Soviet Union. To some in the United States, the ROC became an embarrassment, an attitude reflected by one senior official from the Carter administration, who wrote:

> The strategic relationship with China, not Taiwan, is the main issue, with global and historic importance. That it has been submerged under the Taiwan issue only illustrates anew that trivia can command center stage while great issues wait in the wings.[1]

As long as a strategic alliance with the PRC was possible against the Soviet Union, the United States was willing to progressively downgrade its relations with the ROC. However, Beijing's determination after the August 1982 communiqué to improve relations with Moscow reduced China's strategic value to Washington. As U.S. strategic interests in China declined, so did U.S. incentives to make concessions over Taiwan. During the 1983–1991 period of the Reagan and Bush administrations, the United States sought to preserve its interests in both Chinas through a carefully balanced "dual track" policy of maintaining friendly official ties with Beijing and friendly unofficial ties with Taipei.

During the latter half of the 1980s, internal developments in both Chinas and changes in the international system began to have an effect on U.S. interests in Taiwan. Beginning around 1986, Taipei started to make tremendous progress in liberalizing its economic and political systems. These reforms resulted in the "new" Taiwan described in the first part of this book. These internal developments on Taiwan and the ROC's more pragmatic foreign policy were well received by the U.S. government.

At the same time, the PRC began to experience difficulties in several areas of its reform program. The Tiananmen Square incident in June 1989 was a major setback to U.S. interests, as was Beijing's retreat into more conservative political, economic, and social policies. These developments on the mainland were viewed with great concern by the United States, although American interests in maintaining contact with the PRC were not negated.

International developments in the latter part of the 1980s and early 1990s also had an important impact on U.S. interests in Taiwan. The end of the Cold War and the collapse of communism in most countries of the world produced systemic changes that made developments on Taiwan appear to be more in harmony with international change than did developments on the mainland.

This chapter will examine U.S. interests in the "new" Taiwan, especially in the early 1990s. For the most part, the analysis will use U.S. interests as defined by the Bush administration. The chapter will conclude with speculation on how U.S. interests might be affected under various scenarios for Taiwan's future.

U.S. Interests Defined

U.S. interests derive from fundamental values held by the American people.[2] These values include human dignity, personal freedom, individual rights, and the pursuit of happiness, peace and prosperity. As a reflection of these values, the United States promotes an

international order characterized by self-determination, democratic institutions, economic development through private property and free
enterprise, and respect for basic human rights. The goal of U.S. foreign
policy is to foster the emergence of independent centers of democratic
power, especially in Europe and Asia. Since World War II, the United
States has assumed the primary responsibility for maintaining the
international balance of power.

According to the formulation of the Bush administration, the major
interests and objectives of the United States in 1991 were, first, the
survival of the United States as a free and independent nation, with
its fundamental values intact and its institutions and people secure.
Principle objectives serving this interest were said to include:

- the deterrence of any aggression that could threaten the
  security of the United States and its allies; and defeat of the
  aggressor should deterrence fail on terms favorable to the
  United States and its allies

- effectively counter threats to the United States, its citizens,
  and interests short of armed conflict, such as terrorism

- improve stability by pursuing equitable and verifiable arms
  control agreements, modernizing the U.S. strategic deterrent,
  developing anti-ballistic missile systems, and enhancing
  conventional military capabilities

- promote democratic change in the Soviet Union, while
  discouraging new temptations for military advantage

- foster restraint in military spending and discourage military
  adventurism

- prevent the transfer of advanced military technologies and
  resources to hostile countries, especially chemical, biological
  and nuclear weapons and high-technology means of delivery

- reduce the flow of illegal drugs into the United States.

A second fundamental interest was a healthy and growing U.S.
economy to ensure opportunity for individual prosperity and resources
for national endeavors at home and abroad. Objectives to serve this
interest included:

- promote a strong, prosperous and competitive U.S. economy

- ensure access to foreign markets, energy, mineral resources,
  the oceans and space

- promote an open and expanding international economic system, based on market principles, with minimal distortions to trade and investment, stable currencies, and broadly respected rules for managing and resolving economic disputes .

- achieve cooperative international solutions to key environmental challenges.

A third U.S. interest was the maintenance of healthy, cooperative and politically vigorous relations with allies and friendly nations. U.S. objectives serving this interest included:

- strengthen and enlarge the commonwealth of free nations that share a commitment to democracy and individual rights

- establish a more balanced partnership with U.S. allies and a greater sharing of global leadership and responsibilities

- strengthen international institutions like the United Nations to make them more effective in promoting peace, world order and political, economic, and social progress

- support Western Europe's greater economic, political, and security unity, and nurture a closer relationship with the European Community

- work with North Atlantic allies to help bring about reconciliation, security and democracy throughout Europe.

A fourth interest was in a stable and secure world, where political and economic freedom, human rights, and democratic institutions flourish. Objectives to serve this interest included:

- maintain stable regional military balances to deter powers that might seek regional dominance

- promote diplomatic solutions to regional disputes

- promote the growth of free and democratic political institutions as the best guarantors of both human rights and economic and social progress

- aid in combatting threats to democratic institutions from aggression, coercion, insurgencies, subversion, terrorism and illicit drug trafficking

- support aid, trade and investment policies that promote economic development and social and political progress.

After 1989–1990, the principal threat to the United States shifted from a global conflict with the Soviet Union to diverse and usually unrelated crises in various regions of the world. U.S. strategy correspondingly changed from countering the global challenge posed by the Soviet Union to responding to threats in major regions, with highest priority being assigned to Europe, Southwest Asia, and East Asia. Europe remained the central strategic arena for the United States, but relations with Japan assumed global strategic importance as well.

In terms of U.S. regional interests, East Asia and the Pacific assumed great importance to the United States because the region was home to many of the world's most dynamic societies and also home to most of the remaining communist regimes.

As defined in the *Strategic Framework* report previously reviewed, U.S. regional interests in Asia were:

- protecting the United States from attack
- supporting the U.S. global deterrence policy
- preserving the U.S. political and economic access to the region
- maintaining the balance of power to prevent the rise of any regional hegemony
- strengthening the Western orientation of the Asian nations
- fostering the growth of democracy and human rights
- deterring nuclear proliferation
- ensuring freedom of navigation.

In regards to U.S. interests in China and Taiwan, the Bush administration stressed the importance of maintaining close ties with China, even though the United States assumed the PRC was moving toward major systemic change. Consultation and contact were thought useful to prevent PRC isolation and repression of the Chinese people. In the August 1991 statement of U.S. national security strategy, however, China's position was noticeably reduced in importance from previous years, while Taiwan was mentioned for the first time. The statement noted that the United States "maintains strong, unofficial, substantive relations with Taiwan where rapid economic and political change is underway." The statement went on to say that one of the goals of the United States was "to foster an environment in which Taiwan and the People's Republic of China can pursue a constructive and peaceful interchange across the Taiwan Strait."[3]

Another important statement of U.S. interests in the Western Pacific and in Taiwan which retained its relevancy in 1991 was the Taiwan Relations Act (TRA). According to the TRA, U.S. security, political, and economic interests were served by peace and stability in the Western Pacific region. The TRA linked these regional U.S. interests with a peaceful solution to the Taiwan issue. The TRA made clear that any attempt by the PRC to determine the future of Taiwan by force would be a threat to U.S. security interests in the Western Pacific.

In addition to national security, the TRA referenced other U.S. interests in Taiwan. Section 2(c) stated that the United States maintained an interest in the human rights situation on Taiwan. Sections 4 through 7 and 9 through 14 contained detailed provisions ensuring that U.S. political and economic interests in Taiwan would not be harmed because of Washington's lack of formal diplomatic ties with Taipei.

As a reflection of its political, economic, and security interests in the Pacific, the United States maintains a strong military presence in the region. According to General Colin Powell's testimony before the House Appropriations Committee on September 25, 1991, the Pacific is essentially an maritime theater, necessitating strong U.S. naval capabilities backed by air and ground forces to ensure deterrence and immediate response to crises.[4] The Chairman of the Joint Chiefs of Staff described the Asian Pacific region as an economy of force theater in which the United States would deploy the following forces:

- The Army's Second Division headquarters would remain in Korea, along with one or two tactical fighter wings.
- Japan would be the home port of one carrier battle group, one amphibious readiness group, a Marine Expeditionary Force, and one or two tactical fighter wings.

These minimal forward deployed forces would be backed by a substantial base force ready to respond to regional crisis. Crisis response forces in the Pacific would include:

- More than one Army Division and a tactical fighter wing based in Hawaii and Alaska.
- Five carrier battle groups based on the U.S. West Coast allowing for constant rotation in the Western Pacific.

Powell stated that in FY 1991, the Navy had a total of 15 aircraft carriers and some 536 ships. By FY 1995, these would be reduced by 25 percent to 12 aircraft carriers and 448 ships. According to the 1991 Defense Report submitted to the Congress, the Pacific fleet assignments in 1995 would be:

- the Seventh Fleet in the Western Pacific and Indian Ocean, comprised of four carrier battle groups, two amphibious ready groups, and four underway replenishment groups

- the Third Fleet in the Eastern Pacific, comprised of two carrier battle groups and one underway replenishment group.[5]

Thus, by 1995 half of the U.S. aircraft carrier battle groups and underway replenishment groups would be assigned to the Pacific, as well as two-thirds of the U.S. amphibious ready groups—a substantial military commitment reflecting U.S. interests in the Asian Pacific Rim.

U.S. Interests in Peace
in the Taiwan Strait

One of the best ways to understand U.S. interests in a peaceful resolution of the Taiwan issue is to consider how those interests might be harmed if the PRC attacked Taiwan.

First, a PRC use of force against the ROC would undermine peace and stability in East Asia. The preservation of regional peace and stability is important to the United States because trade, prosperity, peaceful political evolution, and crisis management in Asia are made possible by such an environment. War in the Taiwan Strait would likely cause adverse economic and political conditions elsewhere in the region.

Second, a PRC attack against Taiwan might draw the United States into a military conflict with China, something both Washington and Beijing have tried to avoid since the Korean War. The consequences of a Sino-American military confrontation in East Asia would be extremely serious, especially if either of the two sides determined to use the conflict to re-order the East Asian balance of power in ways more favorable to itself and at the expense of the other.

Third, a PRC attack on Taiwan would dramatically increase tension throughout the region. Neighboring states would view Beijing as much more threatening to their own security. Japan might speed up the expansion of its power projection forces. A regional arms race, already underway in 1991–1992, might escalate to dangerous levels. The shift in the regional balance of power would probably require difficult adjustments in U.S. policy toward East and Southeast Asia.

Fourth, a PRC use of force against Taiwan would harm U.S. trade, investment, and other commercial interests in the region. Sea lanes around Taiwan would be imperiled, major ports on both Taiwan and China would be closed, petroleum imports into Japan and Korea would have to be rerouted, and neutral ships might be damaged.

Fifth, a Chinese attack would have serious and unpredictable effects on the people of Taiwan. A strong movement toward Taiwan independence might develop; social stability would be adversely affected; investment capital and talented individuals would take flight; panic might reign in the streets as families tried to hoard food and other necessities; civil strife might occur. Under these conditions, the delicate mainlander-Taiwanese relationship on the island might disintegrate with severe social repercussions.

The U.S. Response to a PRC Military Threat

The likely U.S. response to a PRC use of force against Taiwan would be of far-reaching consequence to Sino-American relations.[6] Initially, there might be a tendency within the U.S. government to look at the causes of the PRC decision to use force. Was it provoked by Taipei, such as a move toward independence, or was it unprovoked aggression? The United States would probably condition its initial response to the specific circumstances of the crisis. However, a PRC attack against Taiwan would probably swing American public opinion solidly behind Taipei. From the point of view of Congress, such PRC action would immediately call into operation the security provisions of the Taiwan Relations Act (TRA).

It is unlikely such a crisis would catch Washington by surprise. Because of U.S. interests in a peaceful resolution of the Taiwan issue, the United States closely watches military developments in the Taiwan Strait. The United States would probably perceive PRC preparations to use force fairly early, especially if large-scale PLA operations were planned. Having detected these preparations, the United States would send very clear messages to Beijing that should the PRC change its policy of peaceful reunification, Washington might change its position on the August 17 communiqué. It would be noted that the entire process of normalization of Sino-American relations has been predicated on a peaceful resolution of the Taiwan issue.

Since the United States wants to avoid a military confrontation with the PRC, Washington's efforts would first of all concentrate on political and economic pressures to dissuade Beijing from pursuing a military option. If these failed and the PRC demonstrated its intention to actually use force against Taiwan, then the United States would seek to increase the costs to Beijing in a significant way. There is a wide range of actions the United States could take in this respect, such as public condemnation of the PRC, efforts to forge an international coalition to impose political and economic sanctions against Beijing, and restrictions placed on PRC exports to the United States.

In addition, Washington would no doubt step up arms sales and defense technology transfers to Taipei. These would be designed to ensure that the ROC would be able to defend itself. As the threat to Taiwan's security increased, the need to supply Taipei with more advanced defensive equipment would increase as well. If, as the situation developed, Taipei proved unable by itself to deter a PRC attack or to defeat the PLA, then the United States might consider more active involvement in the crisis.

U.S. armed forces are capable of a vast array of supporting activities which would multiply the defensive capabilities of Taiwan while minimizing risk to American service personnel. These activities include escorting ROC convoys off Taiwan's east coast, deployment of AWACS and ASW platforms to help ROC air defense and anti-submarine efforts, and stationing one or more aircraft carrier battle groups off Taiwan as a demonstration of U.S. concern and resolve. If the PRC attacked U.S. forces, the United States would destroy the offending PLA units and prepare for wider involvement in the conflict.

Other U.S. Interests in Taiwan

Preserving peace in the Taiwan Strait is a fundamental, long-term U.S. interest, but the United States has other interests in Taiwan as well.

Geopolitical Interests

Taiwan has lasting geostrategic value because of its location astride the Taiwan Strait and Bashi Channel, two key sea lines of communications linking Northeast Asia with Southeast Asia and the Middle East. Having a friendly government in Taipei serves U.S. interests in keeping these sea lanes open. Japan views Taiwan as essential to the security of its southern flank, and the Philippines considers Taiwan important for the security of Luzon. Taipei has offered the use of its military facilities to the United States should it be necessary in a regional crisis. Having Taiwan as a potential base of operations in the

Western Pacific is a strategic asset U.S. military planners find compelling.

Second, U.S. credibility in Asia is strengthened by American ties to Taiwan. The strength of the U.S. commitment to Taiwan convinces other U.S. friends in the region that Washington intends to remain in East Asia and that its commitments can be counted on. U.S. credibility is especially important at this time because of concerns over declining U.S. power and the reduction of U.S. military forces in the region.

Third, U.S. balance of power interests are served by a strong Taiwan. Other Asian nations do not want to see China reunited under the communists, since it is apt to be hegemonic. Also, the noncommunist nations of Asia would prefer to see a democratic Taiwan remain as a potential model for China's future development.

In addition to these strategic concerns, the United States has substantial interests in the political, economic, foreign, and national security policies adopted by the "new" Taiwan in recent years.

Democratization and Liberalization

The dominant political trends on Taiwan are democratization and liberalization. These trends are clearly in the U.S. interests, although the decisions reached by the people of Taiwan through democratic means may not always please the United States. For example, the majority of the Taiwan people may decide at some time in the future that they want to be an independent nation, completely separate from mainland China. Depending upon conditions prevailing at the time, such a decision might place the United States in the awkward position of having to choose between respect for Taiwan's self-determination and friendly ties with the PRC.

U.S. interests in democracy have been served by the emergence of meaningful opposition parties to the KMT. Thus far, however, the DPP has been a mixed blessing in this regard. The DPP has been responsible for many needed political reforms, but it often does not follow democratic rules in pressing its demands. Democracy cannot work in an environment of political chaos. How the opposition parties handle themselves is of concern to the United States, because their behavior will strongly influence the future of democracy on Taiwan.

Economic Policies

Most economic trends on Taiwan are also in the U.S. interest, especially at the level of ROC government policy. Taiwan is liberalizing its domestic economic system, privatizing most state-owned enterprises, demonstrating greater concern for the protection of the environment, and becoming a more advanced industrialized nation. Internationally, Taipei is removing most tariff and non-tariff trade barriers; negotiating in good faith with American and other trading partners to establish an equitable, balanced trading system; encouraging foreign investment on Taiwan and Taiwan investment abroad; broadening participation by foreign firms in the domestic service sector of the ROC economy; and appreciating the New Taiwan Dollar to bring it into alignment with its true value. U.S. global interests in the expansion of free enterprise and fair trade are also furthered as Taiwan's economy becomes a model for other developing countries.

Another way in which Taiwan supports U.S. interests is assisting mainland China to develop its market economy. Taiwan is one of the largest sources of trade, investment, and foreign exchange for the PRC. These financial contributions to the modernization of China, coupled with the establishment of many Taiwan-owned or managed factories on the mainland, are helping southern and eastern coastal areas to develop rapidly. There is reason to believe that these market-oriented regions constantly lobby the PRC central government to moderate its economic, political, and social policies.

Although relatively modest in size, Taipei's foreign assistance program also serves U.S. interests. In most cases, the ROC extends its economic assistance to nations in Latin America, the Philippines, and other ASEAN states. Taipei's contribution of $30 million to countries adversely affected by the Persian Gulf War has already been mentioned. Taiwan also provides a considerable amount of assistance to Eastern European countries and newly independent republics from the Soviet Union to help these nations make the transition from a planned to a market economy.

The ROC's Six-Year National Development Plan provides many opportunities for American businessmen. A sizeable percentage of the $303 billion plan to restructure Taiwan's economy is open to U.S. bids. Moreover, as reflected in discussions over the sale of F-16s to Taiwan in mid-1992, a more direct benefit to the U.S. economy is Taipei's purchase of big-ticket items, such as aircraft, which keep U.S. production lines open and Americans on jobs that would otherwise be lost.

Like other countries, Taiwan's economy has significant problems. In 1991–1992, for example, Taiwan businessmen often complained about an acute labor shortage, overly stringent environmental protection requirements for plants, rising wages, problems in acquiring new industrial land, reluctance of local investors to put capital into research and development for high-tech industries, and restrictive government regulations regarding business with the mainland.

Issues of concern to the United States included copyright protection and a persistent trade imbalance. Taipei gave high priority to finding an acceptable solution to these problems, however, and differences over these issues were greatly narrowed through 1992.

Another problem area is that Taiwan's "dollar diplomacy" has made the PRC nervous. Beijing is not pleased with Taiwan's use of its economic strength to increase its international presence. The PRC has warned the United States and other countries not to go too far in allowing Taipei to participate in the international community. The impact of this issue on U.S. interests was seen in the 1990–1991 debate over whether Washington should support Taiwan's entrance into GATT and whether China should be given another year of unconditional MFN. As it turned out, Congress and the administration sought to balance both sets of U.S. interests by supporting Taiwan's participation in GATT and extending MFN to China. The interplay between these two sets of interests will probably increase in complexity in the future as Taiwan becomes stronger economically and attempts to gain entrance into more international economic organizations.

Foreign Policies

Taipei's flexible diplomacy furthers U.S. interests in several ways but also makes Washington's efforts to maintain good relations with Beijing more difficult. On the positive side, flexible diplomacy brings Taiwan's foreign policies into greater harmony with pragmatic trends in global politics. Taiwan's wider participation in the international community makes the international political and economic systems more efficient. Moreover, Taiwan's more open policy toward mainland China helps to reduce tensions in East Asia and to moderate PRC behavior.

There are some negative aspects of Taiwan's flexible diplomacy from the point of view of U.S. interests in maintaining a stable, friendly relationship with the PRC. Beijing has become irritated at Taipei's diplomatic success, believing it undermines the PRC strategy of isolating the ROC from the international community. Beijing sees flexible diplomacy as prolonging the process of reunification and increasing the possibility of "two Chinas" or "one China, one Taiwan."

To counter flexible diplomacy, the PRC has assumed a diplomatic offensive of its own, steadily reducing the number of important countries maintaining official ties with Taipei. With the termination of diplomatic relations between the ROC and Republic of Korea (ROK) in August 1992, Taiwan no longer retained official relations with any country in Asia. Taipei's diplomatic success in gaining the recognition of countries like Niger could not compensate for the loss of allies such as the ROK or Saudi Arabia.

Taiwan's flexible diplomacy has caused Beijing to make Taiwan an issue in several bilateral relationships, including Sino-American relations. Beijing characterized the U.S. decision to support Taiwan's participation in GATT as interference in China's internal affairs and as contributing to "two Chinas" or "one China, one Taiwan."

Flexible diplomacy may increase the probability of a U.S.-PRC confrontation over Taiwan. On the other hand, Taiwan's wider participation in the international community is justified on pragmatic grounds. It is in the U.S. interest to draw a major trading partner like Taiwan into the framework governing international trade.

By reversing a process of diplomatic isolation, flexible diplomacy has increased self-confidence on Taiwan, strengthened social stability, and attracted foreign investment. At the same time, however, Taipei's partial diplomatic success has encouraged those calling for Taiwan independence. Their confrontational style of politics has contributed to social division on Taiwan and may have increased the possibility of PRC military intervention.

From the U.S. point of view, the most positive result of flexible diplomacy has been Taipei's rapidly expanding contact across the Taiwan Strait. As specifically noted in the 1991 statement of U.S. national security strategy, the United States favors such contact. Washington believes cross-Strait exchanges reduce tensions between the two Chinese sides, help to moderate policies in Beijing, and make more manageable the Taiwan issue in Sino-American relations.

Security Policy

ROC security policies since 1987 have furthered U.S. interests in at least three ways. First, increased contact across the Taiwan Strait has given Beijing reason to believe that reunification may eventually come through peaceful means. This perception has reduced incentives for the PRC to use force in the Taiwan Strait.

Second, Taipei contributes to regional peace and stability by maintaining a strong deterrence in the Taiwan Strait. Taiwan helps to ensure local freedom of the seas, attempts to be operationally congruent with U.S. forces in the Pacific, has offered the use of its military facilities to the United States in the event of a regional emergency, and willingly contributes to international peace-keeping missions.

Third, the development of Taiwan's indigenous defense industry has reduced the need for many U.S. weapons sales. This has given the

United States an opportunity to be supportive of Taiwan through technology transfers and sale of design packages and components, yet circumspect in its relations with the PRC.

The International System

The international system in Asia has changed in ways that have made the "new" Taiwan more important to U.S. interests. ROC policies allow Taiwan to participate effectively in an interdependent, multipolar world, trends which the United States supports on a global scale.

Under conditions of superpower rivalry in the Cold War, it was thought mandatory that the United States limit its relations with Taiwan in order to protect American strategic interests with Beijing. This perception meant that China's real or imagined reactions weighed heavily in Washington's calculations of its policies toward Taipei. Now that the Cold War has ended, these limitations on U.S. relations with Taiwan may be discarded. A new calculus must be devised which weighs the relative value of Beijing and Taipei to U.S. interests.

The end of the Cold War has had another impact on American interests in Taiwan. A sharply reduced Soviet threat means that U.S. world leadership is based less on American military power and more on its political and economic strength. In these areas of national power, the United States faces stiff competition from other major powers, including Japan and China. To maximize its influence, Washington needs to cooperate with friendly countries to pursue common objectives.

In this regard Taiwan can contribute to U.S. interests in several ways. First, both countries want to open the Japanese market and to see U.S. commercial activities in Asia competitive with those of Japan. Second, both countries want China to continue its political and economic reform and to pursue peaceful regional policies, including greater openness to the West. And third, both countries want to see the expansion of free enterprise, free trade, and democracy in Asia.

The United States can depend upon friendly relations with Taipei, because it is in Taiwan's interests to sustain a special relationship with Washington. Taiwan will be receptive to many American suggestions, such as financially assisting the Philippines, helping to moderate policies on the mainland, and pressuring Japan to further open its markets and buy more foreign products.

The unexpected collapse of communism in the Soviet Union in August 1991 created yet another incentive for the United States to be supportive of developments on Taiwan. Unlike the Soviet Union, the Chinese Communist Party has not allowed the emergence of a rival political figure, such as Boris Yeltsin, around which the Chinese people can rally in a time of crisis. Moreover, the CCP does not allow rival political parties. Hence, the "Taiwan Experience" is one of the few alternative models to socialism which exists for the modernization of China.

Bush Foreign Policy Operating Principles and Taiwan

The previous chapter identified several operating principles which seemed to guide President Bush's foreign policy in the early 1990s. Many of these parallel closely policies being pursued by Taiwan.

First, the United States under Bush supported wider economic integration in East Asia through consensus among Pacific Rim countries. Taiwan's policies through 1991 were supportive of this goal. Taipei played an important role in the economic growth of the region, worked to internationalize its own economy, and sought to participate in a constructive way in regional and global economic organizations.

Second, the Bush administration believed that nations should cooperate to solve specific problems through peaceful means. Taiwan demonstrated its agreement with this principle through its formal ending of the state of war between itself and mainland China in May 1991.

Third, the United States believed the use of force was justified at times to resist hegemony and to restore international balance and stability. Generally speaking, Taipei has been very supportive of U.S. military operations, as demonstrated in the Korean, Vietnam, and Persian Gulf wars.

Fourth, the Bush administration sought to expand democracy and free enterprise to create a growing community of democratic nations. This principle included the encouragement of peaceful change in authoritarian states such as the PRC, North Korea, and Vietnam. The ROC also holds democracy and free enterprise as national values; these were principles Taipei incorporated in its domestic and foreign policies in the early 1990s. Taiwan's support of peaceful change in the PRC and in other socialist countries could be seen in ROC trade, investment, and even foreign assistance program policies.

Fifth, the United States was willing to play a leadership role in bringing about the new world order, while working in a non-ideological, pragmatic way with all countries to realize this goal. Taiwan has traditionally supported the United States in its role as world leader. Moreover, Taiwan's flexible diplomacy is based on a willingness to work with all states, including former communist adversaries, to help stabilize the international system.

U.S. Interests in Taiwan's Alternative Futures

Because of Taiwan's unique diplomatic status and uncertain relationship with mainland China, there are several alternative futures for Taiwan which should be noted: a continuation of the status quo, peaceful reunification, unification by force, Taiwan independence, or political instability. U.S. interests in these alternative futures are discussed in the following paragraphs.

Maintenance of the Status Quo

Under conditions prevailing through the early 1990s, U.S. interests were well served by the status quo in the Taiwan Strait. In this context, status quo means a de facto separation of Taiwan and the mainland into two distinct areas and governments with which the United States maintains a separate relationship. Indeed, a central element of U.S. policy toward the Taiwan issue from 1950 through 1991 was to preserve the status quo until such time as a peaceful resolution of differences between Taipei and Beijing could occur.

If the status quo holds for the remainder of this century, Taiwan's political and economic systems and its foreign policies will likely continue along current lines. The ROC will probably expand its contacts with the mainland on the basis of mutual benefit and necessity. The status quo scenario assumes that Washington will maintain its "dual-track" China policy, maintaining friendly relations with Taiwan but not at the expense of undermining Sino-American relations.

Although the status quo is in fact constantly evolving, a continuation of this scenario over the next decade would seem to give Washington the best of two worlds: formal relations with the PRC and substantive relations with Taiwan. As long as peace is maintained in the Taiwan Strait and a "dual track" U.S. China policy can be pursued, U.S. interests are served by the status quo.

Peaceful Reunification

Under this scenario, Taipei and Beijing would work out their differences over the next five to ten years and agree upon conditions for unification, perhaps along the lines of "one country, one nation, two systems, and two governments" (a North Korean formula for Korean unification which the PRC supports).

If the United States could continue its substantive relationship with Taiwan, benefit from the removal of the Taiwan issue from Sino-

American relations, be assured that the people of Taiwan and their lifestyle would not be harmed, and see moderate policies take permanent hold on the mainland, then peaceful reunification would not be against U.S. interests.

The difficulty is the uncertainty involved with this scenario. Given the relative power of Beijing and Taipei, reunification is likely to be on PRC terms. Beijing would no doubt want to reduce U.S. political influence in Taiwan, although the PRC might not deliberately harm U.S. economic interests.

But Beijing could pursue policies highly detrimental to U.S. interests. For example, despite their promises not to intervene in Taiwan affairs, PRC leaders could do so, especially if they feared a Taiwanese uprising or island-wide protest movement. The PRC could also impose socialism on Taiwan much more rapidly than promised. Under these circumstances, the United States would see not only its influence diminish, but also its political, economic, and human rights interests harmed. Once peaceful unification occurs, the United States would have little moral or legal authority to intervene on behalf of the Taiwan people.

If reunification did turn out badly for Taiwan, there would be criticism that the United States had "lost another China." Accusations of responsibility would fly in Washington, and there might be major repercussions in American politics. Thus, the risks for the United States in actively supporting peaceful reunification are great enough to warrant skepticism about this scenario.

Unification by Force

As indicated earlier, U.S. interests would be harmed by a PRC use of force to resolve the Taiwan issue. The Taiwan issue is sensitive in American politics, so pressure in Washington to intervene on Taiwan's behalf would be difficult for any administration to ignore. Once the initial step of military involvement was taken, it would be hard to avoid a "slippery slope" situation in which the United States would be progressively drawn into the conflict—especially if Beijing was determined to press its military objectives.

If the PRC did achieve reunification through force, the United States would have to recalibrate its interests in China and Taiwan. Much would depend upon policies adopted by Beijing. For example, U.S. economic and human rights interests would be severely harmed if the PRC appropriated U.S. property, made it difficult for Taiwan to continue trading with the United States, or abused the Taiwanese population. On the other hand, these U.S. interests might not be too greatly harmed if Beijing protected U.S. property and investments in

Taiwan, encouraged trade with the United States, and did not oppress the Taiwan people.

The probability of damage being done to U.S. interests is far higher than the likelihood of damage not being done, however. For this reason alone, the United States since June 1950 has consistently adopted policies designed to discourage Beijing from using force against Taiwan.

Taiwan Independence

Many American analysts view Taiwan independence as being against U.S. interests, because a move in that direction could trigger a PRC military response. However, this conclusion needs to be reexamined in view of changes that have occurred on both sides of the Taiwan Strait and in the international environment. If the people of Taiwan or their duly elected government wish to pursue independence, why should the United States oppose that decision or refuse to recognize Taiwan's right of self-determination?

This is a highly debatable issue. In the case of the Baltic Republics, the United States did not extend full diplomatic recognition until it was approved by Moscow. The most important U.S. interest was to maintain good relations with the Soviet Union and to prevent instability in the USSR, not to recognize Baltic self-determination. After the Soviet Union collapsed, however, the United States was free to extend diplomatic recognition to various parts of the former Soviet bloc.

If this experience is taken as a guide, then it can be inferred that if the PRC granted Taiwan its independence, the United States would establish diplomatic relations with Taipei. But, as long as the PRC remains strong and does not grant that independence, it is unlikely Washington will recognize Taiwan as an independent nation. The most important U.S. interest is cooperative relations with a modern China, not recognition of Taiwan's right of self-determination.

Given democratic trends on Taiwan, however, this issue deserves closer analysis. Specifically, Taiwan independence might be against U.S. interests if:

1. a declaration of Taiwan independence led to a PRC attack on Taiwan, involving the United States or at minimum harming its political, economic, and security interests
2. such an attack would lead to long-term antagonistic Sino-American relations
3. such antagonism resulted in a shift in the balance of power in Asia in ways unfavorable to the United States.

On the other hand, Taiwan independence might not be against U.S. interests if:

1. the PRC recognized the independence of Taiwan or allowed it to have formal diplomatic ties with other countries
2. the PRC was already deeply antagonistic to Washington, and the United States cared little for Chinese concerns over Taiwan
3. Beijing was weakened to the point where it could not adversely affect the strategic balance of power in Asia.

In other words, whether or not U.S. interests would be harmed by Taiwan independence is situationally determined. For the foreseeable future, independence would seem to be against U.S. interests in preserving friendly relations with Beijing. However, as events in Eastern Europe and in the Soviet Union have demonstrated, the unthinkable can occur. It is possible, although not likely, that new leaders in Beijing might accept a close federation arrangement with Taiwan, such as that now existing between most of the former Soviet republics, which would allow the United States to upgrade diplomatic relations with Taipei.

Hence, while it remains prudent for the United States not to support Taiwan independence, it is even more prudent to keep all options open in order to respond to changes in the future positions of Beijing and Taipei on this issue. For Washington to attempt to play a leading role in the future of Taiwan is probably the worst of all U.S. policy options.

Political Instability

Another scenario for Taiwan's future is short-term political instability. This could occur under several circumstances, such as irreconcilable differences between the KMT and a strong coalition of opposition parties, a panicked reaction of the Taiwanese people to threats from the PRC, or a severe weakening of the island's economy due to a global economic depression or uncontrolled flight of capital out of the country. U.S. interests would be harmed by instability on Taiwan because of its possible negative repercussions. For example, the PRC might follow through on its warning of intervention should social instability occur, or martial law might be reimposed.

Conclusion

Despite the break in U.S. diplomatic ties with the ROC in 1979, Washington continues to maintain friendly and supportive relations with Taiwan because it is in the U.S. interest to do so. These interests include strategic and security concerns to maintain peace and stability in East Asia, political interests in seeing democracy work on Taiwan, economic interests in maintaining strong U.S.-Taiwan trade and investment ties, and human rights interests in seeing civil liberties continue to improve on the island.

These U.S. foreign policy interests are solidly anchored by U.S. domestic political concerns. In the wake of Tiananmen, any effort to reduce U.S. support for Taiwan, such as curtailing legitimate arms sales or pressuring Taipei to negotiate reunification with the mainland, would undermine the already weakened consensus on U.S.-China policy. As seen in the case of MFN for China, the Congress demanded equal treatment for Taiwan in the form of U.S. support for Taipei's entrance into GATT.

As the "new" Taiwan emerges, U.S. interests in Taiwan will likely increase. This is because trends on Taiwan are in a direction favorable to American interests in the East Asian and Pacific (EAP) region as a whole and in harmony with U.S. efforts to create a new international system. Taiwan's greater military self-reliance and openness toward mainland China are also in the U.S. interest since they tend to strengthen peace in the Taiwan Strait and help to moderate policies in Beijing.

The most difficult challenge posed to U.S. interests by the "new" Taiwan remains, as it has since June 1950, in Taiwan's impact on Sino-American relations. But the prioritization of U.S. interests toward the PRC and toward Taiwan has shifted over the years. Since 1989, this shift in priority has in some ways favored Taipei, although U.S. interests in maintaining official ties with the PRC remain sacrosanct.

But if the most difficult challenge to U.S. interests comes from the unique relationship between Washington, Taipei, and Beijing, so that relationship also provides the greatest asset to U.S. interests. Of all the nations in the world, Taiwan has the best chance to influence the course of modernization in China along lines serving U.S. interests.

It remains a basic U.S. interest that China be stable, prosperous, democratic, and open to the outside world. Taiwan has proven that a Chinese society can have these characteristics and thrive. It is not the U.S. objective to weaken China, nor to separate Taiwan from China. However, the existence of the Taiwan model for Chinese modernization is extremely valuable to U.S. interests.

There are many trends which support the thesis that the Taiwan issue may heat up during the 1990s. From Beijing's point of view, it is a matter of grave concern that global trends toward democratization and free enterprise are on the ascendancy, that communism has collapsed in most countries of the world, that Taiwan is thriving and its model is being given greater credibility as the correct path for China's modernization, that Western nations are selling more advanced weapons to Taiwan, and that Taiwan might be moving in the direction of too much independence and making too much of a comeback in the international community.

The view among current leaders in Beijing is that they must preserve socialism in China at all costs, and that the greatest threat to Chinese socialism is individual freedom. These perceptions may lead to a dangerous confrontation between Beijing, on the one hand, and Taiwan and the United States, on the other. This is especially true in an era, such as presently exists, in which the central Chinese government is beginning to acquire power projection capabilities to reassert China's traditional role as regional hegemon.

Beijing's possible willingness to increase pressure on the Taiwan issue in the 1990s has important policy implications for both Taiwan and the United States. The final chapter of this book will examine those implications and make several policy suggestions as to how Washington might frame its China policy for the remainder of this century.

Notes

1. Richard Holbrooke, "Reagan's Foreign Policy: Steady As She Goes," *Asian Wall Street Journal,* April 8, 1980, p. 4. Holbrooke was President Carter's Assistant Secretary of State responsible for East Asian affairs.

2. The following discussion of basic U.S. values and interests is taken from *National Security Strategy of the United States* (Washington, D.C.: The White House, January 1988, March 1990, and August 1991).

3. *National Security Strategy of the United States,* August 1991, p. 9.

4. Notes taken during C-Span live coverage of Powell's testimony, September 25, 1991.

5. *Annual Report to the President and the Congress* (Washington, D.C.: Office of the Secretary of Defense, January 1991), p. 68.

6. The following is summarized from Parris H. Chang and Martin L. Lasater, eds., *If the PRC Crosses the Taiwan Strait: The International Response* (Lanham, MD: University Press of America, 1993), pp. 178–181.

8

Policy Recommendations and Conclusions

The United States and the "New" Taiwan

Over the years the United States has had to deal with several different kinds of Taiwan.[1] During the 1950s and 1960s, Taipei was a bulwark against communism in Asia. In the 1970s and 1980s Taiwan became an important economic model for development in the Third World. In the late 1980s Taiwan became a strong trading nation with which the United States had an enormous trade deficit. And in the 1990s Taiwan has become a democratic nation seeking a larger international role.

According to American Institute in Taiwan (AIT) director Natale Bellocchi, U.S.-Taiwan relations in the early 1990s were determined by certain factors. These included the cultural and economic ties between the two countries, the fundamental changes taking place in Taiwan's domestic politics and economics, Taiwan's presence in the international community, and its relationship with the PRC.

Cultural and Economic Ties

The amount of interchange between the United States and Taiwan has grown rapidly since the breaking of diplomatic relations in 1979. In 1990, for example, the number of non-immigrant visas for the United States from Taiwan were the third largest in the world (almost 230,000). As many as two percent of the entire population of Taiwan may have travelled to the United States in 1990.

The U.S. cultural impact on Taiwan has been enormous, ranging from the large number of people who speak English, to the clothes people wear and the music they listen to. One of the most popular radio stations on Taiwan is ICRT, an English-language station broadcasting from Taipei and featuring American pop music.

Over 33,500 Taiwan students were in the United States in 1990, one of the largest overseas student populations in the world. More than 90 percent of Taiwan's students attending graduate schools overseas come to the United States. Approximately five percent of all of Taiwan's students of higher education attend American schools. A large percentage of members of the National Assembly and Legislative Yuan are American educated, as are many Taiwan business leaders. In 1990 over half of ROC cabinet officials were educated in the United States, including President Lee Teng-hui.

In spite of the lack of diplomatic relations, the United States and Taiwan have an enormous amount of governmental exchange through their respective representative offices, the American Institute in Taiwan (AIT) and the Coordination Council for North American Affairs (CCNAA). More than forty scientific agreements have been signed between Washington and Taipei since 1979, and the already large number of high-tech joint ventures between the two countries is rapidly growing as the two economies become increasingly interdependent.

The United States is Taiwan's largest trading partner, its largest export market and second largest supplier of imports after Japan. In 1991 Taiwan sold $22.3 billion to the United States and imported $14.1 billion. That equated to about $1,800 worth of trade for each of Taiwan's 20.5 million citizens—one of the largest per capita trade figures in the world.

While trade between the United States and Taiwan remains very large, Taiwan is making significant changes in the nature of its trade toward more service industries, intra-industry trade, and two-way investment flows. During the 1990s, the United States will have an enormous potential stake in Taiwan's Six-Year National Development Plan. The $303 billion plan includes nearly 800 projects, and 15–20 percent of the spending will be foreign procurement. Many aspects of the plan are open to U.S. bids and sale of equipment, although competition from Japan and Europe for these contracts is stiff. The expanding and diverging economic interchange between the United States and Taiwan has created a more competitive market for both countries, along with more complex and wide-ranging issues of contention.

These cultural and economic ties are the cement of the U.S.-Taiwan relationship which have transcended Cold War politics and the changing state of U.S.-PRC relations. Close people-to-people ties are a reality that necessitates efficient and wide-ranging contacts between Washington and Taipei, regardless of the level of officiality of the relationship.

Democratization

U.S.-Taiwan relations are also heavily influenced by political trends on Taiwan. One of the most significant developments in recent years has been the democratization of Taiwan's political system. Political power is being redistributed away from the mainlanders to the majority Taiwanese population, as well as from an older to a new generation of leaders. As a result, government institutions are becoming more representative and government officials are more accountable to the public. There is also a redistribution of political power between the various branches of the central government, although this remains a constitutional issue yet to be legally resolved.

The public has very few restrictions on what it may now openly discuss, including the pros and cons of Taiwan independence. The print media discusses almost any subject, sometimes with little responsibility. The electronic media is still under the control of the KMT and government, but its reporting is more balanced and it is under intense pressure to liberalize further. Additional television or cable licenses are probable in the near future, and some of these new channels will probably be controlled by the opposition.

Taiwan is in the midst of political change. In December 1991 a new National Assembly was elected with the majority of seats popularly elected on Taiwan for the first time. At year's end, the remaining senior parliamentarians retired, leaving the Legislative Yuan during its 1992 session with about 130 members, most of whom were elected on Taiwan. The December 1992 Legislative Yuan elections brought to office an active group of KMT and opposition legislators determined to have a greater say in the direction of their country.

These political developments have had a very positive impact on U.S. relations with Taipei. Both the administration and the Congress had urged greater democratization for many years. The fact that Taiwan's democratization has occurred at the same time that the PRC has reversed political liberalization has sharpened the contrast between Taipei and Beijing to the benefit of Taiwan.

Taiwan's democratization has resulted in Taipei becoming increasingly recognized as a legitimate representative government by the international community. This recognition, coupled with Taiwan's growing economic power, gives Taipei an excellent opportunity to expand its participation in the world community.

Democratization has benefitted Taiwan in its relations with the United States and with other countries, but there are costs as well. As the ROC government structure and policy change in fundamental ways, there is considerable anxiety generated within Taiwan's society. Chinese on Taiwan are demanding more personal freedom and individual fulfillment; society is becoming much more open and permissive. This is creating sharp tension between traditional Chinese values and the pursuit of individual goals.

Greater democratization has also increased social instability, as various political parties and interest groups often take to the streets to press their demands. Given Taiwan's delicate international position, instability can be very harmful to Taiwan's interests. The PRC has threatened to intervene if society becomes too disorderly, domestic and foreign investors may be frightened away, and the international community may be hesitant to respond to Taipei's appeals for greater recognition. Whether the demands for Taiwan's survival are great enough to discipline the emotions involved in Taiwan's democratization is a critical question which will largely determine the island's future.

The seriousness of the challenges facing Taiwan are important incentives for both the ruling and opposition parties to define mutually acceptable "rules of the game" permitting democracy to work effectively on the island. Extremism from any perspective is not in Taiwan's interests; nor is it in the interest of the United States.

Economic Restructuring

Current U.S. relations with Taipei are also influenced by economic developments on Taiwan. The success of Taiwan's economy provides a measure of social stability on the island and helps to create conditions supportive of greater democracy. It has been Taiwan's economic success which has provided the national power and resources enabling Taipei in recent years to reverse two decades of diplomatic retreat. Other nations need to deal with Taiwan because of its economic status and find pragmatic ways of doing so, despite Beijing's opposition in many cases.

But Taiwan's economy, centered mostly around trade, is in serious need of restructuring to continue a reasonable rate of growth. Thus, one of the most critical challenges facing Taiwan is adjustment of its economy to accommodate rising labor costs, large financial reserves, offshore competition for investment capital, and a more representative political system.

The Six-Year National Development Plan is the government's principal strategy to achieve this restructuring, but the plan depends heavily on financial participation by the private sector. Many potential investors have been reluctant to make large investments in Taiwan at a time when it is more profitable to locate factories elsewhere to take advantage of cheaper labor, land, and other operating costs. Moreover, the future of Taiwan is unclear, so many investments are short-term rather than the long-term investments necessary to restructure the economy.

If restructuring is successful, Taiwan's economy will probably become far stronger domestically and internationally, providing both challenges and opportunities to U.S. economic interests. If the restructuring fails, then Taiwan's economy may slow down considerably. Since Taiwan's economic success has played an essential role in most of the island's progress at home and abroad, failure to restructure the economy could have strongly negative effects on Taiwan's future. This could, in turn, harm U.S. interests in a prosperous, stable, democratic, and peaceful Taiwan.

Participation in International Affairs

Taiwan's standing in international politics is undergoing great change, with important implications for U.S. policy, not only with Taiwan but also with the People's Republic of China.

The thrust of Taiwan's new foreign policy is to enhance ROC bilateral relations and to expand Taiwan's participation in international organizations. "Dollar diplomacy" and "flexible" or "pragmatic" foreign policy are strategies to achieve these goals. In recent years, Taiwan has used with considerable effectiveness its growing economic strength to increase its stature in the international community. Taiwan is given credibility by other nations because it is the world's thirteenth largest trader and an evolving democracy. As of mid-1992, Taiwan had official relations with about thirty countries and substantive relations (mostly trade related) with most of the rest of the world.

Taiwan's pragmatic foreign policy is not intended to isolate or anger the PRC. Taipei's short-term objective is to break out of its isolation from the rest of the international community. In the mid-term, Taiwan is attempting to broaden its level of relations with other nations and to expand its participation in international organizations. In the long-term, Taipei hopes to be reunified with a democratic mainland China and to help China play a major role in international affairs. From the U.S. point of view, this formulation usually gives Washington adequate room for accommodating both Taipei's desire to expand its international presence and Beijing's demands that it be recognized as the sole legal representative of China.

The economic importance of Taiwan has caused other Asian governments to give Taipei a larger voice in regional affairs, despite lack of official relations. In recent years, significant increases in trade have occurred with Indonesia, Malaysia, Singapore, and Thailand. Taiwan is the largest foreign investor in Malaysia and one of the largest in Indonesia, Thailand, and the Philippines. Economic links are growing rapidly with Australia. Taiwan's economic ties with both Seoul and Tokyo remain very strong.

In addition to its close economic relations with the United States, Western Europe, and Asia, Taiwan is using its economic strength to build fairly strong ties with both former and current members of the communist bloc. Taiwan is very active in developing the Vietnam market and has been in the forefront of negotiating trade and investment agreements with the former Soviet Union and Eastern Europe. Like West Germany's "Ostpolitik" and South Korea's "Nordpolitik," these efforts are intended not only to diversify Taiwan's markets but also to weaken Beijing's united front aimed at isolating Taipei internationally.

In terms of international organizations, Taiwan participates as a full-fledged member in the Asian Development Bank (ADB) and a number of other multilateral institutions. Taiwan has applied for admission into the GATT and has received backing from the United States and many other Western countries. Taipei is actively seeking membership in such international organizations as the World Bank. Many on Taiwan are advocating that the ROC seek to rejoin the United Nations, although the government views these efforts as being premature.

Taiwan's strength as a trading partner necessitates including Taiwan in the international community. Democracy on Taiwan adds to its government's legitimacy. The fact that the PRC has lost credibility and legitimacy as a result of the Tiananmen incident and persistent human rights violations strengthens Taipei's case for wider international recognition and participation.

Taipei has carefully defined its foreign policy as keeping within the framework of "one China." As long as that principle is affirmed, few countries hesitate to deal with Taipei on substantive, pragmatic issues. It appears likely, if current trends continue, that Taiwan's presence in the international community will grow.

The United States recognizes the need to include Taiwan in broader international forums, as well as to be cautious in not upsetting Beijing. The 1990–1991 debates over MFN for China and GATT for Taiwan may have set the policy guidelines for Washington in this regard: The United States will back Taiwan's participation in international organizations, but only when U.S. interests are served or where substantial lobbying efforts on Taiwan's behalf take place from the Congress. Where possible, the United States will try to do something positive for Beijing at the same time to weaken any adverse impact on Sino-American relations. The fundamental U.S. policy expressed in the three U.S.-PRC joint communiqués will remain in place.

In the future, Taiwan will likely pursue foreign policies which seek an expanded diplomatic presence as well as more formalized relations with other nations. Taiwan will work hard to rejoin international organizations, particularly financial and regional organizations where Taiwan has influence due to its economic strength. To achieve these goals, Taiwan's diplomacy will become increasingly flexible and pragmatic.

As part of its strategy, Taipei will publicize its experience in modernization. Taipei will also expand its assistance to developing countries. Of particular interest to Taiwan are regional countries such as Malaysia and the Philippines. Taiwan will use economic assistance to the Third World to increase its own importance to major countries such as the United States and Japan.

Taiwan will continue to assume the position that substance is more important than name or title in foreign relations; although, as Taiwan gains respect internationally, its feelings of national pride may surface more often and be piqued at diplomatic slights. The perspective adopted by the ROC government will be to pursue policies serving not only Taiwan's interests but also the interests of a united, democratic China.

There no doubt will be occasions when the interests of Taipei and Washington conflict, but these will mostly be over specific issues, not strategy. The general thrust of Taiwan's strategy to win wider participation in international affairs through flexible diplomacy is not against U.S. interests, although this aspect of the "new" Taiwan is sometimes challenging to U.S. policy.

The challenge stems mostly from the fact that the PRC has not viewed Taiwan's new foreign policy with favor. Indeed, Beijing looks aghast at the "new" Taiwan and does not appear to have devised an adequate policy toward the rapidly changing society across the Taiwan Strait, other than to increase its pressure.

Taiwan expects that PRC pressure will increase still further as Taiwan moves forward with its reforms. But pressure is a sword that cuts both ways. PRC attempts to pressure Taiwan economically might backfire to Beijing's disadvantage. Since 1987 Taiwan has invested billions of dollars on the mainland, and trade has reached the level where Taiwan is one of China's most important trading partners. If Beijing applies too much pressure on Taipei, this investment and trade may dry up. This would harm PRC interests as well as those of Taiwan.

Beijing will likely use diplomatic pressure against Taiwan more freely. The PRC routinely demands that other countries not improve relations with Taiwan and not support Taiwan's participation in most international organizations. But because of Taiwan's economic clout, other countries find it in their interests to maintain high levels of contact with Taiwan. It is unlikely that PRC protests will stop these expanding contacts.

Taiwan feels it can weather PRC protests over its flexible diplomacy, because Beijing's leaders must always ponder whether too strong a pressure might cause Taiwan to move toward independence. The unspoken threat from Taipei to hold a national referendum to determine Taiwan's future is sufficiently damaging to Beijing's interests that PRC moderation might prevail.

Thus, even if the PRC objects, Taiwan's international standing will probably improve over the next few years. Taipei does not believe its flexible policy will solve its diplomatic problems overnight, but it does believe that its long-term prospects are good. With some caution, the United States will probably be supportive of much of this process.

Taiwan-Mainland Relations

Relations between Taiwan and mainland China are also important factors in U.S. relations with Taipei. The United States seeks to foster an environment in which peaceful interchange between the two Chinese sides can take place. The fundamental U.S. interest served by this policy is an eventual peaceful resolution of the Taiwan issue.

Over the past few years exchanges across the Taiwan Strait have grown enormously. The official positions of the two Chinese governments, however, are still far apart except for agreement on eventual reunification. Beijing insists on its "one country, two systems" formula, while Taipei insists upon the process described in its Guidelines for National Unification.

The expansion of contact across the Taiwan Strait will likely remain a fundamental policy of Taipei, as long as Beijing does not attempt to undermine Taiwan through the process. Tension between Taipei and Beijing will likely continue, however, because both sides intend to bring about unification under terms favorable to itself. One of the main objectives of Taiwan's flexible diplomacy is to postpone reunification until conditions are more favorable to the ROC.

Taiwan's policies toward the mainland serve a complex set of purposes. These include the easing of tensions across the Taiwan Strait; an indirect response to the peace initiatives undertaken by Beijing since 1979; humanitarian concerns to allow long-separated families to reestablish contact; efforts to influence thinking on the mainland by transferring knowledge of Taiwan's experience in modernization; bowing to public pressure on Taiwan to expand contact with the mainland and to assist in some way with China's modernization; pressure from Taiwan businessmen to expand their markets and to profit from trade and investment with the mainland; and efforts to improve Taiwan's international image by appearing more reasonable in its policies toward mainland China.

The ROC government hopes that expanding contact with the mainland will cause the PRC to abandon its threat of force against Taiwan, persuade the PRC to permit greater freedom and eventually give up communism, and convince the mainland Chinese people that the KMT has the better system. ROC officials say that if the mainland develops along the lines of Taiwan, then there will be few differences between the two systems and reunification will be relatively easy to accomplish. From Taiwan's perspective, the most pressing task for reunification is internal development within the Chinese mainland. Taiwan officials express the hope that in ten or fifteen years enough change will occur on the mainland to make a peaceful resolution of Taiwan-mainland differences possible.

In private, the future relationship between Taiwan and the mainland is subject to intense debate, with differences of opinion being expressed within the KMT and ROC government. One fundamental problem is that over the past forty years the two sides have evolved very distinct identities. These separate identities may become even more distinctive in the future, if policy directions in Beijing and Taipei continue to diverge.

At present a consensus does not exist on Taiwan for its future, although few argue for immediate reunification or immediate independence. It is debatable whether the majority of the Taiwanese people agree that reunification of Taiwan and the mainland should eventually occur. The "status quo," with all its uncertainty, seems the preferred choice. This means that Taiwan's international status is still evolving, a situation made more complex by Taiwan's domestic and international changes.

Future U.S. Policy Toward Taiwan

Current trends suggest that over the next ten years the situation in the Taiwan Strait will likely be a continuation of the status quo or perhaps greater progress toward peaceful reunification. As seen in the preceding chapter, these scenarios for Taiwan's future are generally in the U.S. interest. But it would be a mistake to rule out a growing movement toward Taiwan independence or even a PRC use of force. This is because Taiwan is under intense domestic and international pressure, and China is on the brink of great change. Under such circumstances, there can be unexpected reversals in policy.

If it is to survive as an international entity, Taiwan's vital interests are: security from external threat or internal instability, a growing economy, access to international markets, and cooperative interaction with the rest of the world. As long as these basic interests are met, then the uncertainties which accompany independence are probably sufficiently great to exclude it as a viable alternative for the majority of Taiwan's people. If, however, these essential interests are threatened, then many on Taiwan might feel they have no choice but to risk independence.

A case in point occurred in August 1992. As a result of South Korea switching diplomatic relations from Taipei to Beijing, a number of high-ranking KMT and DPP legislators joined together to ask the ROC government to reexamine its "one China" policy and to pursue either dual recognition or an independent Taiwan.[2] To borrow a phrase from Yang Shangkun, for the PRC to pressure Taiwan too much is to play with fire.

From the point of view of U.S. interests, the key variable in whether to support Taiwan independence is the attitude and capabilities of the PRC government. It must be noted, however, that in an era of strong U.S. support for democracies worldwide, the principle of self-determination for Taiwan looms very large. At present, U.S. interests are best served by continuation of the status quo in the Taiwan Strait until conditions change substantially.

U.S. Influence over the Taiwan Issue

U.S. policy toward Taiwan reflects the desire of the American people to treat Taiwan as a legitimate international entity with which the United States should maintain friendly relations. Since 1979 the U.S.-Taiwan relationship has evolved in ways that have bonded the future of the two societies ever more closely together. Indeed, the United States through its security, political, economic, and psychological support has helped to create a peaceful and prosperous environment necessary for the "new" Taiwan to emerge.

At the same time, the United States acts with considerable restraint on the Taiwan issue, preferring its resolution to be worked out by the Chinese themselves. At times this under-utilized American influence is a source of frustration to Taipei and Beijing. Chinese on both sides comment privately that the United States is too pragmatic, too flexible, and too unprincipled on this issue.

Two simple guidelines frame much of U.S. policy toward Taiwan: try to avoid a military confrontation with the PRC, and try to ensure that a friendly government remains in control on Taiwan. From this perspective, U.S. interests are well-served by having friendly, unofficial relations with the existing government on Taiwan. The other options— having the PRC exercise jurisdiction over Taiwan or having a pro-independence government controlling the island—are much more risky to U.S. interests. Given these basic realities, it is likely that current U.S. policy will remain in place throughout the 1990s, barring major developments which completely change the domestic and international context of U.S. China policy.

To this end, the United States will continue to encourage democratic developments on Taiwan and to support some expanded participation for Taiwan in international organizations. But the United States is unlikely to restore diplomatic relations with the ROC or encourage Taiwan independence. At the same time, the United States will seek to deter the PRC from using force in the Taiwan Strait, while encouraging the liberalization of the mainland's political, economic, and social institutions. As long as Beijing adheres to a "one China" principle, the United States will continue to recognize the PRC as the sole legal government of China. This, essentially, is the "dual track" China policy pursued by the United States in its present form since 1983. There are, however, some adjustments to U.S. policy which should be made in view of developments discussed in this book, particularly in the area of security.

Adjustments in U.S. Security Policy

One fundamental tenet of U.S. China policy is the interconnection between Beijing's policy of peaceful reunification and the U.S. policies of normalized relations with the PRC and limitations on arms sales to Taiwan. If China's policy of peaceful reunification were to change and the use of coercion toward Taiwan were adopted, then U.S. policy toward both mainland China and Taiwan would undergo rapid change as well.

Despite the obvious dangers involved in a PRC use of force in the Taiwan Strait, there are certain trends which suggest that increased tensions in Sino-American relations over the Taiwan issue might be possible over the next decade. These include the increased strength of the PLA, including the acquisition of advanced Soviet fighters and other means of power projection; Beijing's growing concerns about democratic Taiwan moving away from the mainland and becoming too strong internationally through flexible diplomacy; the reduction of U.S. forces in the Pacific; and the focus of most Americans on domestic problems rather than foreign policy issues.

The overarching U.S. security interest is to avoid a military confrontation with the PRC by deterring a PRC use of force in the Taiwan Strait. Given this interest and recent developments in East Asia, the United States should do the following:

1. Do not sell to the PRC any weapon systems or technologies that might be used to increase the PLA's military superiority in the Taiwan Strait.
2. Limit where possible the transfer of advanced weapons and defense technology to the PRC from third countries.
3. Reaffirm the viability of the Taiwan Relations Act and clearly signal U.S. intentions to intervene on Taiwan's behalf if coercion is used by the PRC.
4. Maintain sufficient U.S. forces in the Pacific to permit intervention in the Taiwan Strait if necessary.
5. Improve Taiwan's defense capabilities to the point where any potential PRC use of force would be prohibitively expensive. Key areas of needed improvement remain in aircraft, missiles, ASW, command and control, air defense, early warning radars, and surface and subsurface naval warfare.
6. Remain constructively engaged with the PRC to urge a peaceful resolution of the Taiwan issue and to encourage China's economic modernization and integration into the world community.
7. Do not become involved in the reunification issue, other than to support a peaceful resolution of Taiwan's future.
8. Do nothing to encourage Taiwan independence.
9. Be supportive of Taipei's efforts to expand its participation in international organizations on a case-by-case basis consistent with U.S. interests.

Conclusion

A major dilemma faced by the PRC is that peaceful reunification cannot work without fundamental economic and political reform on the mainland. The extent of these needed reforms is such that, if they are implemented, the CCP's own leadership might be challenged. At the same time, the democratization and Taiwanization in ROC politics and society are resulting in a polity less, not more, likely to want to unify with a communist-led mainland China. Thus far, the PRC has not been able to devise a policy that can convince the people of Taiwan to reunify with the mainland and, at the same time, preserve the power of the Chinese Communist Party. One way out of this dilemma may be the use of force.

U.S. policies which deter such action are clearly in American interests. These policies include a careful program of arms sales and technology transfers to Taiwan, as well as continuous diplomatic urging of Beijing to resolve the Taiwan issue through peaceful means. As an ultimate deterrent to a PRC attack against Taiwan, it is vitally important that the United States maintain powerful forward deployed military forces in the Asian Pacific region and that successive administrations express determination to use those forces if necessary.

A continuation of the status quo in the Taiwan Strait or peaceful reunification are two scenarios for Taiwan's future that seem best suited to U.S. interests. Of these, the status quo is the preferred option at this time. Nonetheless, the United States supports peaceful evolution in the Taiwan Strait. This will require periodic adjustments in U.S. policy, such as that now needed toward Taiwan, but the basic principles inherent in the "dual-track" approach to China policy remain sound.

Since the collapse of the Soviet Union, some PRC leaders view the United States as China's main adversary. This is not because of an American military threat, but rather because American ideals of democracy and free enterprise threaten the authoritarian power of the Chinese Communist Party. Suspicion of U.S. motives for dealing with China, coupled with concerns about self-determination on Taiwan and growing support for Taipei's participation in international organizations, may result in increased tensions over the Taiwan issue in Sino-American relations, at least until the old guard passes from the scene in Beijing.

The balancing of U.S. interests in Taiwan and mainland China has always been a difficult task for Washington. Most American analysts now believe that, in pursuit of its own interests, the United States should maintain a relationship with Taipei that is not separate from considerations of its impact on Sino-American relations, but not hostage to U.S.-PRC relations either. U.S. experience in the 1970s and 1980s proved that if the United States conditions its relations with Taipei on the proviso that Sino-American relations not be harmed, Beijing will attempt to manipulate U.S. policy in a way calculated to weaken Taiwan's domestic and international position.

With the end of the Cold War, the United States seems prepared to adjust its China policy to reflect the new realities on Taiwan, the mainland, and the international environment. This shift in U.S. policy will likely be in a direction favorable to Taiwan, although Taipei will no doubt want the United States to move further in the direction of officiality than might be in the U.S. interest. As of 1991–1992 there was little reason to disregard the principles spelled out in three U.S.-PRC joint communiqués, but the developing arms race in the Taiwan Strait threatened the relevancy of some provisions of the August 17 communiqué.

While many problems face Taiwan, its experience in national development prove that a democratic, free market approach can succeed in a Chinese context. That the people of Taiwan, along with those of Hong Kong and Singapore, enjoy a standard of living comparable with that of Westerners is not lost to the mainland Chinese—a fact which mass communications has spread widely throughout China. If the CCP does not carefully handle the rising expectations of the mainland population, there may be other Tiananmen-like confrontations between the Chinese people and the PRC government. The preservation of the Taiwan model and its success may be the best chance the United States has of influencing the PRC to adopt the free market model of economic development and to broaden the base of political participation by the Chinese people.

Notes

1. The following discussion draws upon the many published speeches of AIT Chairman and Managing Director, Ambassador Natale Bellocchi. These include "The U.S.-Taiwan Relationship: The New Realities," given to the Lan Ting Club in Washington, D.C., September 29, 1991; "American Business and the Four Tigers of Asia," given to the APSA Conference in Washington, D.C., September 23, 1991; remarks given at the 30th anniversary luncheon of the Houston-Taipei Sister City celebration, Houston, Texas, July 26, 1991; "U.S. Perceptions of Taiwan's Democratization and Reunification," given at the conference on "Democracy in Mainland China and Taiwan: Prospects for Unification," The Pennsylvania State University, July 17, 1991; speeches given in San Francisco and Los Angles, June 20 and 21, 1991; speech given to the Thunderbird American Graduate School of International Management in Phoenix, Arizona, April 29, 1991; speech before the American Chamber of Commerce in Taipei, Taiwan, March 27, 1991; speech given at the Sino-American Cultural Society Dinner on December 2, 1990; and the speech given at Harvard University on October 24, 1990.

2. See *China News*, August 25, 1992, p. 1.

Bibliography

Barnett, A. Doak. *The FX Decision*. Washington: Brookings Institution, 1981.

——. *U.S. Arms Sales: The China-Taiwan Tangle*. Washington: Brookings Institution, 1982.

—— and Ralph N. Clough. *Modernizing China: Post-Mao Reform and Development*. Boulder: Westview, 1986.

Bonds, Ray. *The Chinese War Machine*. London: Salamander Books Ltd., 1979.

Bullard, Monte R. *China's Political-Military Evolution*. Boulder: Westview, 1985.

Bullock, Mary Brown and Robert S. Litwak, eds. *The United States and the Pacific Basin: Changing Economic and Security Relationships*. Washington: Woodrow Wilson Center Press, 1991.

Bunge, Frederica M. and Rinn-sup Shinn. *China: A Country Study*. Washington: American University, 1981.

Carpenter, William M. *Long-Term Strategic Forecast for the Republic of China*. Arlington: SRI International, 1980.

Carter, Jimmy. *Keeping Faith: Memoirs of a President*. New York: Bantam Books, 1982.

Chaffee, Frederick H. *Area Handbook for the Republic of China*. Washington: American University, 1969.

Chang, Gordon H. *Friends and Enemies: the United States, China, and the Soviet Union*. Stanford: Stanford University Press, 1990.

Chang, Jaw-ling Joanne. *United States–China Normalization: An Evaluation of Foreign Policy Decision Making*. Baltimore: University of Maryland School of Law, 1986.

Chang, King-yuh. *A Framework for China's Unification*. Taipei: Kwang Hwa Publishing Co., 1986.

China: U.S. Policy Since 1945. Washington: Congressional Quarterly, Inc., 1980.

Ching, Frank. *Hong Kong and China: For Better or For Worse*. New York: China Council of The Asia Society and the Foreign Policy Association, 1985.

Clough, Ralph N. *Island China*. Cambridge: Harvard University Press, 1978.

Cohen, Warren I. and Akira Iriye, eds. *The Great Powers in East Asia: 1953–1960*. New York: Columbia University Press, 1990.

Copper, John F. and George P. Chen. *Taiwan's Elections: Democratization and Political Development in the Republic of China*. Baltimore: University of Maryland School of Law, 1984.

Deng, Xiaoping. *Selected Works of Deng Xiaoping: 1975–1982*. Beijing: Foreign Languages Press, 1984.

Domes, Jurgen. *The Government and Politics of the PRC.* Boulder: Westview, 1985.

Downen, Robert L. *The Taiwan Pawn in the China Game.* Washington: Georgetown University Press, 1979.

——. *To Bridge the Taiwan Strait.* Washington: Council for Social and Economic Studies, 1984.

Ellison, Herbert J. *The Sino-Soviet Conflict: A Global Perspective.* Seattle: University of Washington Press, 1982.

Fairbank, John K. *The United States and China.* Cambridge: Harvard University Press, 1979.

Furuya, Keiji. *Chiang Kai-shek: His Life and Times.* New York: St. John's University Press, 1981.

Garrett, Banning N. *Soviet Perceptions of China and Sino-American Military Ties.* Arlington: Harold Rosebaum Associates, 1981.

Garver, John W. *China's Decision for Rapprochement with the United States, 1968–1971.* Boulder: Westview, 1982.

Gelber, Harry G. *Technology, Defense, and External Relations in China, 1975–1978.* Boulder: Westview, 1979.

Gilbert, Stephen P. *Northeast Asia in U.S. Foreign Policy.* Beverly Hills: Sage Publications, 1979.

——, ed. *Security in Northeast Asia: Approaching the Pacific Century.* Boulder: Westview, 1988.

—— and William M. Carpenter, eds. *America and Island China: A Documentary History.* Lanham: University Press of America, 1989.

Godwin, Paul H. B. *The Chinese Defense Establishment: Continuity and Change in the 1980s.* Boulder: Westview, 1983.

——. *Development of the Chinese Armed Forces.* Maxwell Air Force Base: Air University Press, 1988.

Gold, Thomas. *State and Society in the Taiwan Miracle.* Armonk: M.E. Sharpe, 1985.

Goldwater, Barry M. *China and the Abrogation of Treaties.* Washington: Heritage Foundation, 1978.

Gordon, Bernard K. *New Directions for American Policy in Asia.* New York: Routledge, 1990.

Gottlieb, Thomas M. *Chinese Foreign Policy Factionalism and the Origins of the Strategic Triangle.* Santa Monica: Rand Corporation, 1977.

Gregor, A. James. *The China Connection.* Stanford: Hoover Institution, 1986.

—— and Maria Hsia Chang. *The Republic of China and U.S. Policy.* Washington: Ethics and Public Policy Center, 1983.

——, and Andrew B. Zimmerman. *Ideology and Development: Sun Yat-sen and the Economic History of Taiwan.* Berkeley: University of California Press, 1981.

Harding, Harry and Yuan Ming, eds. *Sino-American Relations 1945–1955: A Joint Reassessment of a Critical Decade.* Wilmington: Scholarly Resources, Inc., 1989.

Heaton, William R., Jr. *A United Front against Hegemonism: Chinese Foreign Policy into the 1980s.* Washington: National Defense University, 1980.

Hinton, Harold C. *Communist China in World Politics.* Boston: Houghton Mifflin Co., 1966.

——. *Peking–Washington.* Beverly Hills: Sage Publications, 1976.

——. *The Sino-Soviet Confrontation.* New York: National Strategy Information Center, 1976.

——. *The China Sea.* New York: National Strategy Information Center, 1980.

Hsiung, James C. *Contemporary Republic of China: The Taiwan Experience 1950–1980.* New York: American Association for Chinese Studies, 1981.

Jacobsen, Carl G. *Sino-Soviet Relations Since Mao.* New York: Praeger, 1981.

Jencks, Harlan W. *From Muskets to Missiles: Politics and Professionalism in the Chinese Army, 1945–1981.* Boulder: Westview, 1982.

Joffe, Ellis. *The Chinese Army After Mao.* Cambridge: Harvard University Press, 1987.

Johnson, Stuart E. *The Military Equation in Northeast Asia.* Washington: Brookings Institution, 1979.

Johnson, U. Alexis, George R. Packard, and Alfred D. Wilhelm, Jr. *China Policy for the Next Decade.* Washington: Atlantic Council, 1984.

Kenny, Henry J. *The American Role in Vietnam and East Asia.* New York: Praeger, 1984.

Kim, Samuel S. *China and the World: Chinese Foreign Policy in the Post-Mao Era.* Boulder: Westview, 1984.

Kintner, William R. *A Matter of Two Chinas.* Philadelphia: Foreign Policy Research Institute, 1979.

Kissinger, Henry A. *White House Years.* Boston: Little, Brown and Co., 1979.

Klintworth, Gary. *China's Modernization: The Strategic Implications for the Asia-Pacific Region.* Canberra: Australian Government Publishing Service, 1989.

Kuo, Shirley W. Y. *The Taiwan Economy in Transition.* Boulder: Westview, 1983.

——, Gustav Ranis, and John C. H. Fei. *The Taiwan Success Story.* Boulder: Westview, 1981.

Lardy, Nicholas R. *China's Entry into the World Economy.* New York: The Asia Society, 1987.

Lasater, Martin L. *The Security of Taiwan.* Washington: Georgetown University Press, 1982.

——. *The Taiwan Issue in Sino-American Strategic Relations.* Boulder: Westview, 1984.

——. *Taiwan: Facing Mounting Threats.* Washington: Heritage Foundation, 1987.

——. *Policy in Evolution: The U.S. Role in China's Reunification.* Boulder: Westview, 1988.

——. *A Step Toward Democracy: The December 1989 Elections in Taiwan, Republic of China.* Lanham: University Press of America, 1990.

——, ed. *Beijing's Blockade Threat to Taiwan.* Washington: Heritage Foundation, 1985.

—— and Parris H. Chang, eds. *If the PRC Crosses the Taiwan Strait: The International Response.* Lanham: University Press of America, 1993.

Li, Kwoh-ting. *The Evolution of Policy Behind Taiwan's Development Success.* New Haven: Yale University Press, 1988.

Lieberthal, Kenneth. *Sino-Soviet Conflict in the 1970s.* Santa Monica: Rand Corporation, 1978.

———. *The Strategic Triangle.* Colgne: Federal Institute for East European and International Studies, 1979.

Lin, Chong-pin. *China's Nuclear Weapons Strategy: Tradition Within Evolution.* Lexington: Lexington Books, 1988.

Manning, Robert. *Asia Policy: The New Soviet Challenge in the Pacific.* New York: Priority Press, 1988.

Nelson, Harvey. *Power and Insecurity: Beijing, Moscow, and Washington 1949–1988.* Boulder: Lynne Rienner Publishers, 1989.

Nixon, Richard M. *RN: The Memoirs of Richard Nixon.* New York: Grosset and Dunlap, 1978.

Pollack, Jonathan D. *The Sino-Soviet Rivalry and Chinese Security Debate.* Santa Monica: Rand Corporation, 1983.

———. *The Sino-Soviet Summit—Implications for East Asia and U.S. Foreign Policy.* New York: The Asia Society, 1989.

——— and James A. Winnefeld. *U.S. Strategic Alternatives in a Changing Pacific.* Santa Monica: Rand Corporation, 1990.

Pye, Lucian W. *Chinese Commercial Negotiating Style.* Cambridge: Oelgeschlager, Gunn and Haig Publishers, 1982.

Rabushka, Alvin. *The New China: Comparative Economic Development in Mainland China, Taiwan and Hong Kong.* Boulder: Westview, 1987.

Rees, David. *Soviet Border Problems: China and Japan.* London: Institute for the Study of Conflict, 1982.

Robinson, Mary Ann. *The American Military and the Far East.* Colorado Springs: USAF Academy Library, 1980.

Robinson, Thomas W., ed. *Democracy and Development in East Asia: Taiwan, South Korea, and the Philippines.* Lanham: University Press of America, 1991.

Rothenberg, Morris. *Whither China: The View from the Kremlin.* Miami: University of Miami Press, 1977.

Schive, Chi. *The Foreign Factor: The Multinational Corporations Contribution to the Economic Modernization of the Republic of China.* Stanford: Hoover Institution, 1990.

Segal, Gerald. *Defending China.* London: Oxford University Press, 1985.

Shaw, Yu-ming. *The Prospects for ROC-U.S. Relations Under the Reagan Administration.* Taipei: Asia and World Institute, 1983.

Shen, James. *The U.S. and Free China.* Washington: Acropolis Books, 1983.

Simon, Sheldon. *The Future of Asia-Pacific Collaboration.* Lexington: Lexington Books, 1988.

Snyder, Edwin K., A. James Gregor, and Maria Hsia Chang. *The Taiwan Relations Act and the Defense of the ROC.* Berkeley: University of California Press, 1980.

Solomon, Richard H. *The China Factor: Sino-American Relations and the Global Scene.* Englewood Cliffs: Prentice-Hall, 1981.

——. *Chinese Political Negotiating Behavior: A Briefing Analysis.* Santa Monica: Rand Corporation, 1985.

Spence, Jonathan. *In Search of Modern China.* New York: Norton, 1990.

Stuart, Douglas T. and William T. Tow. *China, the Soviet Union, and the West.* Boulder: Westview, 1982.

Sullivan, David S. *Redressing the Strategic Nuclear Imbalance in Northeast Asia.* Arlington: SRI International, 1982.

Sutter, Robert G. *Future Sino-Soviet Relations and Their Implications for the United States.* Washington: Library of Congress, Congressional Research Service, 1982.

——. *The China Quandary.* Boulder: Westview, 1983.

——. *Taiwan: Entering the 21st Century.* Lanham: University Press of America, 1988.

Swanson, Bruce. *Eighth Voyage of the Dragon.* Annapolis: Naval Institute Press, 1982.

Tien, Hung-mao. *The Great Transition: Political and Social Change in The Republic of China.* Stanford: Stanford University Press, 1989.

Tow, William T. *Encountering the Dominant Player: U.S. Extended Deterrence Strategy in the Asia-Pacific.* New York: Columbia University Press, 1991.

U.S. Department of Defense. *A Strategic Framework for the Asian Pacific Rim: Looking Toward the 21st Century.* Washington: U.S. Government Printing Office, 1990.

Wheeler, Jimmy W. and Perry L. Wood. *Beyond Recrimination: Perspectives on U.S.-Taiwan Trade Tensions.* Indianapolis: Hudson Institute, 1987.

Whiting, Allen S. *The Chinese Calculus of Deterrence: India and Indochina.* Ann Arbor: University of Michigan Press, 1975.

——. *China Eyes Japan.* Berkeley: University of California Press, 1989.

Wich, Richard. *Sino-Soviet Crisis Politics.* Cambridge: Harvard University Press, 1980.

Winckler, Edwin A. and Susan Greenhalgh, eds. *Contending Approaches to the Political Economy of Taiwan.* Armonk: M.E. Sharpe, 1988.

Wolff, Lester L. and David L. Simon. *Legislative History of the Taiwan Relations Act.* New York: American Association for Chinese Studies, 1982.

Yager, Joseph A. *Transforming Agriculture in Taiwan: The Experience of the Joint Commission on Rural Reconstruction.* Ithaca: Cornell University Press, 1988.

Zagoria, Donald Z. *The Sino-Soviet Conflict: 1956–1961.* Princeton: Princeton University Press, 1962.

——, ed. *Soviet Policy in East Asia.* New Haven: Yale University Press, 1982.

About the Book and Author

Moving into the 1990s, the United States is faced with a remarkably fluid international environment that poses significant challenges, risks, and opportunities. In Asia, one of the most intractable issues that continues to engage U.S. policymakers is the future of Taiwan.

Since 1986 the scope of political, economic, and foreign-policy developments has been so substantial as to create, in essence, a "new" Taiwan. Most of these changes are in the U.S. interest. However, the new Taiwan also poses a major challenge to the Sino-American relationship, particularly in the climate of uncertainty and transformation that characterizes post-containment U.S. strategy toward East Asia in general.

Martin L. Lasater analyzes the major areas of transformation in the new Taiwan and explores its future prospects. He considers the implications for U.S. relations and interests on both sides of the Taiwan Strait and offers concrete policy recommendations.

Martin L. Lasater is a research associate with the Center for East Asian Studies, Pennsylvania State University. A visiting associate professor at National Chengchi University in Taipei during 1992–1993, Dr. Lasater is author of *The Taiwan Issue in Sino-American Relations* (1984) and *Policy in Evolution: The U.S. Role in China's Reunification* (1989).

Index